PARTITION LITERATURE AND CINEMA

This book studies literary and cinematic representations of the Partition of India. It discusses Partition as not just an immediate historical catastrophe but as a lingering cultural presence and consequently a potent trope in literary and visual representations. The volume features essays on key texts – written and visual – including *Train to Pakistan*, "Toba Tek Singh", *Basti*, *Garm Hava*, and *Pinjar*, among others.

Partition Literature and Cinema will be indispensable introductory reading for students and researchers of modern Indian history, Partition studies, literature, film studies, media and cultural studies, popular culture and performance, postcolonial studies, and South Asian studies. It will also be of interest to enthusiasts of Indian cinematic history.

Jaydip Sarkar is Associate Professor at the Department of English, University B.T. & Evening College, West Bengal, India. He has edited and co-edited several books including *Writing Difference: Nationalism, Identity and Literature* (2014), *Unmasking Power: Subjectivity and Resistance in Indian Drama in English* (2014) and *A Handbook of Rhetoric and Prosody* (2018).

Rupayan Mukherjee is Teaching Assistant at the Department of English, University B.T. & Evening College, West Bengal, India. His research interests include modernism, postmodern studies and South Asian literature.

PARTITION LITERATURE AND CINEMA

A Critical Introduction

Edited by Jaydip Sarkar and Rupayan Mukherjee

LONDON AND NEW YORK

First published 2020
by Routledge
2 Park Square, Milton Park, Abingdon, Oxon OX14 4RN

and by Routledge
52 Vanderbilt Avenue, New York, NY 10017

Routledge is an imprint of the Taylor & Francis Group, an informa business

© 2020 selection and editorial matter, Jaydip Sarkar and Rupayan Mukherjee; individual chapters, the contributors

The right of Jaydip Sarkar and Rupayan Mukherjee to be identified as the authors of the editorial material, and of the authors for their individual chapters, has been asserted in accordance with sections 77 and 78 of the Copyright, Designs and Patents Act 1988.

All rights reserved. No part of this book may be reprinted or reproduced or utilised in any form or by any electronic, mechanical, or other means, now known or hereafter invented, including photocopying and recording, or in any information storage or retrieval system, without permission in writing from the publishers.

Trademark notice: Product or corporate names may be trademarks or registered trademarks, and are used only for identification and explanation without intent to infringe.

British Library Cataloguing in Publication Data
A catalogue record for this book is available from the British Library

Library of Congress Cataloging-in-Publication Data
A catalog record has been requested for this book

ISBN: 978-0-367-14386-2 (hbk)
ISBN: 978-0-367-49274-8 (pbk)
ISBN: 978-1-003-04537-3 (ebk)

Typeset in Bembo
by Taylor & Francis Books

In loving Memory of Dr. Ratnadip Mitra

CONTENTS

List of contributors	*x*
Preface and Acknowledgements	*xii*

Introduction: Literature and film: an alternative archive of the Partition of India	1
Mosarrap Hossain Khan	

PART I
Historical reality: texts of response   19

1 Political mayhem and the moment of rupture: Bhisham Sahni's *Tamas*	21
Arnab Roy and Jaydip Sarkar	
2 Ideology of hatred and the violent making of nations: Khushwant Singh's *Train to Pakistan*	34
Shirsendu Mondal	
3 Partition and the shattered familiar: Bapsi Sidhwa's *The Ice-Candy Man*	45
Rupayan Mukherjee	
4 Saadat Hasan Manto's "Toba Tek Singh": A nation split by trauma and madness	56
Kritika Nepal	

viii   Contents

5   Translating trauma into sublime: Gulzar's response to Manto's
    "Toba Tek Singh"   62
    Tuhin Sanyal

PART II
Memory and mnemonic: of homeland and homelessness   **71**

6   Politics of memory and the myth of homelessness: Intizar
    Husain's *Basti*   73
    Mitarik Barma

7   Redrawing the borders of nostalgia: A reading of Ritwik
    Ghatak's selected short stories   85
    Somasree Sarkar

8   Memory of home and the impossibility of return: Reading
    Jibanananda Das's "I Shall Return to This Bengal" and "I
    Have Seen Bengal's Face"   92
    Madhuparna Mitra Guha and Rupayan Mukherjee

9   Tracing erasure and re-mapping the memory lane: Partition
    movies of Ritwik Ghatak   101
    Rajadipta Roy

10 From home to homeland: Negotiating memory and
    displacement in Dibyendu Palit's "Alam's Own House"   112
    Rupayan Mukherjee and Kritika Nepal

PART III
Body politics: the woman in question   **119**

11 Decentrification and gendered perspectives in Partition
    narratives: An analysis of *Garm Hava*   121
    Soumik Hazra and Shubham Dey

12 Honour, woman's body and marginalisation: A study of
    Amrita Pritam's *Pinjar*   134
    Anisha Ghosh

13 History versus (her)story: A study of Jyotirmoyee Devi's *Epar
    Ganga Opar Ganga*   143
    Jaydip Sarkar

Contents ix

14 Immanent needs, immediate solutions: Body and reconciliation
    in Manik Bandopadhyay's "The Final Solution"   152
    Rupayan Mukherjee and Somasree Sarkar

15 The aporiac self: Feminine and the poetics of silence in
    Sabiha Sumar's *Khamosh Pani*   161
    Sankha Ghosh

Postscript: Inverted prisms, imperfect histories: towards a
Dalit historiography of India's Partition   167
Jaydip Sarkar

Index   *175*

CONTRIBUTORS

Mitarik Barma is Assistant Professor of English at Basanti Devi College, West Bengal, India. His research interests include Postmodern fiction and Indian writing in English.

Shubham Dey is an M.Phil. scholar at the Department of English, University of North Bengal, India. His research interests include Postcolonial studies and studies in visual arts.

Anisha Ghosh is Assistant Professor of English at Inspiria Knowledge Campus, Siliguri, West Bengal, India. Her research interests include Modernism, Postmodernism and Feminism.

Sankha Ghosh is Teaching Assistant at Aliah University, Kolkata, India. His research interests include Historiography, Neo-historicism, and Indian writing in English.

Madhuparna Mitra Guha is Associate Professor of History at University B.T. & Evening College, West Bengal, India. Her research focuses on Feminist historiography of Indian Partition.

Soumik Hazra is an M.Phil. scholar of Film Studies at Jawaharlal Nehru University, New Delhi, India. His areas of interest include Historiography, Neo-historicism and Gender Studies.

Mosarrap Hossain Khan is Assistant Professor of English at Jindal Global Law School, O.P. Jindal Global University, Haryana, India. He is a founding editor of *Café Dissensus*.

Shirsendu Mondal is Assistant Professor of English at Barasat College, West Bengal, India. His research interests include culture and media Studies and Postcolonial literature.

Contributors **xi**

Kritika Nepal is a Ph.D. scholar at Sikkim University. Her research interests include Modernism, Trauma studies and Feminism.

Arnab Roy is an independent researcher. His research interests include Historiography, Neo-historicism, Postmodern fiction and Indian writing in English.

Rajadipta Roy is Associate Professor of English at Maynaguri College, West Bengal, India. His research areas include Postcolonial studies and studies in visual arts.

Tuhin Sanyal is Assistant Professor of English at Tufanganj Mahavidyalaya, West Bengal, India. He is a renowned Indo-Anglian poet and a translator.

Somasree Sarkar is Assistant Professor of English at Ghoshpukur College, West Bengal, India. Her research interests include Modernism and Feminism.

PREFACE AND ACKNOWLEDGEMENTS

We are indebted to our histories irreconcilably. History governs and frames us not just through the discursive certitudes of what it is, but also in speculating what is to arrive. This is the inescapable shadow that history posits. It is the nightmarish burden which Sisyphus cannot unburden. Through expulsions, denials and redemptive stratagems at times, the Indian subcontinent has been engaged in relentless endeavours to unburden the catastrophic history of Partition since 1947. Yet, the "underside of its history" has been sneaking in time and again, like smoke, through the fissures of silence. Representation, the truant child of culture, often steals away from the red-eyed surveillances of historiography and manages to inhale these forbidden smokes.

History of Partition has been influentially shaped by the facts and fictions of Representation. The historicity of Partition, its lingering influence on the social and collective consciousness, has often been drawn into context by the discourse of representation, shaping and formulating that dubious discursive economy called 'postmemory', which can be simultaneously doubted and relied upon. That way, Representation has been influential in two distinct ways. It has substantiated, authenticated, voiced and at times imagined the sacrosanct paradigm of lived reality. Simultaneously, it has also produced subsequent generations of historical subjects, who unlike their predecessors, are not historically burdened. They are, instead, historically conscious subjects, endowed with a critical objectivity towards history.

This is not to deny the perennial debate that encumbers the nexus between history, reality and representation. How much of representation is ideologically driven and haunted by the impending shadow of the artist? Isn't representation – a preconceived, systematically (no matter how avant-garde it is) designed aesthetic endeavour– much like Hegel's 'owl of Minerva', which takes its flight only after the descent of darkness? How does representation deny the epistemic violence of appropriation which is involved in the transmutation of suffering and loss into aesthetic? And thus begins the tussle between three neighbours who are not in good terms with each other and are yet irrevocably curious about each other. Each of them is ever ready to claim and legitimise its autonomy and yet at the slightest of provocations and sometimes without any, they expose their fidelities to and dependencies on the neighbouring referentials. The average Indian man will often hear colourful gossip about how a particular region in Kolkata celebrates after Pakistan wins against India in a cricket match. Such discussions will inevitably end with the 'erudite' observation: Should have made this a Hindu nation! Daily newspapers, with their incessant reports on honour killing, continually compel us to face this question of utter discomfort: How much of this do we owe to our histories? History has clearly refused to stay within the frameworks of the happened and has proliferated (or is still proliferating) into the happening present. Reality, in its own way to date, is justifying its misgivings under the grand narrative of 'History Repeats Itself'.

Representation is the third musketeer, who has the autonomy of the aesthetic to its name. It can allude to reality and then surpass the real, it can be both imbibed in history and yet be critical of history. Engaging the reader/audience in a 'wilful suspension of disbelief', representation seeks to indulge not in faithlessness but a critique of faith – the unconditional faith in historical and the real. And in doing so, it lays bare the other histories and other realities, all valid, true and relevant.

The present volume seeks to analyse a few literary and cinematic representations of Indian Partition discursively as we do not intend to generate a historiographic canon which would chronologically record the changing dynamics of representation, or politics of representation of Partition in the literary and visual medium. In our opinion, canon is a formulated historiographic apparatus, governed by the systematics of segregation and we believe that, uncovering the silence of Partition ought to be non-hermeneutic. Hence, along with representative and oft-cited Partition texts, this volume includes texts which are not direct, contextualised responses to Partition but are haunted by its long reclining shadows.

We are grateful to our contributors, who have generously offered their academic labours for the book. Our families have always been a constant support and we take this modest opportunity to thank them, which is only half of what they deserve. We also offer our sincere gratitude to Routledge for its genuine interest in the project. Mr Aakash Chakrabarty, Senior Commissioning Editor of Routledge and Ms Anvitaa Bajaj, part of the Editorial team of the book, deserve specific mention as without their significant observations and interventions, the book would not have acquired its present shape. We earnestly hope that the book will be beneficial to the students and scholars interested in Partition literature and films.

Jaydip Sarkar
Rupayan Mukherjee
9 September 2019

INTRODUCTION

Literature and film: an alternative archive of the Partition of India

Mosarrap Hossain Khan

Introduction

On 30 July 2018, the first draft of the National Register of Citizens for the State of Assam was released to identify people who had been supposedly staying illegally in the state. Nearly 40 lakh (4 million) people were marked as infiltrators, many of whom were Bengali Muslims in origin, whose ancestors had once migrated from Bangladesh. However, with the publication of the final Register on 31 August 2019, it is found that the citizenship claims of nearly 21 lakh (2.1 million) people, which were rejected earlier, have now been included. The relatively higher percentage of inclusion of names in the Bengali-speaking Muslim migrant majority districts of the State has been alleged by the leading political parties of Assam as a "flaw in the process"[1].

The long displacement of Bengali Muslims from Bangladesh was initiated by the British colonial government[2] in the mid-19th century, under projects such as 'Grow More Food,' which aimed to settle more people for cheap agricultural labour in the sparsely populated North Eastern region of India. While Gopinath Bordoloi, the premier of Assam in the 1940s, evicted thousands of Muslims as illegal immigrants, such xenophobia assumed a much larger proportion during the Partition of India. Post-independence, the Muslim community faced extensive riots in 1950, when as many as 53,000 Muslim families crossed over to the then East Pakistan to avoid persecution and later returned under the Nehru–Liaquat Pact. The first National Register of Citizens was prepared the very next year to weed out illegal immigrants (read, Muslims of Bengali origin) from Assam.[3] The NRC controversy foregrounds the continuing legacy of Partition in the North East of India,[4] a legacy that haunts our memory, significantly shaping India's current society and politics in other parts of the country, echoing Jisha Menon's words, "The Partition simultaneously possesses and dispossesses its survivors" (2013: 5).

While the dearth of serious scholarship on Partition literature from the North East of India could be understood as an elision of marginal voices, such a paucity of studies[5] on Partition literature and films from Bengal could be attributed to the 'muted' nature of Partition in the eastern part of India. Unlike Punjab, the Partition violence in Bengal never assumed an air of finality, that is, a moment of complete rupture after Radcliffe arbitrarily drew the borders between India and Pakistan. In order to understand the interventions made by literary and cultural texts surrounding an event that uprooted around 10 million people, killed another million, and resulted in the rape and abduction of around 75,000 women, we must recount a brief history of the key events leading up to 15 August 1947.

A Brief Political History of Partition of India

In the last few years prior to the official rupture of the Indian subcontinent in 1947, the demand for Indian self-government was complicated by the Muslim League demand for a separate home of Muslims following the Lahore Resolution of March 1940. However, in the elections held in early 1946, Muslim League failed to form a ministry in the Muslim-majority provinces of the Punjab and the North Western Frontier Provinces (NWFP) and barely managed to win in Sindh, despite winning in most Muslim constituencies in the subcontinent. This election was considered to be a legitimating factor in Jinnah's quest for Pakistan as a separate Muslim homeland. Once the talks between the Congress and the Muslim League failed after the Cabinet Mission Plan's effort to divide independent India into three loosely federated units, violence erupted between Hindus and Muslims in Calcutta on 16 August, 1946, known as the 'Direct Action Day,' leaving thousands dead in a span of four days. While the violence further spread to Bombay, East Bengal, Bihar, Uttar Pradesh and NWFP, the March 1947 Punjab violence came to signal the inevitability of Partition, as violence spread from Lahore and Amritsar to rural areas of Rawalpindi and Multan, killing around 80,000 by the end of April 1947. Historian Gyanendra Pandey has perceptively observed that the Partition of India in 1947 contained within it at least three different conceptions of Partition: first, the Muslim League demand for Pakistan from 1940 onwards; second, the splitting up of the Muslim-majority provinces of Punjab and Bengal, which many Hindu and Sikh leaders wanted to remain undivided; third, the unprecedented uprooting and displacement of Hindu, Muslim, and Sikh population that moved within the nations and across borders (2001: 25–43).

While the standard historiography of Partition points to Jinnah and Muslim League as solely responsible for the Partition of India and the creation of Pakistan, there is a growing oppositional view that Punjabi and Bengali Hindus were equally complicit in demanding Partition when it became clear that they would be reduced to minorities in the newly created nations. As historian Neeti Nair writes (2011), the controversial Punjab Land Alienation Act of 1907 which amended the earlier act of 1900 and further restricted the ownership of land to agricultural tribes, who happened to be mostly Muslims, homogenised an already agitated urban middle-class Hindu community in Punjab on religious lines. Following the Morley–Minto reforms, which advocated separate Muslim electorates, Lala Lajpat Rai concentrated his energy behind the first Punjabi Hindu Sabha to be held in October 1909, founded with the sole purpose of safeguarding the interests of endangered Hindus: "the passage of the Land Alienation Act and the Morley–Minto reforms compelled certain Punjabi Hindus led by Lajpat Rai, Lal Chand, and Munshi Ram to formulate a discourse of Hindus in danger" (Nair 2011: 46). Subsequently, the Congress faced considerable opposition from the Sabha in its 1909 Lahore session. As a conciliatory gesture, Pt. Malaviya, the president of the Congress session, pointed out how the Morley–Minto reforms acted as an exclusionary factor for Hindus in Punjab, Eastern Bengal, and Assam. The minoritisation of the Hindu Punjabi community in the Punjab became more accentuated following the Kohat riot in NWFP in September 1924, in which hundreds of Hindus were displaced, encapsulating "the failures inherent in a politics that coalesced around sangathan, or the strengthening of the interests of the Hindu community, at the cost of inter-community interactions" (Nair 2011: 52). In her seminal work, *Bengal Divided: Hindu Communalism and Partition, 1932–47*, Joya Chatterji similarly writes that the Partition of Bengal was largely a result of the quest for a homeland by the Hindu elites. During the last decade and a half, the *bhadralok* (the landed genteel upper-caste Hindu Bengalis) politics in Bengal turned communal and inward-looking, concerned with its own minority position in the event of an undivided Bengal. This sense of an inferior position in an undivided Bengal was strongly informed by their memory of earlier domination, a consequence of "wealth and powers as a landed elite, their position at the top of the caste hierarchy, their privileged access to urban employment and to some measure of authority under colonial rule … " (Chatterji 1994: 12). While its wealth and professional background allowed the *bhadralok* to dominate other communities in Bengal, the *bhadralok* represented a curious mix of sensibilities derived from western education and a religion-inflected tradition at home. The Communal Award of 1932, which contributed to an increase in Muslim representation in provincial legislatures, was the first major development in *bhadralok* resentment against the growing political power of Muslim Bengalis. The upper-caste Hindus organised extensively against the award with a view to convince the colonial powers that the culturally, economically, and intellectually superior Hindu Bengalis deserved to rule in Bengal. The Muslim Bengali community, though initially reluctant to accept the Communal Award, gradually came out in strong support of the award in an attempt to assert their growing influence in the province. The Award drove a permanent wedge between the two communities that were engaged in a tussle for power in the decades to come, finally leading the Hindu Bengalis to expend most of their energies in advocating the division of Bengal in order to preserve their interests.

Pandey writes that Partition historiography in the Indian subcontinent has elided the violence of the event that is "seen in the main as being an illegitimate outbreak" (2001: 3), which goes against the fundamentals of Indian (or Pakistani) tradition and history. As Yasmin Khan suggests, this elision could largely be attributed to a lack of

4 Mosarrap Hossain Khan

distance and objectivity in the way the event is still comprehended in the wake of continuing bitter relations between India and Pakistan (2017: 7). In the absence of any serious attempt in historiography to hold the perpetrators of violence accountable, the violence and victimhood in the form of displaced and impoverished refugees have been captured most poignantly in creative writing and films: for example, in Khushwant Singh's novel *Train to Pakistan*, in Saadat Hasan Manto's short stories, in countless films, and in the photographs of long caravan of people trudging across borders.

Literary and Filmic Representation of Partition of India

Contemporary debates on citizenship and belonging in India and south Asia are constantly haunted by the Partition, which becomes "the condition of possibility for the gendered ethnicisation of citizenship and belonging in postcolonial South Asia" (Daiya 2008: 5). Despite its continuing presence in public memory, the violence and trauma have been mostly effaced as the Indian state has refused to memorialise the event in any manner (Butalia 2017). In the absence of formal memorialisation, literature and films on Partition, along with oral testimonies, act as a potent site for memorialisation of the human tragedy, necessitating a reconceptualisation of Partition violence. Whereas the historians provide a larger framework for understanding Partition violence, the nuanced texture of loss, pain, and suffering is often understood better in the works of creative writers and filmmakers, as a counter to official histories, owing to their focalisation of these tales through individual lives. As historian Mushirul Hasan writes, the creative writers

> compel us to explore fresh themes and adopt new approaches that have eluded the grasp of social scientists, and provide a foundation for developing an alternative discourse to current expositions of a general theory on inter-community relations. Their strength lies in representing a grim and sordid contemporary reality without drawing religion or a particular community as the principal reference point.
>
> *(1998: 2667)*

Gayatri Spivak suggests that the "procedure of fiction can give us a simulacrum of the discontinuities inhabiting (and operating?) the ethico–epistemic and the ethico–political" (Spivak 2019: 6) and the genre of Partition literature explores these discontinuities, by universalising the particular and vice versa.

In the larger oeuvre of Partition literature, Saadat Hasan Manto's short stories – "Toba Tek Singh," "Tetwal ka Kutta," "Khol Do," "Thanda Gosht" "Kali Shalwar," "A Tale of 1947," "Ram Khilavan," to name a few – depict the moral complexities of subjects at the receiving end of an event whose political implications were beyond their control. Eschewing an explicit representation of violence in his stories, Manto delves deep into the psyche of seemingly ordinary individuals capable of extraordinary violence in the throes of a cataclysmic event. His protagonists are testament to "his belief that human depravity, though real and pervasive, can never succeed in killing all sense of humanity. His faith lay in that kind of humanity" (Jalal 2013: 24). Amrita Pritam's Punjabi novel, *Pinjar* (1950), literally meaning skeleton, depicts the trauma of Partition violence through the viewpoint of Pooro, whose prosperous Hindu merchant family abandons her after she is abducted by a rival Muslim family 11 years before the Partition in order to settle an old enmity between two families. During Partition, she encounters other women, including her own sister-in-law, who have fallen victim to everyday violence and exclusion by their own families in the name of honour. Pritam's novel foregrounds questions of family/community honour and elision of women's rights as their citizenship is undermined by patriarchal notions of communal ownership of women's bodies in the newly independent nations. Khushwant Singh's novel *Train to Pakistan* (1956) critiques the nationalist celebration of independence by foregrounding the dark underbelly of fratricidal violence and insanity during the transfer of population. The train becomes a metaphor of reluctant mobility and death, turning on its head the idea of romantic adventure, which very much encapsulated Nehru's speech at midnight (Daiya 2008: 25). Attia Hosain's *Sunlight on a Broken Column* (1961) narrates how Partition divides families on ideological grounds, tearing them as under across borders, and how nostalgia ignites memories of a privileged Muslim life in feudal United Provinces. Bhisham Sahni's Hindi novel *Tamas* (1973), a reflective response (in the words of filmmaker, Govind Nihalani), written 25 years after Partition, accounts for the irrational murder and mayhem between communities caught in the vortex of violence. In the tradition of Singh's novel, Sahni doesn't shy away from depicting the rawness of violence and trauma, interspersed with memories of tolerance and syncretism, albeit inflected with a class dimension. Narrated from the perspective of a young Parsi girl Lenny in Lahore, Bapsi Sidhwa's *Ice-Candy Man* (1988), like Pritam's *Pinjar*, tells the story of her Ayah's abduction by a Muslim man in the wake of Partition. By focusing on Lenny's gradual loss of innocence, the novel "offers a counter-history to the dominant national history of partition" (Rastegar 2006: 32) and allows a space to comprehend the trauma of gendered violence. Amitav Ghosh's *The Shadow Lines* (1988) recounts how the long shadow of Partition continues to recur in multiple other moments of violence, such as the riots in Calcutta in 1964 and Tridib's death in the riots in Dhaka. These fictions, as a representative of the larger oeuvre of Partition literature in different languages, highlight the human dimension of the tragedy – a breakdown of social contract of civility and syncretism and a loss of ethical imperatives in everyday life.

Films help in confronting trauma by a collective mourning in a public space such as theatre (Viswanath and Malik, 2009). In the early years of independence, films emerged as an important means of representing and constituting ideas of Nation and nationalism, largely eliding Partition from the Indian filmscape. Paradoxically, a large swathe of the film audience came from the rootless urban population that sought to engage as modern Indian citizens and longed to be part of the idea of the nation.[6] Such omission of the violence and trauma of Partition from Hindi films could be attributed to a fear of censorship and a lack of aesthetic distance from the event (Chakravarty, 1996). Despite problems of censorship and the raw wound of Partition, there were several films that addressed the issues of Partition violence and refugee problem, however folding them into the narrative of nation-building. M.L. Anand's film *Lahore* (1949) didactically depicts the plight of Radha and Neela, who are abducted by Muslim men during Partition. Neela's final recovery from Lahore and Radha's final acceptance by Ramesh are enfolded within the larger project of building a secular progressive nation, albeit undergirded by Hindu values. Despite being critical of the social exclusion of abducted, the film "still relies on the Hindu woman's submissive performance of tradition and subjection to male patriarchal power" (Daiya, 2008: 96). Yash Chopra's *Dharmaputra* (1961) is one of the earliest films to depict the role of Hindu fundamentalism in Partition and like *Lahore*, this film too uses archival footage of long caravans and trains to provide a reality effect. M.S. Sathyu's *Garm Hava* (1975), the first and the best attempt at depicting Partition in parallel cinema, captures the dilemma of Salim Mirza (played by Balraj Sahni), a shoe manufacturer from Agra, about migrating to Pakistan after all his friends leave.[7] Govind Nihalani decided to adapt Bhisham Sahni's novel *Tamas* into a television series after bearing witness to the Bhiwandi riots (1984). Bhaskar Sarkar (2009) argues that the tele-serial, like Sahni's novel, embodies a secular-humanist nationalist historiography, absolving ordinary people of the responsibility for unprecedented violence of Partition. As Viswanath and Malik (2009) note, a spate of films – *Mammo* (1994), *Train to Pakistan* (1998), *Earth 1947* (1998), *Hey Ram* (2000), *Gadar* (2001), *Pinjar* (2003), and *Veer Zaara* (2004) – from 2000 onwards directly depict the trauma of Partition in the domain of mainstream cinema. Shyam Benegal's *Mammo* narrates the impact of Partition on the lives of ordinary people whose desire to cross borders is thwarted by immigration procedure. Kamal Hasan's *Hey Ram* connects the founding violence of the Partition with the communal violence in the aftermath of riots following the demolition of Babri Mosque, foregrounding the continuing bloody legacy of the event. By focusing on gendered perspectives, ruptured family relations, vicious communal hatred, Partition films, thus, challenge the official nationalist historiography of the event. In the next couple of segments, this chapter will dwell on the representation of Partition in Bengali literature and films.

Territory, Space, and Gender in Bengali Partition Literature

While there exists a sizeable corpus of Partition literature and attendant scholarship on the Partition of Punjab, the encoding of Partition experience in Bengali literature has been either negligible or fleeting at best (Chakravarty 2002; Ghosh 2013). In the "Introduction" to the second volume of their pioneering book, *The Trauma and Triumph of Partition: Gender and Partition in Eastern India*, Jasodhara Bagchi and Subhoranjan Dasgupta argue that what is lacking is not a body of creative writing on the Partition, rather an "absence of a dedicated critical engagement" (2009: xi) with this body of literature in Bengali. As Debali Mookerjea-Leonard's (2017) recent study demonstrates, the paucity could well be a definitional question: what really counts as Partition literature? While Partition literature from Punjab narrativises the grim violence of the event and a complete breakdown of inter-communal solidarity,

Bengali Partition fiction from India examines the predicament of the people, the continuous population flows into West Bengal, refugees surviving on the platforms of railway stations, life in squatters colonies, the intense competition for economic opportunities, women's victimisation both sexual and psychological, middle-class Bengali Hindu women's emergence as wage laborers, and the memories of loss.

(Mookerjea-Leonard 2017: 7)

Some of the prominent examples of Bengali Partition fiction encapsulating these themes are Jyotirmoyee Devi's *Epar Ganga, Opar Ganga* (The River Churning, 1967), Sunil Gangopadhyay's *Arjun* (1971), Atin Bandopadhyay's *Nilkantho Pakhir Khonje* (In Search of the Blue-throated Bird, 2006), Narayan Sanyal's *Bakultala P.L. Camp* (1955), Sabitri Roy's *Swaralipi* (The Notations, 1952) and *Bwadip* (The Island, 1972), to name a few. Taking into account Mookerjea-Leonard's more expansive definition of Partition literature,[8] this section provides a brief analysis of few works of fiction and non-fiction in Bengali, accounting for space, territory, loss, displacement, nostalgia and gendered violence.

Territory and Homeland-making in Gour Kishore Ghosh's *Prem Nei* ("Love Lost")

Dipesh Chakrabarty's "Remembered Villages: Representation of Hindu-Bengali Memories in the Aftermath of the Partition" analyses *Chhere Asha Gram* (The Abandoned Village), a collection of essays written by Hindu-Bengali refugees of Partition in West Bengal. The traumatic memory of the narrators reminisces the past within the context of a secure 'home' located in the East Bengal villages. As Chakrabarty writes, the Hindu-Bengali memory invests the 'homeland' with values of sanctity and antiquity:

The 'native village' is pictured as both sacred and beautiful, and it is this that makes communal violence an act of both violation and defilement, an act of sacrilege against everything that stood for sanctity and beauty in the Hindu–Bengali understanding of what home was.

(1996: 2145)

However, this sacred and aesthetic manifestation of the homeland elides the Muslim past of Bengal as the traditions of Muslims are 'not part of the sacred or of the beautiful.' In the sacred Hindu–Bengali imaginary, Muslims of Bengal could at best be guests. The process of Hindu–Bengali homeland-making is, thus, exclusionary in nature and constructs boundaries along community lines. Similarly, in "Whose Homeland? Territoriality and Religious Nationalism in Pre-Partition Bengal," Reece Jones analyses Bengali nationalist leader Bipin Chandra Pal's writings and argues "that the development of territorialized identities and the designation of homelands are… strategies employed to develop a sense of national membership within a population"

8 Mosarrap Hossain Khan

(2006: 116). By "presenting the land as the embodiment of a Hindu mother goddess, and Hinduism as the true expression of love for the land" (Jones 2006: 117), the Hindu-Bengali refugees engage in an act of territorialisation of the ethnic Bengali identity. The process of homeland-making is intimately linked with the territorialisation of the ethno-religious identity; this territorialisation is symbolically and physically an act of drawing boundaries between the Hindu and Muslim populations.

Gour Kishore Ghosh's novel, *Prem Nei* ("Love Lost"), the first in his Partition trilogy, set against the backdrop of 1937 provincial elections in Bengal, foregrounds the construction of a differential Muslim-Bengali identity at the turn of the 20th century, which came to be territorialised in the process of homeland-making under the nationalist impulse. The novel narrates the story of Shafikul, a poor Muslim peasant's son, who struggles to complete his education at the village madrassa and is assisted by his Hindu teachers and neighbours in obtaining a law degree from Calcutta. The oppressive poverty of Muslim peasants, the tyrannical hold of dogmatic Islam over the lives of semi-educated and illiterate Muslim masses, Muslim women's resigned existence under claustrophobic patriarchy, an increasing communalisation of public life among the Hindu and Muslim communities, an emergent antagonistic political consciousness among the Muslim middle classes in rural Bengal and a growing alienation among liberal-minded Muslims like Shafikul are some of the key themes in the novel. By focusing on a growing communal divide, the novel represents complex religious and political configurations which shrink the secular space for individuals as well as secularised political struggles under the umbrella of Krishak Praja Party.

The economic deprivation of poor Muslims was seen as a consequence of the exploitation by Hindu money-lenders and zamindars. The impoverished farmers started aligning themselves with Fazlul Huq's Krishak Praja Party (KPP), which was set up by "some Muslims in the Legislative Council who were spurred by the Bengal Tenancy Act of 1928 to form a pressure group to protect the tenants and the labourers" (Chatterji 1994: 72). The objectives of the KPP were abolition of the zamindari system, remission of rents, and paying off debts, with the main focus of the party being the abolition of the zamindari. As the *jotedars* or small landholding class came into prominence in the rural areas, the interests of the poor farmers were hegemonised by this emergent class, which came to play a dominant political role in the rural areas. For a while, KPP succeeded in projecting itself as a confluence of different ideological positions. However, it gradually started promoting a distinct Muslim consciousness. The KPP started losing the support of Hindu farmers as the meetings started with customary Islamic ritualistic invocations:

> *Bismillah-ir Rahaman-ir Rahim.* Welcome my peasant brothers. We are assembled here because of the generosity of kind Allah … Those who have gathered here are almost all Muslims. I hope the non-Muslim brothers here will not take offence if I speak more about the Muslim brothers. Do not consider this issue as a Muslim and non-Muslim problem; rather consider it as a problem of poor peasants.

(Ghosh 2000: 182)

The empathy of KPP leaders for poor Muslims soon turned into a discourse of nascent Muslim nationalism in Bengal. This territorial rhetoric of homeland-making will be further advanced politically by the Muslim leadership in propounding the demand for a Muslim majority nation called Pakistan where the cultural purity of Islam can be maintained without the intrusions and influences of the Hindus. Gayaram, one of the very few Hindu peasants to retain faith in the KPP, withdraws himself after the arrest of the leaders. He is sceptical about the inclusive nature of the movement,

> I am the only Hindu left in the village. All the others have left. Why did this happen *chacha*? Muslims from the other side are gradually moving to this village. As if an island is formed in the middle of Mother Ganga. How do we succeed in preventing the formation of the island? People from the same village are now divided…Could you ever think that one village will be divided into two? One for Hindus and the other for Muslims.
>
> *(Ghosh 2000: 217)*

The KPP craftily cultivates a communal identity by drawing on the plight of Muslim peasants, ignoring the question of Hindu peasants. This gradual communalisation of a supposedly secular peasant movement finally results in its alliance with the Muslim League after the Bengal provincial elections of 1937. Shafikul is distraught with this opportunistic alliance which betrays the interest of poor peasants in favour of the growing clout of *jotedars* or the land-holding Bengali Muslim middle class. He had hoped that the Congress and the Krishak Praja Party would form an alliance to protect the interests of both Hindu and Muslim peasants. However, the Congress finally backs out of the alliance on the question of prioritising the abolition of zamindari system and the remission of rent. The novel metaphorically ends with the still-birth of Shafikul's child which is akin to the unfulfilled promise of a Congress–KPP alliance suggestive of a solution to communal conflict.

In the novel, Dhaka features prominently in the Muslim imaginary of the 1930s as a place embodying pristine Islamic culture. Yakoob, Shafikul's cousin, a votary of neo-Islamism, is deeply committed to the project of conceiving Dhaka as an alternative cultural space to Calcutta. The discourse of Muslim cultural purity is articulated and shared equally by the orthodox maulvis and the educated urban elite. As Shafikul says,

> There may be a huge gap between the two [Yakoob and Maulavi Din Mohammad Daulatpuri] but both of them are certain that the Muslims of Bengal ought to purge Islam of the influences of Hinduism. Muslims need to evolve an uncorrupted Islamic civilization and culture. Otherwise it will be impossible to revitalize Islam. The orthodox old school and the younger neo-conservative Muslims think alike in this.
>
> *(Ghosh 2000: 228)*

10 Mosarrap Hossain Khan

Such reform movements were essentially based on the conception of a revitalised Islam with origins in the Middle East. This movement towards achieving purity finds resonance among the educated youth in the form of Islamic cultural nationalism. The Muslim students idealise Dhaka as an alternate cultural space to Calcutta which has been traditionally seen as a *bhadralok* Hindu cultural capital. During his student days in Calcutta, Shafikul himself fails to find a place in the Hardinge Hostel for being Muslim, who are lodged at the Carmichael Hostel. The subsequent desire for self-esteem prompts Muslim educated youth to imagine a separate cultural space and Dhaka is imagined to be the counter-cultural space to Calcutta. The idea of creating and consolidating a separate categorical Muslim identity and the territorialisation of that identity is a project that the educated urban Muslims undertake with fervour.

Communalisation of Urban Space in Mijan-ur-Rahman's *Krishna Sholoi* ("The Dark 16th")

The historiographical literature on the experiences of Partition in Bengal predominantly engages with problems of refugee rehabilitation and their struggle for assimilation in the host country, the consequent demographic impact of migration on the host population, the growth and expansion of the city proper as a result of refugee settlement on the outskirts and social tension between the Hindu refugee population and the *bhadralok*. Partition scholarship in Bengal, however, still continues to be marked by its silence about how the urban spatial imaginary progressively becomes communally marked. Mijan-ur-Rahaman's memoir, *Krishna Sholoi* ("The Dark 16th") is an eyewitness account of the riots that rocked Calcutta from 16 to 19 August, 1946, as a consequence of the Direct Action Day call given by the Muslim League. The memoir is narrated from the point of view of a 13-year-old Rahman, whose family lived in Calcutta and left India for East Pakistan after Partition. As the title suggests, the book describes with fidelity what the young boy saw in Calcutta in the first few days after 16 August, when the intensity of the riot was felt most. Rahman frames his memoir with Tagore's remarks about Hindu–Muslim relations in colonial Bengal and narrates an incident that Tagore writes about: how during the anti-Partition movement of 1905, one particular Hindu revolutionary had asked his Muslim colleague to get off the verandah so he could drink water (Rahman 2000: 12). This particular framing challenges much of our contemporary discourse in which communal rhetoric is often normalised and erased under the rubric of liberal *bhadralok* cultural values. Rahman's memoir captures a time-period when the liberal anti-communal posturing of the Congress party was severely challenged by the aggressive communal politics of the Muslim League. The memoir points to certain moments of contradiction in *bhadralok* values as when young Rahman, growing up in a Hindu locality, notices how his Brahmin playmates are asked to bathe after playing with the Muslim boys; how in school, he is not allowed to touch the water jug and has to request his friends to pour water for him to drink; how in the class, a particular history teacher calls Siraj-ud-Daula, a 'nere,' a derogatory term used to address Bengali Muslims. The memoir also notes how he attends Saraswati puja at school; how his father's Hindu friends visit his house to eat food cooked by his mother; how his father's friends send them gifts while they spend their summers in *desh* or ancestral place in East Bengal. In Rahman's young mind, such contradictions raise questions about the putative secular credentials of the *bhadralok*, most of whom were supporters of the Indian National Congress.

Recounting the communal carnage of 1946 in minute details, Rahman notes how the urban space becomes more communalised as Muslims leave the Hindu pockets of Calcutta and cluster around the Muslim localities,

> The Muslim families that lived in the Hindu localities of Bhabanipur, Shyambazar, Behala, and, in other places, were gathering at the Muslim localities such as Park Circus, Taltala, Wellesley, Baithakkhana, Narkeldanga, Khidirpur, Metiabruz. The houses in these areas were rented out fast. People even started renting the verandahs.
>
> *(Rahman 2000: 74)*

Rahman's own family, which has been living in a Hindu locality, is threatened with death and is forced to seek the security of a Muslim locality. In his study on Partition, Pandey corroborates this view, "Hindus and Sikhs were never restricted in their movements to quite the same extent as Muslims, even during curfews and in the worst affected areas" (2001: 131). Joya Chatterji writes that the so-called 'Muslim Pockets' in Calcutta were kept under tight surveillance following the Partition:

> From 1948 at least until 1957, the police maintained surveillance over what they described as "Mohammadan Pockets," which were duly listed, with a careful record kept of any changes in their composition, right down to the number of firearms owned by their inhabitants.
>
> *(2005: 248)*

Madness as Subversion in Shankha Ghosh's *Supuribaner Sari* ("The Rows of Areca Nut Trees")

Shankha Ghosh's Bengali novella, *Supuribaner Sari* ("The Rows of Areca Nut Trees") juxtaposes the putative lunatic figure of a bereft daughter-in-law, Pramila, against the figure of the male revolutionary fighting colonial domination, thereby foregrounding the overt masculine construction of subcontinental nationhood. This image of a mad woman in the attic critiques the masculine notion of political independence which confines women to the gendered domestic space and disciplines them by reducing them to symbols of culture and tradition. The novella is narrated from the viewpoint of adolescent Nilu and is set against the backdrop of Partition of India and the emergence of newly independent nations. Nilu visits his maternal grandfather's house in East Bengal every Durga Puja along with his family, but this turns out to be his last journey to his grandfather's ancestral place.

On this particular journey to the village in a steamer and later by a boat, he remembers one of his previous journeys when he heard a commotion on the deck of the steamer at the dead of night and saw the nebulous bearded figure of a man clad in a shawl. The man, being pursued by the police, jumped into the river and vanished. Nilu gathered from his parents that the man was a member of an anti-colonial secret group fighting British rule in India (Ghosh 1963: 7–8). This parti-cular episode frames a complex multi-layered reality of the nation: the imaginative appeal of the masculine acts of an anti-colonial activist; the natives in the colonial police force, the active collaborators of the colonial state-apparatus; and, the figure of *Bado Mama*, who metaphorically represents the effeminate Bengali *bhadralok*, always anxious to avoid a direct conflict with the British because of material interests. Nilu also discreetly learns about the putative madness of Fulmami (wife of the youngest uncle) from the conversation among the elders:

> Everyone says that Fulmami has gone insane. Nilu tries to remember their previous conversation; he can't belive that she has turned mad …Who is called a mad person? If she is now mad, won't she write poetry any more? Won't he be able to read her poems any more?
>
> *(Ghosh 1963: 11)*

The novella ends with Fulmami's disappearance from home and their final return to Calcutta along with other family members.

When Nilu first goes to meet Fulmami after reaching his grandfather's house, he finds her in the attic, where she spends her whole day writing. However, the other members of the family feel that she spends her day as a reclusive lunatic. She allows Nilu to read from her book of poems. In one of her poems, she writes, "Who do I confess to? /That morning bird/ Invites me to fly! / No one understands / They call me mad/ I keep my secrets to myself" (Ghosh 1963: 29). She requests Nilu to take her one day to the haunted, dilapidated house that could be seen from her window. While Nilu reads her poems, Nilu's mother visits Pramila and admonishes her to be more sociable,

> Why do you spend your whole day in this room? We are all here after a year. You should be with us and look after us … Ma cannot take care of all the cooking alone. Can't you see, she is growing old? You should go to the kitchen.
>
> *(Ghosh 1963: 30)*

Pramila replies, "I don't like to go to the kitchen" (Ghosh 1963: 30). Failing to comprehend why Fulmami is called 'insane,' while she writes wonderful poetry, Nilu questions the constitutive elements in madness by asking why his Sejomama, who is equally given to idealism, should not be called mad, "Ma, why do you call Fulmami mad? Is she madder than Sejomama?" (Ghosh 1963: 45) However, this question subtly points to how not all acts of transgression are termed madness and how the idea of insanity is gendered and linked to the subversion of gender-roles supposed to be performed in a rural *bhadralok* household. The notion of madness, to use the Foucauldian discourse, is one of deviance from the cultural norms and must be thrust into secrecy because they border on unreason. If the figure of Toba Tek Singh could be read, following Todorov (1975), who theorises the fantastic, as a figure of ambiguity at the level of political, the figure of Pramila is subversive, first, by aspiring access to the public/political and second, by deviating from middle-class gender norms. Her confinement denotes a sanctification of the inner/domestic space (Chatterjee, 1989). During Partition, community identities were crystallised around discourses of cultural purity, a particular strand of which was embodied in the recovery operation of the abducted women. The body of the abducted and recovered women became a contested site for inscribing patriarchal values of community honor and shame. The recovery operation, vindicated by a logic of masculinity, served as an act of legitimising the newly formed nation-state. As has been argued by Bhasin and Menon (1998), the recovery operation 'emasculated' the family and the communities as the state infringed on the domain of these two entities. Ghosh's novella foregrounds the surveillance of the 'emasculated' families (and communities) in regulating the bodies of women, in times of crisis, as symbols of culture and tradition. By disappearing at the end of the novel, Pramila not only transgresses gendered roles in the domestic sphere but also manages to subvert the masculine surveillance of the state and the coercive disciplining by the family.

Bengali Partition Films

Whereas Bengali Partition literature traverses a larger landscape between rural Bengal to the metropolis of Calcutta, cinema of Partition maps the city-space as one of habitation and encounter, through the trope of mobility, something that is particularly invested in the body of the refugee attempting to reconstruct her/his life after the traumatic events. The figuration of Partition in Bengali cinema was often covert in the immediate decades following the event: the Uttam–Suchitra popular romances were one way of coping with the trauma of the Partition (Sarkar 2009). In the aftermath of the traumatic events culminating into the Partition of India, Calcutta, the beleaguered city, became the locus of two master filmmakers, Nemai Ghosh and Ritwik Ghatak, who derived their inspiration from the works of European avant-gardes, and their reimagination of the city-space:

> they were witnesses to the sheer and momentous visuality of dispossession that was around them, as Calcutta was seething with the dislocated. It was only a matter of time before the city would inevitably become the locus of their scopic drive.
>
> *(Chowdhury 260)*

Nemai Ghosh's *Chinnamul* ("The Rootless," 1950), like Salil Sen's *Natun Yahudi* ("New Jews," 1953), deeply inspired by European neo-realist and Soviet avant-garde films, experimented with untrained actors, camerawork, and natural approach, integrating elements of documentary and cinema to record the experience of a group of farmer-refugees streaming into Calcutta after Partition. In a classic Italian neo-realist vein, actual refugees themselves were convinced to act in the film, blurring the line between the harsh reality of Partition and cinematic narrative of displacement. Ritwik Ghatak's *Nagarik* ("The Citizen," 1951) similarly bears cinematic witness to a changing post-Partition Calcutta, through the depiction of Ramu's impoverished family, while keeping the real city absent by depending more on theatrical representation via sets. In the film, the "camera leaves this constricted theatrical space only to give an omniscient gaze of the city in turmoil, stock shots that particularise the city, but not the essential narrative space" (Chowdhury, 2015: 265). Ghosh and Ghatak's films visualise a deliberate way of seeing the hitherto non-cinematic city, a way of mapping its middle-class and mundane spaces. Sukumar Sengupta's less remembered film, *Ora Thake Odhare* ("They Live That Side," 1954), similarly captures the experience of impoverishment of the middle class in the aftermath of Partition. The film narrates a conflict between two families, one from West Bengal (*ghoti*) and the other a refugee family from East Bengal (*bangal*), finally resolved in a love affair between members of two families. Of all the filmmakers capturing the trauma of Partition, Ghatak is the most obsessed with dispossession because of his own displacement from Dhaka to Calcutta in his twenties. As a refugee, Ghatak committed himself to recording the implications of this momentous event in his Partition trilogy – *Meghe Dhaka Tara* ("The Cloud-Capped Star," 1960), *Komal Gandhar* ("E-Flat," 1961), and *Subarnarekha* ("The Golden Thread," 1965). *Meghe Dhaka Tara*, an adaptation of Shaktipada Rajguru's short story, "Chena Mukh" ("A Familiar Face"), narrates the story of Nita, a refugee woman settled on the outskirts of Calcutta, who turns out to be the sole breadwinner of the family after her father's retirement as a school headmaster. At the end of the film, Nita is shown to be dying of tuberculosis in a sanatorium, where she utters her most striking statement to her brother, Shankar, "Dada, I wanted to live." In the course of the film, she is represented as the mother–daughter Durga, one who is symbolically turned into a mother-provider figure, yet remaining a sacrificial daughter in a refugee family. Ghatak refuses the closures of social realist cinema by conjoining "Brechtian epic with Bengali mythological epics and offers a narrative that resists the progammed pleasures" (Menon, 2013: 55). By adopting the melodramatic form in *Meghe Dhaka Tara*, Ghatak enfolds, as Paulomi Chakraborty (2018) reminds us, the social and the political into the individual character of a refugee woman, collapsing the national with the familial. In *Komal Gandhar*, Bhrigu and Anasyua, two theater-performers from two rival theatre groups, an allusion to a factional struggle within the Indian Peoples' Theatre Association (IPTA), arrive at an Indian border town on the banks of the Padma and gaze wistfully across the river on the other side, which was once their ancestral land. A sense of longing and nostalgia undercuts the notion of the present, blurring the line between *desh* (home) and *bidesh* (foreign country), present and past, a persistent trope in post-Partition cultural productions. This traumatic and violent rupture with the past is a condition for Ghatak's Partition films (Chakraborty, 2018). Satyajit Ray's *Mahanagar* ("The Metropolis," 1963), adapted from

Narendranath Mitra's novella *Abataranika* (1949), documents the first tentative efforts of Arati, a refugee woman with a desire to save her family from financial ruin, to be part of the labour market in the metropolitan city, Calcutta. The movie deftly explores the complexities involved in gendered labour, the patriarchal expectations imposed by family members, including her husband, Subrata, and the limited mobility women could achieve within a constricted space. Srijit Mukherjee's film *Rajkahini* (2015), remade into Hindi as *Begum Jaan* (2017), revisits in a Mantoesque fashion (whom he acknowledges in his film credits) the experience of Partition from the perspective of a group of sex-workers, whose house falls on the border between India and East Pakistan and is about to be demolished. The film is a welcome departure from Bengali Partition films' obsession with the middle-class economic, political, and cultural crises in and around Calcutta. Mukherjee's interest in Partition, by his own admission, owes much to the tele-serial *Tamas* and Ritwik Ghatak's films.

Partition films in Bengali, mostly located in Calcutta and centred on refugees, recreate the city-space through its encounter with the rootless and dispossessed from East Pakistan. The city-space reorients gender relations, opens up access to labour market for refugee women, and allows them considerable mobility, altering Bengali middle-class women's participation in public life irrevocably in the decades that follow.

Notes

1 Prabin Kalita, "19 Lakh Left Out, Final Assam NRC Elicits Anger & Sense of Betrayal." *Times of India*, 1 September 2019. https://timesofindia.indiatimes.com/india/19-lakh-lef t-out-final-assam-nrc-elicits-anger-sense-of-betrayal/articleshow/70930061.cms (accessed 1 September 2019).

2 Kaustubh Deka, "Bengali Muslims Who Migrated to Assam in 1871 Are Not 'Illegal Bangladeshis'." Scroll.in, 4 June 2014. https://scroll.in/article/664077/bengali-muslim s-who-migrated-to-assam-in-1871-are-not-illegal-bangladeshis (accessed 18 October 2018).

3 Abdul Kalam Azad, "Assam NRC: A History of Violence and Persecution." *The Wire*, 15 August 2018. https://thewire.in/rights/assam-nrc-a-history-of-violence-and-persecution (accessed 18 October 2018).

4 In a recent article, Binayak Dutta and Suranjana Choudhury demonstrate how the debate over predominantly Bengali-speaking district of Sylhet in south Assam brought the North East to the vortex of Partition politics. See "The forgotten partitions of northeast India and its lingering legacies." *Café Dissensus*, 15 August 2017. https://cafedissensus.com/ 2017/08/15/the-forgotten-partitions-of-northeast-india-and-its-lingering-legacies (acces- sed 18 October 2018).

5 Apart from Jasodhara Bagchi and Subhoranjan Dasgupta's pioneering studies on the Par- tition literature of Bengal, *The Trauma and the Triumph: Gender and Partition in Eastern India* (2003), three recent book-length critical studies have contributed significantly to this field: Debjani Sengupta's *The Partition of Bengal: Fragile Borders and New Identities* (2016); Debali Mookerjea-Leonard, *Literature, Gender, and the Trauma of Partition: The Paradox of Independence* (2017); Paulomi Chakraborty's *The Refugee Woman: Partition of Bengal, Gender, and the Political* (2018).

16 Mosarrap Hossain Khan

6 Kavita Daiya further refers to Girish Karnad to observe that the next wave of Indian films expressed the anguish of this audience in terms of recording their anger at being uprooted and their sentimentality for the family.
7 Tanvir Mokammel's Bengali film, *Chitra Nodir Pare* (Quiet Flows the River Chitra, 1999), makes a similar effort to depict the plight of a Hindu family, Senguptas, in Bangladesh in the wake of 1964 riots. However, this film's comparison with Sathyu's film, by Mokammel's own admission, ends there.
8 In *The Refugee Woman* (2018), Paulomi Chakraborty alerts us to the textual politics of this body of texts, which refuses easy collation on the basis of themes, as it seems to be the case with Debjani Sengupta's critical study, *The Partition of Bengal* (2016).

Acknowledgement

My sincere gratitude to Ms Amanpreet Kaur for her timely research assistance.

Works Cited

Bagchi, Jasodhara and Subhoranjan Dasgupta. *The Trauma and the Triumph: Gender and Partition in Eastern India*. 2 vols. Kolkata: Stree, 2009.

Butalia, Urvashi. *The Other Side of Silence: Voices from the Partition of India*. New Delhi: Penguin, 2017.

Chakrabarty, Dipesh. "Remembered Villages: Representation of Hindu-Bengali Memories in the Afternath of the Partition," *Economic and Political Weekly*, 31:32 (10 August1996), 2143–2151.

Chakraborty, Paulomi. *The Refugee Woman: Partition of Bengal, Gender, and the Political*. New Delhi: Oxford University Press, 2018.

Chakravarty, Sumita. *National Identity in Indian Popular Cinema*. New Delhi: Oxford University Press, 1996.

Chakravarty, Tapati. "The Paradox of a Fleeting Presence," in *Pangs of Partition*, vol. 2, ed. S. Settar and Indira B. Gupta. New Delhi: Manohar, 2002.

Chatterji, Joya. *Bengal Divided: Hindu Communalism and Partition, 1932–47*. Cambridge: Cambridge University Press, 1994.

Chatterji, Joya. "Of Graveyards and Ghettoes: Muslims in Partitioned West Bengal 1947–1967" in Mushirul Hasan and Asim Roy (eds) *Living Together Separately: Cultural India in History and Politics*. New Delhi: Oxford University Press, 2005, pp. 222–249.

Chatterjee, Partha. "The Nationalist Resolution of the Women's Question," in K. Sangari and S. Vaid (eds) *Recasting Women: Essays in Indian Colonial History*. New Delhi: Kali for Women, pp. 233–253, 1989.

Chowdhury, Sayandeb. "The Indian Partition and the Making of a New Scopic Regime in Bengali Cinema," *European Journal of English Studies*, 19:3 (2015), 255–270.

Daiya, Kavita. *Violent Belongings: Partition, Gender, and National Culture in Postcolonial India*. Philadelphia, PA: Temple University Press, 2008.

Ghosh, Gour Kishore. *Prem Nei (Love Lost)*. Calcutta: Ananda Publishers, 2000.

Ghosh, Semanti. "Silence: A Deliberate Choice?" *Seminar* 645 (May2013). http://www.india-seminar.com/2013/645/645_semanti_ghosh.htm (accessed 2 November 2018).

Ghosh, Shankha. *Supuribaner Sari*. Calcutta: Aruna, 1963.

Hasan, Mushirul. "Memories of a Fragmented Nation: Rewriting the Histories of India's Partition," *Economic and Political Weekly*, 33:41 (10–16 October1998), 2662–2668.

Jalal, Ayesha. *The Pity of Partition: Manto's Life, Times, and Work across the India–Pakistan Divide*. Princeton, NJ: Princeton University Press, 2013.

Jones, Reece. "Whose Homeland? Territoriality and Religious Nationalism in Pre-Partition Bengal," *South Asia Research*, 26:2 (2006), 115–131.

Kalita, Prabin. "19 Lakh Left Out, Final Assam NRC Elicits Anger & Sense of Betrayal," *Times of India*, 1 September2019. https://timesofindia.indiatimes.com/india/19-lakh-left-out-final-assam-nrc-elicits-anger-sense-of-betrayal/articleshow/70930061.cms (accessed 1 September 2019).

Khan, Yasmin. *The Great Partition: The Making of India and Pakistan*. New Haven, CT: Yale University Press, 2017.

Menon, Jisha. *The Performance of Nationalism: India, Pakistan, and the Memory of Partition*. New York: Cambridge University Press, 2013.

Menon, Ritu and Kamla Bhasin. *Borders and Boundaries: Women in India's Partition*. New Brunswick, NJ: Rutgers University Press, 1998.

Mookerjea-Leonard, Debali. *Literature, Gender, and the Trauma of Partition: The Paradox of Independence*. New York: Routledge, 2017.

Nair, Neeti. *Changing Homelands: Hindu Politics and the Partition of India*. Cambridge, MA: Harvard University Press, 2011.

Pandey, Gyanendra. *Remembering Partition: Violence, Nationalism and History in India*. Cambridge: Cambridge University Press, 2001.

Rahman, Mijan-ur. *Krishna Sholoi*. Dhaka: Sahana Publishers, 2000.

Rastegar, Kamran. "Trauma and Maturation in Women's War Narratives: The Eye of the Mirror and Cracking India," *Journal of Middle East Women's Studies*, 2:3(Fall 2006), 22–47.

Sarkar, Bhaskar. *Mourning the Nation: Indian Cinema in the Wake of Partition*. Durham, NC: Duke University Press, 2009.

Sengupta, Debjani. *The Partition of Bengal: Fragile Borders and New Identities*. New Delhi: Cambridge University Press, 2016.

Spivak, Gayatri C. *Ethics and Politics in Tagore, Coetzee and Certain Scenes of Teaching*. New Delhi: Oxford University Press, 2019.

Todorov, Tzvetan. *The Fantastic: A Structural Approach to a Literary Genre*. Ithaca, NY: Cornell University Press, 1975.

Viswanath, Gita and Salma Malik, "Revisiting 1947 through Popular Cinema: A Comparative Study of India and Pakistan," *Economic and Political Weekly* 44:36 (5–11 September2009), 61–69.

PART I

Historical reality: texts of response

1

POLITICAL MAYHEM AND THE MOMENT OF RUPTURE

Bhisham Sahni's *Tamas*

Arnab Roy and Jaydip Sarkar

The modern Nation state, as opposed to the more indigenous paradigms of community, is founded on an ethos of transcendence. The universalised ideal of a homogeneous commune indeed tends to incorporate and simultaneously transcend the "phantasms of the lost community" (Nancy 1991: 12), i.e., those more fundamental and material conditions of race, colour, religion, language etc. In his celebrated philosophical work, *The Inoperative Community*, Jean-Luc Nancy observes that community is an irreducible component of human *being and becoming*, an apriori "given…with being and as being" (ibid.: 35) leading to the genesis of a "culture of immanence." Benedict Anderson's understanding of the modern Nation State is, however, the conception of a "solid community moving steadily down (or up) history" (Anderson 1983: 26) which is marked by the Hegelian notion of "having in another the moment of one's own subsistence" (Nancy 1991: 12).

The evolution of the Modern Nation state in the subcontinent and its consequent arrival into sovereignty is marked by rupture; a rupture that had its progeny in more rudimentary parameters of community such as religion. The conceptualisation and the enactments to ensure the culmination of a transcendental modern spatial paradigm called Nation were interrupted by a non-modern essence of community. The moment of modernity in the subcontinent is thus paradoxically, a movement backwards, a movement into non-modernity, where religion over-ruled other considerations, bifurcating a shared cultural lineage and splitting a geo-spatial paradigm into two distinct political communities: India and Pakistan. The Hegelian notion of progressive history that is central to any considerations concerning the genesis of a modern Nation State is dysfunctional when one takes into account the history of sovereignty and political independence of the subcontinent. Instead, the history of political modernity in India and Pakistan is indissociably associated with an element of the non-modern, when religion and communal considerations over-ruled the progressive advent of modernity.

As such, the Nationalist historiography of India concentrated its attention almost entirely on the unified nature of Indian nationalism and eulogised a progressive narrative of India's struggle for independence (Pandey 2001: 3), consistently denying the 'other side of history' (Butalia 1998: 349), which was a saga of rupture, genocidal massacre and the consequent inception of two independent Nation states. Such a nationalist narrative of history essentially relied on a sequential exposition of a stagist narrative that culminated into independence. But a more serious account of Partition, a moment of split of a unified nationalism, is missed from the ambit of this nationalist historiography, which came under scholarly criticism in the late 1980s from a brand of historians, comprehensively known as the Subaltern school.

Following E.P. Thomson's concept of *history from below*, on one hand, and using a Gramscian framework, on the other, the Subaltern historians have offered a useful critique of Indian nationalism. Instead of focusing on the role of the elites and glorifying the unified nature of Indian freedom struggle and nationalism, it surfaced the role of the subordinate groups and their complex relationship with Indian freedom struggle. Undoubtedly, Subaltern schools searched for an alternative model that problematised the notion of unity and instead, focused on the diversity of Indian nationalist movements. A more radical historiography, in the recent times, has gone to the extent even to challenge a pan-Indian nationalism that claimed to have existed in colonial India.

In these processes, a different account of Partition, an-other side of history, has redeemed significant spaces in the academic engagement of the past three decades. Historians, particularly of the Subaltern schools, have constructed the meanings of Partition for many 'Subaltern' communities, drawing on from the narratives of everyday lives. Shifting its focus away from a nationalist discourse on Partition, the Subaltern scholars have now been able to 'deconstruct' the grand narrative of Partition. As such, later historiography has studied the character of its unprecedented violence. The killing, rape and massive genocide etc. have formed a part of the historiography. Thus, for instance, historians like Pandey (2001) provide accounts of the violence accompanying Partition by focusing on the narratives of the people who had experienced it. This has accounted the story of many individuals and groups, unheard before, and the extraordinary torment that they had to endure during Partition. Not surprisingly, historians have increasingly become interested to turn to oral history that seemed to have helped to bring out the narratives of violence of Partition. This trend towards oral history has taken Subaltern historiography towards the evolving discourses of memory studies where *intimate histories* become an essential component of the greater enterprise to comprehend "history from below" This is most tellingly illustrated in the works of Butalia (1998), Menon and Bhasin (1998) and Roy (2010) and some others.

The engagement with oral histories and the consequent evolution of an alternative historiography often considers texts[1] as authentic chronicles that testify the agony of the age. Partition and its menaces have often been captured in the literary and cultural genesis of what we understand as Partition literature today. Thus, for instance, in the films of Ritwik Ghatak or in the songs of Hemanga Biswas or in the stories of Saadat Hasan Manto the tragic catastrophe of an enormous mass of people during Partition is more tellingly illustrated than in any historical account. It is in this sense that these texts can be considered as important historical evidence.

This chapter attempts a reading of Bhisham Sahni's *Tamas* from the perspective of New Historicism. Since 1980s, New Historicism has evolved as an approach in the study of history with its preoccupation with the historicity of the text and the textuality of history. The phrase was coined by Louis A. Montrose in 1989. The proponents of traditional Historicism focus on the reality of history as more important than literary texts. New Historicism, on the contrary, argues that both history and literature belong to the same semiotic and symbolic system. While text is considered as condensed history, history is viewed as an extended text. Therefore, any literary text seems to disclose different historical events at a particular historical specific situation. It must be noted that in the methodology of New Historicism both literature and history occupy importance and both are given same weight. In other words, the school of New Historicism seems to extend its attention to the particular socio-cultural and historical context in which a literary text is originally produced. At the same time, in this process, such literary works, in the methods of New Historicism, establish its relationship with contemporary social and political institutions and historical events (Veeser 2013).

There is no denying that while history deals with facts and figures, literature has the innate capacity to portray the experiences of the people involved in the event. Thus, any standard account of history, relating to Partition, might not be able to represent the dismay and adversity of the huge mass of people. But literature, at least in the readings of New Historicism, helps one to bring out the experience of the Partition from different viewpoints. It is in this sense of the term that literature represents the complexity and holocaust of the tragedy of the Partition, more than any standard account of history. Thus, any literary text appears to enrich the historical account of Partition. Reflecting upon the necessity to bring out memories of horror involved in Partition, Urvashi Butalia (1998) observes that the historical reality called Partition exists publicly in history books while the particular rests in rather unreliable, dubious narratives in the paradigm of fiction.

It is true that the recent engagement with fiction, i.e., with the 'particular', has exercised a dominant influence on the Partition historiography. The issue of violence, as expressed through the memories etc. has taken a front seat in the more recent account of Partition. Ironically, one of the consequences of this trend is a surprising silence on the political and social events at a larger level that shaped Partition. In their effort to distance themselves from the nationalist historiography, scholars have been increasingly pushed away from the larger political history of the day to day account for Partition. This, however, is not to argue and defend the nationalist school of historiography that eulogised a romantic and unified notion of Indian nationalism and hence, saw Partition as a troubling moment that ruptured the idea of a pan-Indian nationalism. This nationalist perspective, however, in any case, does not problematise the very notion of nationalism in colonial India. The present chapter attempts to bring out both these issues. On one hand, it deals with

24 Arnab Roy and Jaydip Sarkar

the problematic of nationalism in colonial India that led to Partition and simultaneously brings out the violence of Partition, portrayed in the novel.

Colonial rule undoubtedly has had a deep and profound influence that was to shape and fashion the nature of polity, economy and society in the making of modern India. It has played a momentous role in the making of nationalism in India, often marked with religious identities. This is particularly true in the case of formation of a Muslim identity and a distinct Muslim nationalism, as opposed to a pan-Indian view of nationalism, advocated by the Indian National Congress. Nationality became a contested terrain for both the parties which furthered the political trajectory in such a course that would inescapably result in the creation of two separate nations.

The idea of Muslim nationalism, based on a particular culture and religion, did not exist till the end of the Muslim rule in Delhi sultanate. The advent of the colonial rule marked an end of the era of Muslim rulers. The rise of colonial power in the socio-political scenario of India from the middle of the 18th century was simultaneous with the gradual defamation of the erstwhile elite Muslim aristocracy and intelligentsia from their prestigious position. The cultural and communitarian lineage of the Muslims were compromised in favour of an evolving order of political modernity. Farzana Shaikh observes

> Modern liberal representation has, on the whole, tended to assume that the unit of representation consists primarily of the individual and his interests. This quintessentially European view which emerged early in the nineteenth century was vitally related to the principle of individual equality … In Islam, on the other hand, the preoccupation with communal identity has necessarily entailed a focus upon communal claims and the communal group as the basic unit of representation and focus of loyalty.
>
> *(Shaikh 1986: 541)*

Muslim intelligentsia, under the new rule, lost both its material interest and social-cultural status and was systematically marginalised. This social alienation was further deepened by the political reassertion of the Hindu community. With the advent of the colonial rule, the Hindus had quickly accommodated themselves within the European discursive models and frameworks.

This was possible as the many proponents within the Hindu community, from the beginning of the 19th century, had engaged in the reformation project. The introduction of Bengal Renaissance was heavily influenced by the advent of English education in Bengal presidency. Bengal Renaissance was also hybrid in disposition as it continuously promoted the necessity to combine ancient Indian culture with that of modern European civilisation. With the introduction of modern education, Eurocentric thoughts and matrixes like positivism, rationalism and utilitarianism encroached into the non-modern epistemic and cultural models in the Indian social life. (Mittra 2001). The Muslims, however, were apprehensive to the modern education and viewed it as something that would corrupt the Islam and Muslim culture. They maintained a distance from the British culture and modern education that accompanied it. Naturally, the benefit of a modern English education system during the time of Bengal Renaissance was solely enjoyed by the middle-class Hindu Bengalis. Thus, for instance, in 1817, stalwarts like Ram Mohun Roy had founded the Indian College in Calcutta. Many other social reformers, primarily coming from the rank-and-file of middle-class Hindu families, had promoted modern education among the common mass of the Hindu people. On the contrary, the British-Indian Muslims had no similar efforts at that time. According to the data of the British India Board of Education, published in 1883, the number of the Muslim college students was precariously low, as compared to that of their Hindu counterparts. As a consequence of their adverse attitude towards the English educational system, Muslims lost their control and social position from different departments of the British Colonial Government. Thus, for instance, from 1852 to 1862, only one among 240 High Court judges was appointed from the Muslim community. In another such estimate, in 1871, the number of the Muslims in administration, health, police and other departments were abysmally low than that of the Hindus. Only 92 Muslims were appointed in all these positions against 681 Hindus (Jiang 2016).

The knowledge of and acquaintance with the culture of the colonisers helped the Hindus to transform themselves and consequently occupy an important position in the political and social landscape of British India. The anxiety of self-backwardness and a continuous threat of Hindu hegemony might have played a critical role in constructing an identity crisis for the Muslim population. This Muslim identity crisis further led to the construction of a Muslim nationalism.

Faced with identity crises, the Muslims adopted some reform programmes within the community to gain and assert a self-identity. It is in this context that one should look at the magnitude of the educational project of Sir Syed Ahmad Khan in shaping the political aspirations of Muslim upper class. Sir Syed Ahmed Khan (1817–1898) was a pioneer who championed a social reform movement among the Muslim community. He promoted a sense of modernisation among the Muslim community by imparting the English educational system. He realised the necessity to push the Muslim community to participate in the colonial administration. Muslim literary society in Calcutta, established in 1863, was the brainchild of Sir Syed Ahmed Khan. The activity of the Society was not only restricted within the academic debates, but went on to embrace political discourse. This was perhaps an unambiguous indication on the part of the Society to assert Muslim identity in the contemporary political scenario. In order to promote modern science among the common Muslim readers, Sir Syed Ahmed Khan established Scientific Society of Aligarh in 1864. It was in 1875 that Sir Syed Ahmed Khan established the Muhammadan Anglo-Oriental College. It must be noted that Sir Syed was successful in blending the modern education of the Western world with the basic teachings of Islam (Jiang 2016). The influence of such a gigantic project of Sir Syed was not only confined within the narrower circle of the Muslim elites. Rather, it could capture the imagination of the common Muslim middle class and enabled them to claim their identity in the political scenario of the day. A.R. Desai argues that "the Muslim middle classes enthusiastically responded to the Aligarh Movement. The Aligarh College created a modern Muslim intelligentsia which was imbibed with the spirit of political loyalty to the British government and enthusiasm for the western culture" (Desai 2010: 371).

Aspiration to claim and assert a Muslim self-identity gained momentum, especially after the Indian National Congress was formed in 1885. The Congress claimed to function as an all encompassing representative indigenous political party but was in reality dominated by "urban, highly educated Brahmans" (Tudor 2013: 256) and was hegemonic to religious and ethnic minorities. Ahmad Khan was suspicious of the Congress from the outset. In his letter to Budruddin Tyabji, he questioned the legitimacy of Congress as a national platform:

> A Congress can only be called 'national' when the ultimate aims and objects of the people of which it is composed are identical. My distinguished friend himself admits that some of the aims and objects of Mahomedans are different from those of Hindus, while some are similar; and he desires that Congress should put aside those in which they differ and confine itself to those in which they agree. But under these circumstances how can the Congress be a National Congress?
>
> *(Malik 2006: 377)*

Syed Khan was the first one to pronounce with unmistakable clarity of a Muslim Nation. He proposed the theory of 'two Nations.' But one must not forget the fact that at the same time he was an ardent advocate of the unity between Hindus and Muslims. His sole idea was perhaps to champion and protect the interest of the Muslims in colonial time. The concept of the "Muslim nation," as proposed by then Muslim intelligentsia like Syed Khan was not a territorial claim of separate state for the Muslims (Jiang 2016). Muslim intelligentsia believed that Congress could not represent the Muslim community in India. In a speech, Khan made this point in the following words:

> The second thing is this: that some Hindus – I do not speak of all the Hindus but only of some – think that by joining the Congress and by increasing the power of the Hindus they will perhaps be able to suppress those Mohammedan religious rites which are opposed to their own, and, by all uniting, annihilate them.
>
> *(Guha 2018: 68)*

Disdaining this 'Hinduttwa' of Congress, Syed Khan continued:

> Those Mohammedans are quite unaware of what sort of thing the National Congress is. No Mohammedan Rais of Bengal took part in it; and the ordinary Bengalis who live in the district are also as ignorant of it as the Mohammedans.
>
> *(Ibid.: 68–69)*

This animosity and contest between the Hindus and Muslims took a more prominent shape with the genesis of the Muslim League in the first decade of the 20th century. The tussle with Congress finally led the Muslim League to demand for a separate Muslim state on 23 March 1940 in its Lahore Resolution.

Written against the milieu of a ceaseless contest between the Congress and Muslim League, *Tamas* represents the climate of political tension and xenophobia and understands the catastrophe of Partition as an inevitable material outcome of a tradition of political suspicion and antagonism. The novel consists of political conflicts between Congress and Muslim League. While the Congress always claimed to represent all sections of the Indian society, Muslim League supporters and leaders were averse to such claims and instead, echoed the worldview of their leaders like Sir Syed Khan etc. Thus, in a fascinating passage, Sahni brings out a conversation involving both Congress and Muslim League supporters:

> One of them wore gold rimmed glasses and had a Rumi cap on his head. Planting himself in the middle of the lane, he said in a challenging voice: "The Congress party belongs to the Hindus. Muslims have nothing to do with it."
>
> "The Congress belongs to everyone!" an old man from among the singing party replied. "It belongs alike to the Hindus, the Muslims and the Sikhs. Mahmood Saheb, you're forgetting. Once you were also one of us."
>
> Walking up, the old man threw his arms around Mahmood Saheb and hugged him warmly.
>
> Disengaging himself from the old man's clasp, Mahmood said, "Bakshiji, I know your tricks. Whatever you may say, the Congress as a political party belongs exclusively to the Hindus. The Muslim League represents the Muslims. The Congress cannot lead the Muslims."
>
> *(Sahni 1998: 19)*

When Bakshiji challenges such a view by showing instances where different individuals from the Muslim community joined Congress, the answer of Mahmood is even harsher:

> "You can see for yourself," Bakshiji said, "we've Hindus, Sikhs and Muslims among us. There's Aziz standing over there and there's Hakimiji on his right – both Muslims."
>
> "They are the dogs of the Hindus. We don't hate the Hindus but we certainly hate their dogs."
>
> There was so much venom in Mahmood's voice that both Aziz and Hakimji felt deeply upset.
>
> "Is Maulana Azad a Hindu or a Muslim?" Bakshiji asked. "He's the President of the Congress party."
>
> "Maulana Azad is the biggest dog of the Hindus. He follows Mahatma Gandhi everywhere, wagging his tail."

28 Arnab Roy and Jaydip Sarkar

> Bakshiji said with a show of great patience. "Freedom will be for everybody. It will be for the whole of Hindustan."
> "The liberation of Hindustan will benefit the Hindus only. The Muslims can feel free only in Pakistan."
>
> *(Ibid.: 20)*

This unquestionably is a manifestation of the-then political current of the Muslim League which demanded the formation of new states based on religious identity. The hostility reaches to an inconceivable point where even the singing party, led by Congress, is debarred from entering a particular *moholla* that 'belonged' to the Muslims. Thus, the aspiration of the Muslim League to possess its own social and religious constituency is tellingly illustrated in this simple incident. In yet another shocking incident, one finds the heightening of this ensuing tension. The Congress party workers had started the cleaning of drains in Imamdin's *mohalla*. But they are advised to leave the place as their presence might create further hostility and a religious tension between the two communities:

> "Go away from here!" the old man again warned them. "You've already done sufficient mischief. Are you listening? I say, go away." He gave them a threatening look and walked away. A hush fell over the singing party. Mehta and Bakshi looked at each other.
>
> *(Ibid.: 33)*

Thus, *Tamas*, as a novel, presents the readers with a realistic political and social account that loomed large during the time of Partition across the country. The novel encompasses the role and involvement of the four major political organisations in the development of this narrative. Thus, the story of Partition, as depicted in this novel, is not confined within the circle of a Congress – Muslim League debate. Rather, it includes organisations like that of the Hindu Mahasabha, the Communist Party etc. It is undeniable that some of the political leaders of all sides perhaps were busy calculating the narrow and sectarian gains during the time of Partition. Thus, in a most dismal crisis, the religious leaders and the political organisations were not in a state to resolve the conflict between major religious communities. The secular forces and the communist party in turn played an influential role in promoting and maintaining religious harmony among different communities and the novel is strewn with such instances. Readers find a sense of urgency among the local communist party member like Devdutt to conduct a Peace Committee meeting:

> Comrade, if we can prevail upon them to sit together, that by it will have a salutary effect. It will be conducive to the establishment of a Peace Committee in the city. We can propagate the idea in every mohalla through a town–crier. What's happening at present? There's no wholesale rioting. We have only

stray cases of stabbing on both sides. It is essential that representatives of all the communities should sit together and try to resolve their differences …

(Ibid.: 90)

This reminds the readers of a significant role that these secular forces had played during Partition. Even in the meeting of the Peace Committee, when all other political organisations were preoccupied in reclaiming their position within the committee, it is Devdutt who proclaims:

If we argue in this manner we won't transact any business. We must wage a war against the communal elements. It is not necessary to represent each community on the Committee. The point is that the Peace Committee should take care of every interest and we should have faith that its members will be able to speak for the Hindus, the Muslims and the Sikhs alike. Keeping that aspect in view I suggest that Janab Hayat Buksh, Bakshiji and Giani Jodh Singh should be appointed as the Vice- Presidents of the Peace Committee.

(Ibid.: 159)

Bhisham Sahni aptly exposes the vices of communal politics and uncovers the role of different political organisations during Partition. There is no denying that this underlying current of the novel makes *Tamas* a political text. However, it must not be denied that the novel also seems to bring out Sahni's own political commitment. He was initially associated with the theatre group called IPTA. He also served as a translator in 'Foreign Language Publishing House', Moscow. His association with 'the Progressive Writer's Association' and 'Afro-Asian Writers Association' might have played an important role in shaping his political self.

The novel, simultaneously, with an unmistakable clarity, brings out the general nature of violence of Partition. Sahni depicts the climate of mistrust and uncertainty that exists in the town:

The limits of Hindu and Muslim mohallas had suddenly been clearly demarcated. The Hindus and the Sikhs dared not trespass into Muslim mohallas, or the Muslims into Hindu and Sikh lanes. Holding lathis and spears, people guarded the entrances to their lanes. Where Hindus and Muslims happened to live together, only one sentence was heard, uttered again and again, 'It's too bad! It's too bad!' Conversation in any case was spasmodic. Everyone seemed to know that what had happened was only the beginning. What was coming next?

(Ibid.: 79)

In an encumbered climate of hatred and communal intolerance, diverse religious groups were engaged in a culture of violence. It is in resonance with this evolving milieu of hatred that Devbrat examines young Ranvir's ability to nurture and execute violence:

30 Arnab Roy and Jaydip Sarkar

"Ranvir, kill the hen." Master Devbrat said. The chowkidar, handed Devbrat the knife. "Before you're initiated into our fold you must prove that you possess a stout heart."

Devbrat pushed Ranvir forward. "An Aryan youth must be strong in faith, resolute at heart, and determined in action. Take the knife and go and sit there!" He gave Ranvir another shove forward.

(Ibid.: 43)

Ranvir's turn towards a hatred-based politics, however, does not comfort his mother. In the middle of a riot-torn town, Ranvir does not come back home. His lamenting mother, engrossed by fear of riot and concerned about her son's safety, evokes pity in the reader's mind:

In the evening his friend came and told me that all the boys were with Masterji. Didn't I tell you that there was no need to make a brave Arya out of him? This is the time for him to study, eat and have some fun. But, no, you wouldn't listen to me. You drove him out every day to learn the drill, handle the lathi and God knows what else. It's a Muslim city and we have to live among Muslims all our lives. If one has to live in the sea one does not make enemies of the crocodiles. And now you'll rue the consequences.

(Ibid.: 77)

The text thus invokes and depicts a society endangered and engulfed by a culture of fear and the novelist depicts a worldview that is haunted by hatred and mutually directed violence. The vivid descriptions of communal riots explicate this phantasma of cruelty and in one such scene, Sahni represents the horror that persisted in the consciousness of the commoners. While returning from looting the houses of Sikhs, Ramzan sees a Shikh running for his life. This Sikh is none but Iqbal Singh, the son of Sardar Harnam Singh. After his father is brutally attacked, Iqbal Singh, terrified by the incident, attempts to escape by crouching inside a carter. Conversion to Islam is the only possible means of survival for Iqbal and he consequently becomes Sheikh Iqbal Ahmed:

Before nightfall all the signs of Iqbal Singh's Sikhism had been carefully obliterated; in their place were all the external Muslim signs. From an enemy he had been transformed into a friend, not an infidel, but a believer – a Mussalman. The doors of all Muslim houses were now open to him.

Lying on a cot Iqbal Ahmed passed the night in torment.

(Ibid.: 130)

Widespread violence on ethnic grounds was an everyday phenomenon during Partition. The catastrophe that was brought forth on women has been a subject of many narratives and accounts of Partition. Commenting on the nature of violence on women, Arunima Dey notes:

Political mayhems and moment of rupture **31**

This ethnic genocide witnessed two kinds of gender-based violence. Firstly, the violence inflicted on women by men of the opposite religious group that involved kidnapping, rape, and mutilation of the genitalia or public humiliation. The supposed aim of this kind of violence was to abase the men of the rival religion to which the women belonged. A second form of violence against women included the violence inflicted on women by their own family members. This could vary from honour killings to the insistence of male kin that their mothers, daughters, or wives commit suicide in order to safeguard the purity and chastity of the community. Both forms of violence substantiate the claim that women were not treated as humans but rather as markers of communal and national pride.

(Dey 2016: 104)

Women have been vulnerable and frequent victims in the catastrophe of Partition. For instance, in the scene quoted below, the readers find Sikh women in a Gurdwara collectively taking part in suicide to save their 'honour' from assaulting Muslims:

They made no sound as they advanced, oblivious to everything around them. Jasbir Kaur was the first to jump. She did not raise a slogan, or address any one. She simply said Vah Guru! quietly and leaped. As she fell, many more women climbed up on to the parapet of the well. Hari Singh's wife pulled up her four-year-old son after her and they jumped into the well together. Deva Singh's wife followed next, her infant clinging to her breast. Prem Singh's wife also jumped in, but her small son kept standing where he was looking down in utter bewilderment. Then Gyan Singh's wife pushed him in, ensuring that he joined his mother. Scores of women, with their children, followed.

(Sahni 1998: 135)

This incident undoubtedly seems to suggest the anguish that women of any community had to suffer and experience. The greatness of Sahni, as a novelist, resides in the fact that he could bring out this trauma of women during Partition. *Tamas* here transcends the boundary of a mere narrative and appears to authentically represent a historical catastrophe like Partition.

Most importantly, the central character Nathu experiences a psychic disorientation throughout the novel. The story begins with Nathu, a poor *chamar*, who is asked to kill a pig by Murad Ali. Murad lies that the pig is required by the veterinary doctor. Nathu kills the pig. The dead pig is then unceremoniously left on the steps of the mosque, a deliberate incident that entails a riot in the city. Nathu blames himself after such a revelation. All through the riots, he suffers the most and experiences a constant disillusionment. In a conversation with his wife, he laments: "If I had known, I would have kept away from such mischief" (ibid.: 101).

The mischief that would have otherwise caused a possible defamation of a community transforms into an irredeemable stimulant of genocide. It doesn't merely violate the epistemic imperatives and the fulcrum of faith that constitutes the discursive design of community. Rather, it dismantles the irreducible essence of humanity by the perpetration of violence on the bare subject/self. In this unforgiving dystopia, redemption from what has occurred is an impossibility. The irreversibility of the occurred is non-negotiable and the confessing self can only engage in a mourning that is heavily drawn upon the desire to autonomy. Nathu desires sovereignty, his lamentation that is premised on 'what if' foresees the possibility of a self who can exceed the aporia that the collective perennially has in store for the self and which the self in reality, can never transcend. Judith Butler rightly observes "The "I" is always to some extent dispossessed by the social conditions of its emergence" (Butler 2005: 8). This social is a relational arena where the collective and its ethos precede the self as a pre-discursive truth. The self is inescapably confined within the circumstantial limits of community. Thus, Nathu can merely, almost helplessly, observe the unfolding of the catastrophe with no possible agency to intervene and redeem the course of collective history. However, his moral consciousness and ethical sensibility remains unappropriated and unessentialised by the collective. It is in this departure that the possibilities of Nathu's sovereign agency sustain. For Butler, the "ethical deliberation" of the self is often characterised by a difference and "critique" (ibid.) that the self holds in consideration of the pre-dominating social. Nathu is disenfranchised in practice, he cannot yield form to or actualise his departure. Nevertheless, the departure sustains within the psychic contemplations of the self and the sacrosanct logos of regret. Shahni's novel imagines and locates such irreducible potencies and traces of humanity that do not actualise but manage to transgress the infernal real. These transgressions emerge as the repertoire of alternative history which has been excluded from the mainstream historiography of Partition. Nathu iconises millions of dispossessed and disenfranchised subjects who were apparently appropriated by the greater ideological fabric of the collective but whose possibilities of agency survived in the traces of guilt, shame, epiphany and the desire for an impossible redemption.

Note

1 The idea of the text has been problematised by literary and cultural scholars, ranging from Walter Benjamin to Edward Said. The text, as Said describes in his book *The World, The Text and The Critic*, is not a mere literary/ linguistic expression that is predominated by a print culture. Instead, he claims that the text is the result of an immediate contact between the author and the medium and which produces something as lively and transitory as a voice (32–33).

Works Cited

Anderson, Benedict. *Imagined Communities: Reflections on the Origin and Spread of Nationalism.* London: Verso, 1983.

Butalia, Urvashi. *The Other Side of Silence: Voices from the Partition of India.* Delhi: Penguin Books, 1998.

Butler, Judith. *Giving an Account of Oneself.* New York: Fordham University Press, 2005.

Desai, A.R. *Social Background of Indian Nationalism*. Mumbai: Popular Prakashan, 2010.

Dey, Arunima, "Violence against Women during the Partition of India: Interpreting Women and Their Bodies in the Context of Ethnic Genocide," *Revista de FilologiaInglesa*, 37 (2016), pp. 103–118.

Gilmartin, David. "The Historiography of India's Partition: Between Civilization and Modernity," *The Journal of Asian Studies*, 74:01 (February2015), pp 23–41.

Guha, Ramachandra. *Syed Ahmad Khan: The Muslim Modernist*. Delhi: Penguin Books. 2018.

Jiang, Lan and Yang Ya. "The Evolution of the British Indian Muslims' National Identity," *Cross Cultural Communication*, 12:8 (2016), pp. 36–42.

Malik, Hafeez (ed.). *Political Profile of Sir Sayyid Ahmad Khan: A Documentary Record*. New Delhi: Adam Publishers and Distributors, 2006.

Menon, Ritu, and Kamala Bhasin. *Borders and Boundaries: Women in India's Partition*. Delhi: Kali for Women, 1998.

Mittra, Sitansu Sekhar. *Bengal's Renaissance: An era of Multi-faceted growth*. Kolkata: Academic Publishers, 2001, pp. 7–8.

Nancy, Jean-Luc. *The Inoperative Community*. trans. and ed. Peter Connor. Minneapolis: University of Minnesota Press, 1991.

Pandey, Gyanendra. *Remembering Partition: Violence, Nationalism and History in India*. London: Cambridge University Press, 2001.

Roy, Rituparna. *South Asian Partition Fiction in English: From Khushwant Singh to Amitav Ghosh*. Amsterdam: Amsterdam University Press, 2010.

Sahni, Bhisham. *Tamas*. trans. Jai Ratan. New York: Penguin Books, 1988.

Said, Edward. *The World, the Text, and the Critic*. Cambridge, MA: Harvard University Press, 1983.

Shaikh, Farzana. "Muslims and Political Representation in Colonial India: The Making of Pakistan," *Modern Asia Studies*, 20:03 (1986), pp. 539–557.

Tudor, Maya. "Explaining Democracies Origins: Lessons from South Asia," *Comparative Politics*, 45:03 (April2013), pp. 253–272.

Veeser, H. Aram. *The New Historicism*. London: Routledge, 2013.

2

IDEOLOGY OF HATRED AND THE VIOLENT MAKING OF NATIONS

Khushwant Singh's *Train to Pakistan*

Shirsendu Mondal

It is difficult to conceive of Indian Partition as the inescapable event of our cultural inheritance. To acknowledge that the two modern nation states of today were born in bloody bestiality is indeed an unsettling experience. The task of transcribing Partition violence is certainly more painful as the hauntings of history intrude into the transcribing moment of the temporal 'now.' As such, the remonstrating/writing subject lacks the necessary objectivity that one is likely to possess in his/her engagement with the 'occurred.' Instead, the occurred intrudes into the living present and affects the materiality of the now that contains the remonstrating self. The self encounters an impossibility of transcription. Ted Svensson identifies this impossibility as a probable explanation to the relative silence of the post-1947 Indian scholarship on the human dimension of the atrocities during the days of Partition. Referring to Veena Das's essay "The Anthropology of Pain," Svensson suggests that "the magnitude of violence and pain itself partly extinguished language and the possibility to communicate the experience" (Svensson 2013: 50).

Partition and its climate of violence was a regressive age of animalistic primitivism. It was one of those rare occasions when people recognised the inadequacy of imagination to fathom the extent of cruelty human beings were capable of. We would love to have obliterated the chapter from the register of our embittered memory. Erasing the record clean by way of disowning responsibility of the entire course of events would be one way of negotiating with a traumatic past. But this could be justifiable if the violence was undisputedly proven to have been an exception, an aberration, a rarest of the rare phenomenon, experienced at an unusual juncture of human history and most importantly unprecedented. A distinct line of nationalist historiography followed this agenda of portraying the Partition violence as something extraneous to the essential harmony of Indian pluralism. It emphasised the peace-loving nature of Indian people and how the communities, divided by religion, had been continually living with each other since ancient times. Only this time, it claimed, something went seriously wrong, loosening the wildest frenzy of violence which, at a later date, was unthinkable even to the perpetrators of it. This particular period was abnormal and therefore, not representative of history. Gyanendra Pandey perceives that this line of thought aimed at "justifying or eliding, what is seen in the main as being an illegitimate outbreak of violence" by denying the truism that "violence and community constitute one another" (Pandey 2008: 3).

The epoch of Partition was a period of diabolical insanity. To date, people experiencing the cataclysm at close quarters find it impossible to explain the reality in a more comprehensive manner. This description of the time attempts to negotiate with an extremity which unhinges mind and confounds reason. It is, however, entirely different from choosing an expression to disown or at least dissociate from the loot, arson, rape and genocide which were committed by those ordinary, sociable, law-abiding next-door neighbours. That Partition became synonymous with violence and at times surpassed the atrocities of the Holocaust can be substantially accounted for by the complete withdrawal of British administrative control and the failure of Indian politics to assess and manage the fallout of this monumental blunder. Neeti Nair argues that more than religious fundamentalism, Partition violence was "a tragic consequence of a breakdown in political negotiations," involving the British, the Congress and the Muslim League. The absence of martial law and the reluctance of the British to stay until the sharing of resources between the Nations were seen through – the shameful hurried scuttle that Churchill had feared – resulted in havoc (Nair 2011: 9, 179–218). These factors had tremendous impact upon the pervasive anarchy and the ensuing dystopia. Nevertheless, the terror was fundamentally bred in and was inflicted by the savage intolerance of the familiar mass. Consequently, the polarisation of social life into communities governed by religious affiliation was complete.

It is difficult to understand why people of different religions, irrespective of provocation and instinctual survival drive, engaged in such a random, thoughtless killing spree. The perpetrators themselves, in retrospect, found no words to explain their acts except that they had no control over the sweeping hatred (Butalia 1998: 71). Partition violence was an encounter with the darker side of one's own being: in a bizarre defamiliarisation of the stable and the known, an ordinary individual could see the potential murderer within him.

To look into ways in which common citizens recognised the explosive revulsion within them for members of another community and how they were utterly transformed by the disturbed imaginings of near extinction makes a relevant study. It is of momentous importance to know how people, sharing similar social-cultural values, were overtaken by virulent hate and suddenly turned into predators. Reading *Train to Pakistan* from this perspective reveals several fissures and faults along the fabric of social relations. If the much-vaunted legacy of a pluralistic Indian culture has been the spontaneous outcome of a broad-based egalitarian society, the seeds of mistrust and intolerance among the Hindus, Muslims and the Sikhs have also been bred by the dark underside of the same society. The much-vaunted harmony

36 Shirsendu Mondal

of Indian multiculturalism and its copious accommodativeness suddenly appears to be a delusive chimera. Bir Bahadur Singh, one of the many victims of Partition whom Butalia interviewed, recounts how the Hindus of his time would customarily treat the Muslims with utter contempt (Butalia 1998: 39–40).

The situation of East Bengal was no different. Identical responses of repulsion and hostility towards the religious 'other' dominated the prevalent social–cultural milieu of the then Bengali society. Bid Chakrabarty quotes from Mrinal Sen's memoir as the latter's mother faced the uncomfortable questions of poet Jasimuddin who was brought up in Sen's family at Faridpur but was "never integrated with the family as a Hindu would have been" (Chakrabarty 2004: 42). Such humiliations of ostracism and the resultant striving to reclaim an Islamic supremacy over the Hindus definitely had its part in Muslim rigidity and wiliness against Hindu politics in the 1940s. Riots like The Great Calcutta Killing, which is commonly considered to have set in motion the bloodbath, witnessed the all-consuming fire of hatred (Talbot 2007: 193). This perhaps has been our blighted legacy of communal harmony in India.

In independent India, religious and ethnic communities have continued to engage in bloody strife since the days of Partition. Instances are not limited to the large scale massacres of Sikh extermination in 1984 and the Gujarat riot in 1992 following the demolition of Babri Mosque. Religious, communal and ethnic violence has been a routine occurrence in the country. As testified by the Ministry of Home Affairs in the Parliament on 6 February 2018, a staggering 822 violent incidents have occurred in the country in 2017, killing at least 111 people and leaving 2,384 others injured (BS Web Team 2018). Neither the succeeding generation nor the emergence of a vibrant, cosmopolitan youth culture has quite overcome the deadly legacy of mutual hatred and mistrust lying beneath the surface of a general tranquillity. We have been living and still live a perennially partitioned and violent life in the subcontinent (Butalia 1998: 3–26).

Train to Pakistan has held an iconic status in the rich body of Partition literature not merely because it 'documents' the history of carnage that bought independence for the two countries, but because it offers a counter-narrative to the nationalist historiography by revealing the horror of violence unleashed by ordinary people. The novel, rooted in the everyday experience, becomes a site of polyphonic and contested articulation of identity (Didur 2006: 6). More importantly, the novel explains the complex dynamics of social relations through which the trajectories of gnawing suspicion flow into the fury of violence. It follows the gaping fissure along the surface of cross-religious transactions until it bursts open in violent severance.

Yet, *Train to Pakistan* is not history but a work of fiction. Jugga badmush, the rogue, a seasoned criminal with an arbitrary moral behaviour, sacrifices his life for a poor Muslim girl and eventually saves thousands of lives. Jugga's sacrifice can be read as a profound assertion of our belief in humanity in times of adversity, but it does not sufficiently assure us of the inherent goodness of man. The historical reality of Partition violence puts the bare unaccommodated man before stark and crudest ways of surviving, even survival by killing or being complicit to it. In reality, almost all men in the rank of Jugga, would do just the opposite of what Jugga did. It would be a facile observation, as Rituparna Roy did, to assert a triumph of faith over despair as the novel concludes with a note of positivism:

> Unlike other bhasa writers of the time, he (Khuswant) is not completely taken up with just the violence, for he also redeems a sense of faith in essential humanity at the end of the novel through the figure of Jugga. Indeed, it must have been very difficult to take such a stance at the time the novel was written, a difficulty that is borne out by the fact that very few of his contemporaries were able to do this.
>
> *(Roy 2010: 24)*

Jugga's heroism, at best, is part of those stray instances of loving mankind that feature as exceptions to the general fury of the time. The passengers on trains to Pakistan, on most occasions, were massacred in much the same fashion as on the train to India that pulled up at Mano Majra station a few days earlier with 1,500 corpses on board. Nisid Hajari, in *Midnight's Furies*, attempts to recreate by piecing together evidences, the actual derailment of a Pakistan Special train and the massacre of its Muslim passengers on the night of 9 August 1947 near Giddarbaha (Hajari 2015: 8–11). Against the whirlwind of raging hatred, no superhuman saviour like Sardar Juggat Singh and his monumental sacrifice stood before the mayhem to foil it.

If Jugga's heroic sacrifice is an exceptional instance, Mano Majra, remaining unaffected for so long by the communal disturbances all around, is another fortunate exception. I believe one possible explanation is that under a predominant land-owning Sikh community, the Muslim tenants never enjoyed autonomy of articulation. The text is mostly crowded with the confident Sikh members of the village and although Imam Baksh features prominently in the crowd, his poverty, his hoary age and his benignity as a pious, harmless Muslim makes him a subject of pity. The Muslim subject of Mano Majra is archetyped as disenfranchised and dependent on the benevolence of the dominant Sikh clan.

The resounding proclamation of friendship and brotherhood uttered before Imam Baksh soon gives way to a sweeping, generalised hatred against Muslims. The solidarity, nurtured with compassionate camaraderie by a handful of village headmen, is suddenly made vulnerable and is believed to be a fatal weakness of the Sikhs as new and aggressive voices threaten to take over. The notion that the other can go down into a primordial cut-throat antagonism – that the Muslims are acting on a potentially subversive plot of consuming the Hindus – is the persistent anxiety of the majority. Adhering blindly to unwarranted social knowledge of Muslim belligerence and their inherent criminality, this ideology constructs reality for the dominant at the social level. While herd instinct unifies the population, friendship is destroyed by socially engineered mistrust extended to the religious other (Shaban 2018: 1–22). The mass ascribes ubiquitous generalisation of enmity to a community and does not care to distinguish the good from the evil within it. The two constables carrying Jugga and Iqbal have this to say about fellow Muslim police persons:

38 Shirsendu Mondal

"On the day of Independence, the Superintendent sahib disarmed all Muslim policemen and they fled. Their intentions were evil. Muslims are like that. You can never trust them."

"Yes," added another policeman, "it was the Muslim police taking sides which made the difference in the riots. Hindu boys of Lahore would have given the Muslims hell if it had not been for their police. They did a lot of *zulum*."

(Singh 1956: 64)

Later on, for the Muslims of the village, "every Sikh in Mano Majra became a stranger with an evil intent" and the Sikhs reiterate their conviction, "Never trust a Mussulman" (Ibid.: 113). Jugga recounts the retreat of a truckload of Baluch soldiers who rampantly killed Sikh refugees on the way before being killed in an accident near the border. For the common villagers like Jugga and Bhola, this is reprisal administered by God. Iqbal is surprised to note that the same retributive role of God is not invoked when Bhola, the tonga driver, tells them about the armed Sikhs mowing down Muslim refugees as they ambush the hapless members of a trudging Kafila. The condemnation of the act is only muted with a soft platitude that "bad acts yield a bitter harvest."

The undeniable proof of Muslim atrocities (as they send a trainload of corpses) could be enough to instigate the Mano Majra Sikhs against the native Muslims. Yet, some of them still retain the sanity of not implicating the innocent Muslims at home with the crimes of other Muslims elsewhere. The mass, however, smugly continues to identify each Mussulman with the idea of a brutal, complicit community – a ferocious Islamic brotherhood. Every unique inter-religious social relationship, every ceremony of innocence above religion is being drowned by the group identification applied to all and sundry. Bhai Meet Sing, the man of reason and compassion, desperately confronts the rumbling of change in attitudes towards the native Muslims. Clearly he cannot cope with the changing time that subsumes identity under religious affiliation in an extremely polarised society.

"Our problem is: what are we to do with all these pigs we have with us? They have been eating our salt for generations and see what they have done! We have treated them like our own brothers. They have behaved like snakes."

The temperature of the meeting went up suddenly. Meet Singh spoke angrily.

"What have they done to you? Have they ousted you from your lands or occupied your houses? Have they seduced your womenfolk? Tell me, what have they done?"

"Ask the refugees what they have done to them," answered the truculent youth who had started the argument. "You mean to tell us that they are lying when they say that gurdwaras have been burned and people massacred?"

"I was only talking of Mano Majra. What have our tenants done?"

"They are Muslims."

(Ibid.: 115)

Hukum Chand, the Deputy Magistrate of Chundannagore, capitalises on this unbridgeable gulf between the Sikhs and the Muslims to ensure that there is no 'incident' of riot in Mano Majra. It is a sardonic reality that the mutual antagonism responsible for all the bloodshed is now manipulated to avoid bloodshed at Mano Majra and the adjoining areas. In hindsight, Hukum Chand seems aware that rupture, at times, can be infinitely more productive than harmony, especially when the harmony requires the stretching of one's capacity to rise above sectarianism. Harmony and inter-religious friendships, the opposites of rupture, are peace-time affairs, but for wartime exigency, it is best to keep the warring parties separate. Until now, Mano Majra has been untouched by the disturbances all around, but this exceptional status of the habitation is now most likely to be consumed up by eruptions of hatred underlying the surface because it does not fall in line with the reigning separatist ideology. As an administrator, Hukum Chand is oppressed with the burden of saving Muslim lives:

> He believed that an individual's conscious effort should be directed to immediate ends like saving life when endangered, preserving the social structure and honouring its conventions. His immediate problem was to save Muslim lives. He would do that in anyway he could.
>
> *(Ibid.: 93)*

However, Hukum Chand releases the culprits and circulates, through subtle machination, the knowledge that the murder was committed by the notorious Muslim criminal Sultana who has fled to the safety of Pakistan. It testifies that the administration, operating within the blind unscrupulousness of the masses, shared the same ideology of mistrust for the Muslim community. What is perhaps more important is that the little deceit of Hukum Chand reveals the gaping hollow between the communities which, until then, has been hidden under a ramshackle surface. The following excerpts validate the claim:

> Quite suddenly, every Sikh in Mano Majra became a stranger with an evil intent. His long hair and beard appeared barbarous, his kirpan menacingly anti-Muslim. For the first time, the name Pakistan came to mean something to them – a refuge where there were no Sikhs.
>
> *(Ibid.: 113)*

> Now a trainload of Sikhs massacred by Muslims had been cremated in Mano Majra. Hindus and Sikhs were fleeing from their homes in Pakistan and having to find shelter in Mano Majra. Then there was the murder of Ram Lal. No one knew who had killed him, but everyone knew Ram Lal was a Hindu; Sultana and his gang were Muslims and had fled to Pakistan … Muslims were basely ungrateful.
>
> *(Ibid.: 113)*

40 Shirsendu Mondal

The Sikhs and the Muslims are now antagonised within a climate of mistrust where an unbridgeable rift functions within the material and psychic imaginary of Mano Majra. The climactic subversive mission is lent support by the same knowledge of a deeply embedded fissure in the social structure. The young men, who arrive at the dead of the night to incite the villagers to kill a trainload of Muslim refugees, are confident about making a complicit audience out of ordinary people. In India, fanaticism has never been far removed from religiosity, and pride over racial superiority has defined community identity. A good portion of the listeners, roused by the impassioned reproach for cowardice and mythical tales of their Guru betrayed by Muslims, suddenly feel themselves terribly insecure with the Muslims. The Sikh refugees migrating to Mano Majra, who are still strangers to them, are felt closer to heart than an Imam Baksh. An imagined community has popped up, replacing the real community of long-held social relations.

As usual with most hate speech, the speaker presses for greater retribution for the massacre of Sikh and Hindu refugees in Pakistan. In his exchange with Bhai Meet Singh, he avoids contesting the 'legitimacy' of killing the innocent for somebody else's crime. The counter discourse, spiced up with a jingoistic war cry, solely relies on the retributive logic of blood for blood, even if that involves execution of the innocent. Meet Singh interjects:

> "What have the Muslims here done to us for us to kill them in revenge for what Muslims in Pakistan are doing? Only people who have committed crimes should be punished."
>
> The lad glared angrily at Meet Singh. "What had the Sikhs and Hindus in Pakistan done that they were butchered? Weren't they innocent? Had the women committed crimes for which they were ravished? Had the children committed murder for which they were spiked in front of their parents?"
>
> *(Ibid.: 138)*

Historians observe that more often than not, Partition violence reflected an organised and systematic method of annihilation in which both the Hindus and the Muslims carried out the task with meticulous planning. The rioters included a significant number of hardened criminals. The violence provided them with the opportunity to settle personal scores and make fortunes out of loot and plunder. Notwithstanding their presence in the mob, the leaders, without a concern for material gain, were motivated to kill by a sense of sacred duty. The young adolescent leaders on their mission in *Train to Pakistan* are city-bred educated people with money and influence. Presumably they also have the sympathy of the local police and military, and these departments, by now, have been cleared of the presence of Muslim employees. It is likely that the youth neither suffered personal losses nor could directly identify themselves with the cause for retribution. They are outsiders with no knowledge of the delicate ties and conflicts of inter-religious social mixing. They draw upon the stereotypes of masculinity – revenge being interpreted as virility, courage and glorious sacrifice – with a heady dose of clan kinship. That they are more methodical than mad and approach the task with almost a philosophical indifference is a matter of greater concern for an introspecting reader of Partition. The simple village folks prove easily susceptible to the incitement because the threat to survival, imagined or real, from the religious other has traditionally shaped the existential fear of man. The idea that the enemy is lurking at the corner to deliver the fatal blow unmistakably draws a brutal response to eliminate the threat. The young Sikh leader says:

> "For each Hindu or Sikh they kill, kill two Mussulmans. For each woman they abduct or rape, abduct two. For each home they loot, loot two. For each trainload of dead they send over, send two across. For each road convoy that is attacked, attack two. That will stop the killing on the other side. It will teach them that we also play this game of killing and looting."
>
> *(Ibid.: 137)*

Partition violence legitimised itself as the attack of one aggressive religion over a 'tolerant' other and vice versa. Indeed religious difference appeared as the paramount factor behind the outbreak of riot and bloodshed. Yet difference of religion, though more sensitive than most others, is one among a number of differences dividing people. Reading through *Train to Pakistan* and other accounts of Partition violence, one may wonder whether violence requires any self-justifying logic. Wading through the blood and mire with the interminable cycles of bloodshed, the logic of difference actually disappears with the unrestrained indulgence to the bestial and the brute in man. A mob on rampage can be swayed to construct enemies with any or no difference whatsoever so long as it finds an 'other' to vent its anger. The target may shift to Dalits, Adivasis, linguistic minorities, immigrants, migrants and any other social groups that have a distinctive identity. Modern India has been a witness that xenophobia and chauvinism is never limited to religious difference only. Controversies over linguistic right, ethnic identity, territorial demand, economic and social exploitation have frequently led to riots and carnage among people irrespective of religion. D.N. Panigrahi quotes Lord Wavell's cogent assessment that the

> root of political conflict so far as the leaders are concerned lies in the fear of economic domination rather than difference of religion. It has been found that Hindus and Muslims can live together without conflict where there is no fear of economic and political domination, e.g., in the army.
>
> *(Panigrahi 2004: 312)*

The covert British policy in the post-war scenario to carve out a separate favoured nation of Pakistan out of a hostile India, perfectly synchronised with a belligerent Muslim League demand and the British governance had looked for far-reaching benefits to make the most of the opportunity (Sarila 2005: 15–32). The British encouragement and the League propaganda resulted in a cataclysmic disjunction of minds. If the fragile harmony of Mano Majra is wrecked from within by the social ideology of hatred, the narrow politics of wielding power hasten its downfall.

The politics of constructing the 'other' is fundamentally a question of power (Tripathi 2016: 10). The predominant social superiority of the Hindu majority was suddenly under threat in the wake of a demand for a separate Muslim state. The Muslims politics, on the other hand, did all it could to infuse the consternation that a liberated India would crush all aspirations of its minority Muslim inhabitants (Panigrahi 2004: 308). Jinnah, in his bid for political ambition, spearheaded and crystallised the movement with a two-nation theory that drew upon the essential difference of two sets of people (Hajari 2015: 26). Jinnah's political goal and ambition had undergone a complete transformation in the years leading to the transfer of power. A man who had once been a steadfast Congress ideologue, advocating the consolidation of Hindu–Muslim unity that the British had been trying to split, Jinnah suddenly became the principal exponent for a separatist demand (Sarila 2005: 63–96). It is surprising that the alleged differences of the two religious communities, necessitating the slicing up of India, never featured in Jinnah's political outlook two decades back. If differences were so overpowering, they must have been as true in the 1920s as they were in 1940s. The implacable political ideology for the creation of a mythical pure Pakistan was developed, disseminated and fed with in a relatively shorter span of time. Jinnah made minor differences astronomical and encouraged intolerance to conclusively prove that the two communities could not stay together. Of course, this was carefully garbed in anxiety over the feared enslavement of the Muslims by the Hindus relegating them to second-class citizens in a free India. He was encashing hatred in his bargain for power. Violence became the tool for procuring the demand for Pakistan (Khan 2017: 66–80). In *A Bend in the Ganges* (1957), Shafi, the militant revolutionary, is bewildered by hearing Hafiz advise him to reorient his fury against the Hindus instead of the British: "'Our methods remain as they are; only our targets have changed. We have to be ready to use the same methods against the Hindus'" (Malgonkar 1964: 86). When Shafi, in great fear, points out that the changing strategy will only bring civil war to the country, Hafiz laughs arrogantly and says:

> "That is exactly what we have to prepare ourselves for, a civil war. We have to think ahead, one year, two years from now, to a time when the British will leave this country, leaving our fate in the hands of the Hindus. Are we to sit back and take whatever indignities they have in store for us? We must hit back ten-fold."
>
> *(Ibid.)*

The political ideology of violence and hatred thriving on the social rupture suddenly ushers Mano Majra into the whirlwind of genocide. Had the train been attacked, it would have spawned more massacres in the self-perpetuating dynamic of violence and another Rawalpindi or Bhawalpur or Garhmukteswar would have ensued in direct response. The train is saved in this instance, but what could possibly save the permanent partitioning of consciousness? One man and his doctrine of non-violence took up the staggering task of ridding people of the evil of hatred, but failed miserably. Gandhi's non-violence revealed an incapability to fathom the roots of bottled-up violence in the interstices of society. Yet, in spite of the controversy over his leadership in the violent years before the transfer of power, Gandhi had at least fought violence by all means. Against the surging tide of conflagration engulfing the nooks and corners of the vast country; the small, meagre acts of conscious opposition to violence could only have kept the spirit of antithesis alive.

For those who retained sanity in the pervading madness, the incapacity of putting up meaningful resistance to the mayhem did really open up lasting wounds in their guilt-ridden conscience. The realisation that they stopped short of the active intervention which would normally be expected of a sensitive individual plunged them into a despairing trauma. It is easy to sneer at Iqbal's vain, self-gratifying philosophising at a moment of dire crisis, but protecting one's own life, that irresistible penchant for survival, can hardly be labelled as escapism (ibid.: 155–157). In the novel the Deputy Magistrate Hukum Chand and his police are acutely aware of their precarious lack of reinforcement. In the process of evacuating the Chandunnagore refugees safely out of the country, they brave the wrath of thousands of murderous people. The fury of the mob, gathering power with more men volunteering, is about to overpower the puny vestiges of government authority. Even so, Hukum Chand and his subordinates stretch beyond their politically correct positions to foil the attack on the train to Pakistan. And Hukum Chand grieves that their efforts are too small for the onslaught. The question remains: what can one do in such circumstances? How can one possibly justify the inaction to get rid of an overpowering sense of guilt? The Deputy Magistrate observes ruefully:

> "What can we do? Everyone has gone trigger-happy. People empty their rifle magazines into densely packed trains, motor convoys, columns of marching refugees, as if they were squirting red water at the Holi festival; it is a bloody Holi. What sense is there in going to a place where bullets fly? ... No, Inspector Sahib, the only thing a sane person can do in a lunatic asylum is to pretend that he is as mad as the others and at the first opportunity scale the walls and get out."
>
> *(Ibid.: 143)*

Perhaps the only antithesis to the discourse of hatred lies in the irredeemable 'transgressions' of human agents forging emotional ties with the 'other.' Jugga fights for his poor Muslim girl Nooran, his mother's stiff resistance melts and gives way to Nooran's plea and Hukum Chand, the big man of authority, is left languishing with an irredeemable love and affection for an ordinary prostitute girl, Haseena. All the while, at least two persons will be heard praying fervently for love and togetherness, they are Imam Baksh and Bhai Gurmeet Singh.

Works Cited

BS Web Team. "111 People Killed in 822 Communal Incidents in 2017; UP Tops List," *Business Standard*, (7 February2018). https://www.business-standard.com/article/current-affairs/india-not-safe-under-modi-govt-2017-sees-822-communal-riots-up-tops-list-118020700474_1.html (accessed 14 June 2018).

Butalia, Urvashi. *The Other Side of Silence*. New Delhi: Penguin Books, 1998.

Chakrabarty, Bid. *The Partition of Bengal and Assam, 1932–1947*. London: Routledge Curzon, 2004.

Didur, Jill. *Unsettling Partition: Literature, Gender, Memory*. Toronto: University of Toronto Press, 2006.

Hajari, Nisid. *Midnight's Furies*. Boston, MA: Houghton Mifflin Harcourt, 2015.

Khan, Yasmin. *The Great Partition*. New Haven, CT: Yale University Press, 2017.

Malgonkar, Manohar. *A Bend in the Ganges*. London: Hamish Hamilton, 1964. E-book, digitised by Digital Library of India Item 2015.207484. https://archive.org/details/in.ernet.dli.2015.207484 (accessed 16 June 2018).

Nair, Neeti. *Changing Homelands: Hindu Politics and the Partition of India*. Cambridge, MA: Harvard University Press, 2011.

Pandey, Gyanendra. *Remembering Partition*. New Delhi: Cambridge University Press, 2008.

Panigrahi, D.N. *India's Partition: The Story of Imperialism in Retreat*. London and New York: Routledge, 2004.

Roy, Rituparna. *South Asian Partition Fiction in English*. Amsterdam: Amsterdam University Press, 2010.

Sarila, Narendra Singh. *The Shadow of the Great Game: the Untold Story of India's Partition*. New Delhi: Harper Collins Publishers, 2005.

Shaban, Abdul (ed.). *The Lives of Muslims in India*. London: Routledge, 2nd edn, 2018.

Singh, Khuswant. *Train to Pakistan*. New Delhi: Penguin, 1956. E-book in pdf. https://archive.org/stream/TrainToPakistan-English/Train-To-Pakistan#page/n3/mode/2up (accessed 3 June 2018).

Svensson, Ted. *The Production of Postcolonial India and Pakistan*. London and New York: Routledge, 2013.

Talbot, Phillips. *An American Witness to Indian Partition*. New Delhi: Sage Publications, 2007.

Tripathi, R.C. "Violence and the Other: Contestations in a Multicultural Society," in *Perspectives on Violence and Othering in India*, ed. R C. Tripathi and Purnima Singh. New Delhi: Springer, 2016. https://link.springer.com/chapter/10.1007/978-81-322-2613-0_1 (accessed 16 June 2018).

3

PARTITION AND THE SHATTERED FAMILIAR

Bapsi Sidhwa's *The Ice-Candy Man*

Rupayan Mukherjee

> Is there a way to tell your daughter what it is like to sew a few jewels in your petticoat and close the door on a whole life? To hide in ditches, body spread over the babies? To watch a friend be raped and to be silent?
>
> *(Prajna Paramita Parasher, "A Long Walk Out from Partition")*

In his characteristic dark-humoured and austere political response to the Paris massacres of 2015, Slavoj Žižek, the Slovenian psychoanalyst and cultural critic, draws our attention to the impossibility of empathising/sympathising with a sublime narrative of human catastrophe. Žižek remarks

> The formula of pathetic identification "I am" only functions within certain limits, beyond which it turns into obscenity ... Such identification becomes obscene in the case of Muselmanner, the living dead in Auschwitz. It's not possible to say: "We are all Muselmanner!" In Auschwitz, the dehumanization of victims went so far that identifying with them in any meaningful sense is impossible.
>
> *(Žižek 2015: 1)*

Žižek argues that it is impossible to contextualise a 'sublime' human catastrophe and that all renderings of the historical reality in literary and cultural representations disempower history of its intensities of sufferings and misgivings. Ranjan Ghosh, borrowing L.P. Harley's phrase from *The Go-Between*, describes history as a 'foreign country' (Ghosh 2012: 1) and representations, no matter how authentic it claims itself to be, can never accommodate the disturbing surplus of history, that element of the alien within its aesthetic boundaries and fictional territory. For Žižek, the attempt to accommodate this surplus, the inexpressible, only puts the cart before the horse. It changes the dynamics of valorisation as the ecstasy of catharsis silences the tragedy of the real, the actual and the historical. In other words, it is the

46 Rupayan Mukherjee

fictional impressions of the real, the documented, registered, narrativised history that surpasses the historical real. Žižek sensitively points this out in his discussion on Hegel and his (Hegel's) appreciation of the Peloponnesian war and Thucydides' consequent historicisation of it. Hegel praises Thucydides' foundational work *The Peloponnesian War* as a work "of absolute gain which humanity has derived from that contest" (Hegel 2001: 285). Žižek is critical of Hegel's didactic, telocentric ideal of history as he writes:

> One should read this (*The Peloponnesian War* as absolute gain) judgement in all its naivety: in a way from the standpoint of world history the Peloponnesian war took place so that Thucydides could write a book about it. The term "absolute" should also be given its due: from the relative perspective of our finite human interests, the numerous tragedies of the Peloponnesian war (the suffering and devastation it caused) are, of course, infinitely more important than a mere book; from the standpoint of Absolute, however, it is the book that matters.
>
> *(Žižek 2010: 315)*

The Indian Partition and the consequent exodus and the massacre of humanity occupies a historically distinct position in cultural and material history and historiography. While scholars, historians, poets, filmmakers, novelists and critics have rigorously researched on and contributed to the many dimensions, perspectives, implications and effects of Partition, they have also unconsciously incurred upon themselves the responsibility of mythologising Partition. It is no longer a historical happening, which is real, objective and a catastrophe of the distant past, but has become the inextricable ritual of everyday living. Partition, thus borrowing the words of the French thinker Jean-Luc Nancy, can safely be inferred to have been occupying a "mythic status" (Nancy 1991: 48) in the history of the subcontinent. Mythologies do not necessarily de-historicise the historical, the historical can safely reside in simultaneity with the mythic. At times, the historical even trespasses into the discursive corridors of mythologies, without being compromised or robbed of its historicity. Roland Barthes rightly points out "mythology can only have a historical foundation" (Barthes 1972: 108). Myths and histories are not antagonistic or hostile to one another's authenticity and they do not necessarily jeopardise each other; they are rather complementary. The mythic has to do instead with the modes of representation, it is the representational politik that determines the mythicness of myth.

The Partition of India and its subsequent treatment in theory and fiction has mythologised it. But what is interesting to note in this context is the fact that the mythologisation of the Partition of India happened simultaneously in the engaging attempts to historicise the sublime reality of Partition. Peter Novick observes "To understand something historically, is to be aware of its complexity ... to see it from multiple perspectives, to accept the ambiguities, including moral ambiguities, of protagonists, motives and behavior" (Novick 1999: 3–4). These complexities, these unregistered tremors, are experiences that representations (which include visual and textual) on Partition registers.

The historical reality of Partition is thus haunted by an element of an excess imaginary, which can be considered as a *dangerous supplement*, that representation seeks to unveil. The discursive sovereignty of representation and its potential to imagine history provokes the possibility of culmination of the historical as trans-historic. The trans-historic contains an excess that the historical never overtly declares or affirms. This excess isn't necessarily unhistorical, but is also simultaneously conceived, reshaped, discursively formulated and nurtured through the medium of representation. Representation explores the fissures of history and thereby often attempts to invent history, something that is typical of post-structuralism and postmodernism. Pierre Nora, in exploring the postmodern tendencies on historiography coins the idea of the "new historian," who is a new kind of historian, "prepared, unlike his predecessors, to avow his close, intimate, and personal ties to his subject," one who is "entirely dependent on his subjectivity, creativity, and capacity to re-create" (Nora 1996: 5–7). Such ficto-factual renderings of history, which Rigney calls 'imperfect histories' (2001: 2) provoke an "alternative cultural history" (ibid.) and are often a precondition to historicise the sublime tragedy of Partition. It is through these unreliabilities and uncertainities that the historical event of Partition has become a myth.

Urvashi Butalia calls these unreliable histories the 'underside of history' (1998: 10) and argues that they make up the 'human dimensions' (ibid.: 7) of history which explore not just sanctified and validated historical facts but human experience of the great derangement called Partition. These invalid yet provocative, unsound yet true renderings of histories become important in a discourse like Partition, which is not merely a history of occurrence but is also a history of experience. In Butalia's words, this underside of history comprises of micro-histories about

> how families were divided, how friendships endured across borders, how people coped with the trauma, how they rebuilt their lives, what resources, both physical and mental, they drew upon, how their experience of dislocation and trauma shaped their lives, and indeed the cities and towns and villages they settled in.
>
> *(Ibid.: 9)*

All of which "find little reflection in written history." Butalia, in excavating these 'other histories' or the other side of history, becomes Nora's 'new historian.'

Sukeshi Kamra observes that the historicisation of Partition today has started to rely increasingly on personal experiences and that representation has consistently contributed to the growing histories of Partition. She observes,

> There is a significant body of Partition literature, and a number of films have appeared in recent years in which 1947 is remembered primarily for partition. We have learned much from these about the depths of human misery, degradation and of the depravity that defied the symbolically charged moment of independence from colonial rule.
>
> *(Kamra 2015: 156)*

48 Rupayan Mukherjee

But the problem that was hinted at the start of this chapter survives: how does representation translate the unimaginable, the loss and the de-functional humanity within the economy of language and expression? Andreas Huyssen, in a discussion on Art Spiegelman's *Maus* (a graphic novel based on the Holocaust) observes: "Since the 1980s, the question is no longer whether, but rather how to represent the Holocaust in literature, film and the visual arts" (Huyssen 2000: 65).

How does representation translate the horror of a human catastrophe without falling within the pitfalls of sentimental idealisation and cathartic redemptive pretensions? Does representation in its attempt to explore the other side of histories only end up in becoming 'modern forms of catharsis'? Or is representation as disturbing as the reality of the represented, so much so, that it creates a coherent, parallel world of dystopia in which the text gathers a tragic autonomy of its own and in doing so, is able to make the ravages of history relevant even within the unfamiliar and strictly artificial spaces of 'postmemory' (Hirsch n.d.). Through a reading of Bapsi Sidhwa's Partition novel *The Ice-Candy Man*, this chapter attempts to address these questions.

Sidhwa's novel *The Ice-Candy Man* was published in 1988 and is considered a seminal text on Partition. The novel captures the dark, sinister and dystopic world of Partition, where the familiar slithers into the terrain of unfamiliarity, where the self is estranged or exiled at home and the home gradually becomes an unfamiliar 'other.' It sets up a contrast between the small and sensitive, the 'compressed' yet personal world of Lenny and the changing political terrains of the Nation founded on the discourses of power, conflict and violence. Sidhwa's novel follows the structure of a bildungsroman, mimicking or parodying (if not consciously) its generic features. George Lukacs defines the bildungsroman as a genre that reconciles the "problematic individual, guided by his experience of the ideal, with concrete social reality." (Lukacs 1971: 132). Lukacs further extends his generic contemplation and argues that there are two contrasting world orders in the bildungsroman, the world of interiority and the world of reality, which, no matter how opposing, demand reconciliation.

The Ice-Candy Man, following the generic pattern of a bildungsroman, sets up two contrary worlds – the familiar world of Lenny, the protagonist and the conflict-torn, violence-ridden political world of the Nation. Lenny's world is set within the polis of Lahore and as she describes it in the very opening lines of the novel, it is a world that is intersected by Warris Road, Queens Road and Jail Road, "orderly streets at the affluent fringes of Lahore" (Sidhwa 1989: 1) Lenny's world is strictly personal, it is a collage of faces: her parents, her brother Adi, her Ayah and the Ayah's friends, her Godmother, her cousin; in short, it is an imagined community shaped by her phenomenological sense of being. It is also made of stories and songs: stories of Heer and Ranjah, Romeo and Juliet and songs that narrativise forgotten Punjabi folk tales. Lenny's Parsee identity remains uncompromised by these sporadic elements of multiculturalism; it is, in short, the community of possibilities, conceived, moulded and discursively framed on an ideal of secularity. Benedict Anderson argues that communities are to be distinguished "by the style in which they are imagined" (Anderson 1983: 6). Lenny's world is a

Partition and the shattered familiar **49**

community defined, shaped and determined by her. It is geo-politically located in the multicultural milieu of Lahore; the Lahore which in the initial length of the novel is a cosmopolis, an ideal city characterised by the multiplicity of castes, religions, class, where both the native and the migrant, the majorities and minorities (religious and ethnic), the rich and the poor live and with them live their worlds. It is, in other words a 'heterotopia,' where different worlds, even mutually contradictory and contested worlds survive. Foucault (1986a) characterises heterotopias as not completely distinct from the internal space (the space accorded to the individual) but rather formulates an understanding of heterotopias as places which are capable of holding numerous other spaces (which include internal and lived spaces). Lenny's world thus lives in peace in the heterotopic milieu of Lahore, as do many other worlds that Lenny comes across with the gradual progress of the novel. The world of Lenny lives simultaneously with the world of Ayah, the ice-candy man, Godmother and Sharbat Khan.

Lenny's 'contracted' world keeps on expanding as news from the other 'worlds' keep on intruding into it. Lenny's world is sceptical about these other worlds but isn't essentially intolerant to them. The world where Jinnah and Nehru are engaged in political bargains, the world where Subhas Chandra Bose, envisioning India's Independence, allies with the Japanese and consequently forms the Indian National Army, are nothing but redundant supplements to Lenny's world. As the bildungsroman narrator notes: "Mother, father and their friends are always saying: Gandhi said this, Nehru said that. Gandhi did this, Jinnah did that. What's the point of talking so much about people we don't know?" (Sidhwa 1989: 29).

These worlds are excess to Lenny's world for they overlap into her own compressed child's world. This element of excess is, however, a characteristic of the political condition and as such the human and his/her microcosmic world order is often subjected to the excesses that accompany his/ her political condition. Jean-Luc Nancy observes:

> In today's world, excess is not an excess in the sense that it is indeterminant with relation to normative structures; it does not form a monstrous excrescence and, as such, is not doomed to perish ... It indicates not so much the degree or quantum of its magnitude [grandeur] ... but magnitude itself as an absolute which touches upon another propriety of Being (or the human, or meaning – however we want to say it).
>
> *(Nancy 2000: 179)*

The excesses become dangerous, not just intruding into Lenny's world but also violating its essence of innocence. Lahore changes, with the advent of Independence, Lahore begins to burn, it burns endlessly and on Lenny's eighth birthday a new Nation called Pakistan is born. The child narrator remarks: "I am Pakistani. In a snap. Just like that" (Sidhwa 1989: 140). Sidhwa, obeying the generic demands of the bildungsroman, stresses the alteration of identity of the personal subject before she stresses on the historical moment of Partition: "A new Nation is born. India has been divided after all" (ibid.).

50 Rupayan Mukherjee

The personal, within the generic characteristics of a bildungsroman is prioritised; it is the individual that precedes the political. However, the individual is no longer apolitical, she is now a politicised subject. The exterior political starts exerting its influence on the sanctified interior world of the personal as Lenny's birthday euphoria is eclipsed by the collective hysteria that the birth of Pakistan provokes:

> Cousin returns with brown paper bags and a dented cardboard cake box. I blow out the candles and cut the squashed cake. And then we sit around the radio listening to the celebrations of the new Nation. Jinnah's voice, inaugurating the Constituent Assembly sessions on 11th August says: "You are free. You are free to go to your temples. You are free to go to your mosques or any other place of worship in the state of Pakistan. You may belong to any religion or caste or creed, that has nothing to do with the business of State ... etc., etc., etc. Pakistan Zindabad!"
>
> *(Ibid.: 144)*

The trope of politicisation and the understanding of the human condition of existence as an essentially irreducible political condition of being is dominant throughout the text. For instance, let us analyse the conversation that Lenny's mother has with Colonel Bharucha regarding Lenny's polio-infected leg:

> "I don't know where I went wrong," she (mother) says. "It's my fault ... I neglected her – left her to the care of ayahs. None of the other children who went to the same park contracted polio."
>
> "It's no one's fault really," says Col. Bharucha, reassuring her as usual. "Lenny is weak. Some child with only the symptoms of a severe cold could have passed the virus." And then he roars a shocking postscript: "If anyone's to blame, blame the British! There was no polio in India till they brought it here!"
>
> *(Ibid.: 16)*

Lenny's body is thus a site of political contestation and is a marked body where Colonel Bharucha sees the imprints of the colonial history of undivided India. Hannah Arendt argues that since antiquity man has been a political subject, conditioned to live two orders of existence, the 'idion', which is personal and the 'koinon', which is the political (1998: 24). However, Lenny's greater political world isn't the eudaemoniac world of the 'animal rationale' that was valorised by the Greeks. It is instead a highly politicised world where not just actions (praxis) but also gestures, not just words (lexis) but also silences carry political implications. Lenny's body thus becomes a politicised body, a body that is a relic of the British history of colonisation. Lenny, the observing protagonist, reflects: "I feel it is my first personal involvement with Indian politics; the Quit-India sentiment that has fired the imagination of a subject people and will soon sweep away the Raj!" (ibid.: 17).

The body becomes a pertinent discourse in the novel. We have Lenny's deviant body, Godmother's austere body, Ayah's voluptuous/ erotic body, Hari's naked body, cousin's unfamiliar body, the violated body of the women from Gurudaspur, the massacred body of the masseur and finally the partitioned body of the Nation. The body serves as a significant metaphor for the banal, the crude and the non-epistemic, having to do with the immediate rather than the transcendent. Simultaneously, body in the novel serves as a significant objective correlative of the violence that dominate and alienate the humane. Its consistent emphasis depicts a dehumanised world, where the human is reduced to corporeality. Lenny's description of the masseur's body evokes a sensation of estrangement:

> He was lying on one side, the upper part of his velvet body bare, a brown and white checked lungi knotted on his hips, and his feet in the sack. I never knew Masseur was so fair inside, creamy, and his arms smooth and distended with muscles and his forearms lined with pale brown hair. A wide wedge of flesh was neatly hacked to further trim his slender waist, and his spine, in a velvet trough, dipped into his lungi.

> *(Ibid.: 174)*

As Lenny observes the accumulating crowds around Masseur's dead body, she observes:

> Faces bob around us now. Some concerned, some curious. But they look at Masseur as if he is not a person.
>   He isn't. He has been reduced to a body. A thing. One side of his handsome face already buried in the dusty sidewalk.

> *(Ibid.: 174)*

This experience of alienation by the 'coming of age' protagonist in the novel is not something that is essentially a post-Partition experience. Rather alienation by means of deviant bodies is a part of her everyday habitus. The austere, guarded body of the Godmother, with whom Lenny shares an otherwise intimate relationship, only alienates her as she remarks: "In all the years I never saw the natural shape of her breasts" (ibid.: 4).

However, the discourse of body in the novel has other implications as well and it will probably be worthwhile to understand the consistent references to the body beyond the predictable tropes of metaphor and objective correlative. Michel Foucault, in his path-breaking, rigorously researched work *The History of Sexuality*, interrogates the perilous subject called the body and depicts how body shares with the social a relationship of repression and how discourses on the body (which include fictional and visual representation) inevitably involves an element of transgression, a transgression from the established institutions and ideals of power.

In the increasingly hostile political milieu that pervades Lahore in the novel, bodies become not just sites which are appropriated and violated by the overtly increasing masculine displays of violence, they also become sites which oppose the dominant political world of mutual hatred and suspicion. In other worlds, bodies in the novel do not just occupy a space in the economy of possession and violation;

they are also functional in the chequered economy of desire. Hence, Ayah's body isn't just a violated body (which it is at the end of the novel), it is also a body that is subversive to the increasingly hostile political and social milieu born out of the accumulating clouds of Partition. In the initial phase of the novel, Ayah with her tantalising sexuality transgresses the dominant political order as it is desired by diverse and distinct individuals, each belonging to different religious, cultural and economic communities. It is an object of desire for the masseur, Ice-candy man, Sherbat khan and even Imam Din. The promise of physical proximity that is cherished by these men becomes a discourse of universality, i.e., irrespective of their religious, ethnic or political differences they share an element of common-ality – they all nurture sexual fantasies and cherish physical proximity to her. Ayah's body thus becomes a site of contention but it also has the possibilities of becoming a site of transgression which subverts the dominant political order. While the political climate of Lahore gets increasingly strengthened on an ethics of exclusion and difference, Ayah's body is a site that can accommodate differences and multi-cultural hybridities.

This is not to deny that Ayah's body is objectified throughout the novel and within the patriarchy dominated world of Lahore, her body is constantly recog-nised only through or within the discourse of desire. The female and the feminine are consequently objectified and no matter how transgressive her body might appear in the initial half of the novel, it ultimately succumbs to the changing world order, where she is finally commodified into a prostitute, an identity that is foun-ded unconditionally on the discourse of body and sexuality. She is no longer the woman whose sexuality is a means of assertion of subjectivity and agency; it is now commodified by the dominant order of patriarchy and is transfigured from a body of potentialities into a docile body. Foucault defines 'docile body' as a body that "may be subjected, used, transformed and improved"(Foucault 1975: 136). In other words, it is a body that has been robbed of its agency.

Identity and agency are subjects that a bildungsroman usually interrogates and the growth of agency and the assertion of identity is often a stock feature of a bil-dungsroman, which Lukacs describes as "a widening of the soul which seeks ful-fillment in action, in effective dealings with reality, and not merely in contemplation" (Lukacs 1971: 133). *The Ice-Candy Man*, following the patterns of a bildungsroman, also attempts to explore the notions of identity and agency. However, this exploration isn't much about a development of the self which nor-mally occurs in a bildungsroman. Instead, it is more about the conflicts in agency formulation and the consequent dissension in identities. The novel, like a political novel, tends to read the characters in relation to and not in isolation from each other. Often this relation is of opposition, what Levinas would call "a relation without relation" (Levinas 1961: 80). Nevertheless the *building self* is depicted to be deriving its agency from the 'other,' the individual is read and represented as an intrinsic part of the collective. Hence, the individual's identity and agency has numerous categorical imperatives – religion, language, dialect, dress and food habits, all become signifiers of the individual's identity; an identity that isn't just

Partition and the shattered familiar **53**

exclusively a political identity but is also simultaneously a politicised identity. As the clouds of Partition gather in the familiar skies of Lenny's world, she observes:

> "I feel a great swell of fear for Hari: and a surge of loathing for his bodhi. Why must he persist in growing it? And flaunt his Hinduism? And invite ridicule? And that preposterous and obscene dhoti! Worn like a diaper between his stringy legs. Just begging to be taken off!"
>
> *(Sidhwa 1989: 118)*

The incident in the text demands attention for more reasons than one. It is a perfect example of how Partition breaches the familiar world of the self and alters not just the personal world order but also undoes the ethics of the familiar world. Previously Hari, the gardener, who is a Hindu in Lahore, was often ridiculed by the other employees in Lenny's household. Often, on playful evenings, Imam Din and Yusuf would chase him, attempting to undo his dhoti, where the intent was of recreation rather than abuse. But with Partition haunting Lahore, the rules of the game change. It no longer seems like an innocent recreation that is the purpose of the game, instead it is driven by the urge to shame the other, to deride and deject the agency of the other. As the season of Partition intensifies, Hari shaves off his 'bodhi,' the marker of Hindu identity on his body and changes his name to Himat Ali as his penis is circumcised and his dhoti replaced by a drawstring shalwar. The political thus governs the personal, the rigours of koinon is dominant over the natural flourishes of idion and identities are not just about innate characteristics that the self possesses. Instead, they are reliant, almost helplessly dependent, on social and religious markers.

This is where Sidhwa starts complicating the generic features of a bildungsroman and ushers her readers into a world which isn't just about 'coming of age' for the protagonist, it is also about learning the *ways of the world*. The alteration of Hari's identity doesn't occur in a neutral space, it is very much a part of the familiar world of Lenny, the 'I' in the bildungsroman. With the first-person narrative voice relaying the incident to the readers, the episode appears as a lesson for the growing child, who has, in the initial phases of the novel, been obsessed with her narrowed worldview, happy to exist within the comforts of her protected, personal world. Lenny realises that the personal familiar worlds are moulded, often ontologically reshaped by the political.

The Ice-Candy Man, keeping in tune with the great human catastrophe of Partition, depicts the saga of alteration, displacement, dehumanisation and, in a few instances, even the annihilation of the humane. The massacred train from Gurudaspur, the violence inflicted upon the characters like Ayah and the masseur, the ontological alterations of the familiar characters such as Dilnawaz, the ice-candy man – all of them undo Lenny's familiar world. However, Sidhwa relies on an exploration of the climate of violence that haunts the novel rather than sensationalising violence through overt descriptions of murder and rape. It is the economy of fear and unfamiliarity that characterises the climate of violence and violence in the novel doesn't necessarily limit itself to an active (physical) violation of the self. On the contrary, it is more concerned with the violation of the ontological and the

54 Rupayan Mukherjee

epistemic essence of the self. Sidhwa accomplishes that by ushering the self into an unfamiliar world where the familiar world of the self is breached, appropriated and moulded by the political.

Franco Moretti, in his discussion on the bildungsroman, argues that as a genre it tries to negotiate the tension between the individual and the social, the autonomous-sovereign and the normative (which is often determined by the ordains of the collective). In Sidhwa's novel, this reconciliation happens in an atmosphere of violence, or the resulting reconciliation is violent, where it is not a happy consensus between the interior and the outside, rather it is a tale of violation of the individual subject and her world by the political exterior.

The Ice-Candy Man, however, unlike other Partition novels, doesn't end in dystopia. The political milieu of Lahore in the immediacy of Partition appears dehumanised where ethics and morals have been suspended, but it isn't an absolutely unethical world. As such, the possibilities of redemption for the characters remain open. Sidhwa turns the genre of bildungsroman on its head as the conscious reader observes that there is a promised world of reconciliation between the inside and the outside, i.e., the personal and the political in the concluding chapters of the novel, only with the difference that the self doesn't necessarily succumb to her outside, as is the common occurrence in a bildungsroman. Instead, it is the outside of Lahore that promises a world of redemption. It is no longer the Lahore where the spectre of violence haunts the morbid cityscape in form of rapes, murders and mutilations. It is a Lahore where Dilnawaz, the predator who had once mutilated Ayah and coerced her into a forced marriage, seeks redemption. Dilnawaz's songs and his endless wait before the gates of the rehabilitation centre, where the rescued Ayah lives, is a probable confession of the outer political order of its inhumanity. Lenny's learning self doesn't reconcile with the changing dynamics of the city; it is the city that confesses its misgivings and infamy before the humane. In doing so, *The Ice-Candy Man* explores other possibilities within the hermeneutics of a bildungsroman and seeks to valorise the individual over the collective. Unmaking the paradigm of a 'coming of age' novel, *The Ice-Candy Man* seeks to explore the possibilities that survive in this impossibility of reconciliation between the subject and the socio-political, the self and the world. Sidhwa's open-endedness with form serves two purposes; on one hand she explores in fantasy that which is denied in the real or immanent, i.e., the possibility of reconciliation. Simultaneously, the open-endedness explicates the impossibility of aesthetic to represent the pathos of the real. Her refusal to end the unravelled plot and her seeming failure to do so explicates Sidhwa's inability to translate into aesthetic the inexplicable suffering that accompanies the historical reality of Partition.

Works Cited

Anderson, Benedict. *Imagined Communities: Reflections on the Origin and Spread of Nationalism*. London: Verso, 1983.
Arendt, Hannah. *The Human Condition*. Chicago: University of Chicago Press, 1998.

Barthes, Roland. *Mythologies*, trans. Annette Lavers. New York: The NoonDay Press, 1972.

Butalia, Urvashi. *The Other Side of Silence: Voices from the Partition of India*. Viking: Penguin, 1998.

Foucault, Michel. *The History of Sexuality Vol. I: An Introduction*. trans. Robert Hurley. New York: Pantheon Books, 1978.

Foucault, Michel. "Of Other Spaces: Utopias and Heterotopias," trans. Jay Miskowiec. *Diacritics*, 16:1 (Spring1986a), 22–27.

Foucault, Michel. *Discipline and Punish: The Birth of the Prison*, trans. Alan Sheridan. New York: Vintage Books, 1986b.

Ghosh, Ranjan. *A Lover's Quarrel with the Past: Romance, Representation, Reading*. New York: Berghahn Books, 2012.

Hegel, George Wilhelm Friedrich. *The Philosophy of History*, trans. J. Sibree. Kitchener, ON: Batoche Books, 2001.

Hirsch, Marianne. Postmemory.net, n.d. http://www.postmemory.net (accessed 23 August2018).

Huyssen, Andreas. "Of Mice and Mimesis: Reading Spiegelman with Adorno," *New German Critique*, 81 (Autumn2000), 65–82.

Kamra, Sukeshi. "Engaging Traumatic Histories: The 1947 Partition of India in Collective Memory," in *Partition: The Long Shadow*, ed. Urvashi Butalia. New Delhi: Penguin, 2015.

Levinas, Emmanuel. *Totality and Infinity: An Essay on Exteriority*, trans. Alphonso Lingis. Pittsburgh, PA: Duquesne University Press, 1961.

Lukacs, George. *The Theory of the Novel: A Historic-Philosophical Essay on the Forms of Great Epic Literature*, trans. Anna Bostock. Berlin: The Merlin Press, 1971.

Moretti, Franco. *The Way of the World: The Bildungsroman in European Culture*. London: Verso, 2000.

Nancy, Jean-Luc. *The Inoperative Community*, trans. and ed. Peter Connor. Minneapolis: University of Minnesota Press, 1991.

Nancy, Jean-Luc. *Being Singular Plural*, trans. Robert D. Richardson and Anne E. O'Byrne, Stanford, CA: Stanford University Press, 2000.

Nora, Pierre. *Rethinking the French Past. Realms of Memory. Volume I: Conflicts and Divisions*. New York: Columbia University Press, 1996.

Novick, Peter. *The Holocaust in American Life*. New York: Houghton Mifflin, 1999.

Parasher, Prajna Paramita. "A Long Walk Out from Freedom," in *Partition: The Long Shadow*, ed. Urvashi Butalia. New Delhi: Penguin, 2015.

Rigney, Ann. *Imperfect Histories: The Elusive Past and the Legacy of Romantic Historicism*. Ithaca, NY: Cornell University Press, 2001.

Sidhwa, Bapsi. *The Ice-Candy Man*. New York: Penguin, 1989.

Žižek, Slavoj. *Living in the End Times*. London: Verso, 2010.

Žižek, Slavoj. "In the Grey Zone: Slavoj Žižek on responses to the Paris Killings," *London Review of Books* (5 February2015). https://www.lrb.co.uk/2015/02/05/slavoj-zizek/in-the-grey-zone (accessed 23 July2018).

4

SAADAT HASAN MANTO'S "TOBA TEK SINGH"

A nation split by trauma and madness

Kritika Nepal

> He would argue with her about killing themselves; and explain how wicked people were; how he could see them making up lies as they passed in the street. He knew all their thoughts, he said; he knew everything. He knew the meaning of the world, he said.
>
> *(Virginia Woolf,* Mrs. Dalloway*)*

The psychic essence of human consciousness is ambiguous; it is both affected by and apathetic to the stimuli of the exterior. While the events and influences of the surrounding often disintegrate the psychic subject, it also enhances the possibility of resilience in the subject. Great sections of society have survived inhumane conditions like the gruesome Holocaust, the two World Wars, the communal riots during the Partition of India – the list goes on, for violence and suffering go as far back as human history itself, so much so, that it seems that we all exist within a shared trauma inherited from the violent history of our race.

From the Greeks using the term originally to denote "wound" of a physical nature or injury to the physical body, the word "trauma" has greatly evolved in its usage and implications (Caruth 1996b: 3). Trauma is now interpreted as a psycho-logical or psychiatric condition. The literature produced during times of crises have helped us analyse human psychology in disorganised and hostile settings. Victor E. Frankl's *Man's Search for Meaning* is one such literary example of a first-hand account of life in the concentration camps during the extermination of Jews in Nazi Germany. The vitality of resilience is undoubtedly valorised in such survival accounts, but the ones who do emerge are often changed in harrowing ways. The subject of our study, Saadat Hasan Manto's short story "Toba Tek Singh," inspired by the real events of the 1947 Partition of India, is a satirical and distressing account of violence, discrimination, chaos and confusion.

The shift in its meaning from an outward wound to something more internal and primitive in nature has brought the concept of trauma to the present stage where, though its meanings have expanded their horizons, its internal workings are still an enigma. Today, trauma is understood as a reaction to unpleasant events that had occurred in the past like, as Cathy Caruth explains in *Unclaimed Experience*, a "recurring" (Caruth, 1996b: 6–7) echo of something screamed out a long time ago. The central character in "Toba Tek Singh" is a perfect example of such a phenomenon; we could perhaps even read him as a 'human echo.' Trauma is conceived at the moment of an event in the past and forms not immediately but after a certain amount of time has passed and one still can't shake off the recurring memory. The time taken for the realisation of this trauma is termed by Freud in *Moses and Monotheism* as the "incubation period" or "latency" (Freud 1939: 110–137). This is also a psychological reaction towards events that do not normally or automatically fall into the complex web of meanings we have structured for ourselves individually or as a society. Such events are perceived and appropriated by the consciousness as diversions from the familiar and the habitual order and this essence of the unfamiliar is often the source of psychological trauma. Trauma may arise from situations in which the sufferer goes through violence of some sort – be it sexual violence, violence against one's individuality, identity or emotions. For instance, the survivors of Holocaust exhibited mass trauma due to the variety of inhuman conditions they had to live through. What is important and interesting to note in the context of mass or group trauma is that in spite of similar harsh conditions and maltreatments, not all the survivors displayed trauma of the same intensity as everyone else. The asylum inmates in "Toba Tek Singh" are afflicted with mental unease, they are traumatised over and over again, especially after the government announcement regarding their transaction across borders, but not all of them display the same intensity in their trauma. The brain is wired in a way that is full of surprises. Certain individuals go through disturbing or discomforting situations and emerge mildly scathed, while some are troubled by those situations to the extent that they become a part of their identity and a reason for illness.

Manto's "Toba Tek Singh" begins in an absurd reality where one Nation is being split into two and the insane citizens are being divided and transported to either half on the basis of their religious identity. Inspired by real events, the incident forms the icing on the metaphorical cake as an example of collective or mass trauma. The story opens with the government declaration that the asylum inmates are to be exchanged, but the absurd announcement coming from great political leaders questions their sanity. The privileged few who lead a Nation and cause its division seem more unhinged than the residents of the mental asylum. These inmates, who have spent years in the facility and who have come to consider it their home, are confused and afraid upon learning about the transaction. To the irrational government they are nothing more than a statistic; a commodity that can be sent across borders in order to satisfy a political agenda. Already dislocated from their families and brought into the asylum, these inmates are now to be sent off from there as well, completely confusing their sense of identity and belonging. They themselves are the Nation divided in two, the head slashed off from the rest of the body, entities who can no longer determine which part of the body is in fact them. "Lahore could slide to India any moment" – reality is as absurd to the inmates as it is bleak. The possibility that parts of land can be divided and reassigned is beyond the comprehension of these simple people, who cannot fathom how a place can belong to one country one day and can be shifted into another country the next. In a political parody of the great leaders, some inmates abruptly declare themselves Jinnah and Tara Singh. These declarations, however, do not seem too surprising given that the so-called sane leaders have acted in a more extreme manner than the mentally unsound. One of the inmates climbs up a tree in rebellion at the exchange. He believes that doing so will exempt him from being sent into Hindustan or Pakistan; it is a bid to preserve himself and his innocence. Amid all the chaos in the horizontal space, there is a simple wish to remain untainted by violence or deranged authority by climbing upwards to a vertical space and declaring it home. There is a particular incident of an inmate – an M.Sc. Radio Engineer – handing over his clothes to the guards and running stark naked in the garden. The already defenceless and marginalised youth retaliates by showing that under the present situation, his only possible defence is to bare all defences.

"Toba Tek Singh" also mocks the concept of God when, amid inmates declaring themselves as one political leader or another, one of them announces that he is God. When inmate Bishan Singh, in utter desperation, begs to "God" for answers regarding his homeland, the "God" is unable to reply. In spite of this, interestingly, Bishan Singh does not lose faith in a higher power but simply says that if he were a Sikh god, he would have answers. This residual sense of faith is foundational to the ontological essence of Bishan Singh. Simultaneously, however, this faith is in a process of systematic erasure, owing to the experience of the altered materiality, shaped by the tremors of communal divide. In a dystopic social-political milieu, the familiar appears alien and as such Bishan Singh can no longer rely on the familiar logos called God. Instead, he expresses his desire to become God, if only to negotiate the misgoverned institution of religion and its valorised ideal of violence, that has started promoting a homo–hegemonic and exclusivist construct of divinity.

The story places the lunatic Bishan Singh, hailing from a place called Toba Tek Singh, at the centre of all the commotion. Said to have been institutionalised 15 years ago upon going mad "suddenly," he has been standing ever since he arrived, resulting in swollen feet. Even though the guards have spotted him leaning against the wall sometimes, he has not slept a wink for the past 15 years. As is the nature of trauma, the events leading to Bishan Singh's trauma of Partition are not recent. The riots, arrests, communal hatred – all this mental and physical violence has built up to a breaking point which he is now experiencing. The crescendo, upon reaching its highest point, had now begun its descent.

Bishan Singh is a symbol of the endurance and suffering of an entire population prior to Partition, a metaphor of the masses whose patience is finally worn down by the division as they are robbed of their final possession and freedom; their sense of identity. He rarely speaks but when he does, he talks in complete gibberish, which can be read as his complex subconscious being externalised in an attempt to proclaim and reclaim his internal territory. It can also be interpreted as his reply to the chaos in the outside world and a surreal hope that madness understands madness. His sentences are difficult for others to make sense of, as is his personal suffering and the complicated maze of trauma created by it.

Even though his family have moved to India, Bishan Singh longs to go back to Toba Tek Singh, which now belongs to Pakistan. He experiences an extreme necessity to connect to his roots, his birth place, as it is to him the only salvation he requires and the only way to find peace. In the end when put in a position where he absolutely has to choose, Bishan Singh runs into no-man's-land and collapses there. Before doing so, however, he declares that the piece of land between India and Pakistan, a land untouched by either parts of the divided nation, is in fact Toba Tek Singh. The desperation of a mind tormented by the echoes of violence for 15 years is made clear as day in the character of Bishan Singh.

"Toba Tek Singh" gives voice to the unheard, the marginalised of the society, the outcasts who have been shunned as insane but who can also be read as the voice of reason presented in a satirical way. As in any major socio-political upheaval, the general masses underwent great violence during the Partition of India in 1947. Termed the biggest mass migration in human history, the reshuffling of borders was tainted with religious frenzy, a madness which robbed people of their conscience. Neighbours killing neighbours, friends against friends – that which people had known all their lives as an honourable way of living seemed somehow to have been traded for a new alien code of conduct which thrived on violence. As William Dalrymple notes, "People who a year before would've attended each other's wedding parties … are murdering each other, raping each other's daughters, roasting each other's babies on spits" (quoted in Chao 2017: n.p.; see also Dalrymple 2015).

Violence in any form creates terror, which in turn gives birth to trauma, and the brutality of physical and mental violence that occurred during the Indian Partition of 1947 has left deep scars. Manto's "Toba Tek Singh" can be read as a study of existence in a state of perpetual trauma. As mentioned earlier, traumatic memory presents itself in a haphazard manner which is often so confusing that the individual struggles greatly in his/her attempt to decipher the basic nature of his/her trauma. In that process, trained to find meaning and structure in events, things or entities, the human mind often projects one thing on the other while striving to make sense. A group or society, where everyday life smoothly follows a psychological semantic, is suddenly turned on its head by events such as war. Consequently, the entire order previously maintained and engrained in the people's minds is now reshuffled beyond the point of recognition. The mind takes time to arrange this new order or turn of events into information that makes sense.

In Cathy Caruth's collection of writings, *Trauma: Explorations in Memory*, the theme of trauma has been explored, keeping in mind the wide spectrum that reality encompasses. Trauma is described as a different reality altogether in the sense that the subtlety and abstraction of traumatic memories drive the victim from mental norms in his or her attempts to find meaning in life (Caruth 1996a: 3–11). An event of traumatic nature is seen as a jolt from the regularity of everyday life and memories, opening up another portal through which the victim views the event in hindsight. A sense of dissociation occurs in the mind of the victim, creating a fracture in perceived reality and the recurrence of this fracture is the experience of trauma where the event is experienced anew with every echo. Traumatic memories are tricky in this sense, for the natural reaction of human mind to something that can't be understood or explained in the context of normal circumstances is to attempt to place it in a meaningful way, be it in hindsight or in the way the particular memory is processed.

The essence of being human relies greatly on memories – historical as well as personal. How a character is formed in real life or in works of literature depends on the memories they have and the placement of these memories in the social and ethical context. Since traumatic experiences are an entirely different entity, the human mind reacts to them by negating and attempting to forget them initially. However, oblivion only complements remembrance and the void or gaps between the event, the negation or forgetting of the event and its re-experience as a fresh wound is what gives core power to the trauma. As such, trauma is characterised by the "return of the repressed' (Lacan 1989: 67) where a psychic re-enactment of the happening constantly re-fashions the actual event, often intensifying it with every rehearsal and making it an essential post-truth. This "crisis of truth" (Felman 1992: 6) is distinctive of traumatic events and is arguably the power source of the recurrence of trauma.

Saadat Hasan Manto's short story has painted a gaping wound on paper, a portal to the 1947 turmoil that tore away major parts of the Indian subcontinent. With "Toba Tek Singh," Manto satirises political leaders who have made a mockery of human sentiment and peace, and in under ten pages, he puts up for examination the innumerable issues plaguing society and the human mind. It is a study into the human psyche and, with its multiple symbolisms, a treasure trove for scholars of Trauma Studies.

Works cited

Baron, Robert A. *Psychology*. Boston, MA: Allyn and Bacon, 2000.

Caruth, Cathy. *Trauma: Explorations in Memory*. Baltimore, MD and London: Johns Hopkins University Press, 1996a.

Caruth, Cathy. *Unclaimed Experience: Trauma, Narrative and History*. Baltimore, MD and London: Johns Hopkins University Press, 1996b. Chao, Steve. 'Remembering Partition: "It Was Like a Slaughterhouse",' Al Jazeera News Feature (15 August2017). Retrieved from https://www.aljazeera.com/indepth/features/2017/08/remembering-partition-slaughterhouse-170810050649347.html (accessed 13 February 2020).

Dalrymple, William. "The Great Divide (The Violent Legacy of Indian Partition)," *The New Yorker* (22 June2015). Retrieved from https://www.newyorker.com/magazine/2015/06/29/the-great-divide-books-dalrymple (accessed 13 February 2020).

Felman, Shoshana. *Testimony: Crises of Witnessing in Literature, Psychoanalysis and History*. New York: Routledge, 1992.

Frankl, Victor E. *Man's Search of Meaning*, rev. edn. London: Rider Books, 2011.

Freud, Sigmund. *Moses and Monotheism*. Letchworth, Herts: Hogarth Press and The Institute of Psycho-Analysis, 1939.

Lacan, Jacques. *Ecrits: A Selection*, trans. Alan Sheridan. London and New York: Routledge, 1989.

Scaer, Robert C. *The Trauma Spectrum: Hidden Wounds and Human Resiliency*. New York: W. W. Norton and Company, 2005.

Woolf, Virginia. *Mrs. Dalloway*. Oxford World's Classics. Oxford: Oxford University Press, 2009.

5

TRANSLATING TRAUMA INTO SUBLIME

Gulzar's response to Manto's "Toba Tek Singh"

Tuhin Sanyal

> Mujhe Wagah pe Toba Tek Singh wale 'Bishan' se jake milna hai.
>
> *(Gulzar, "Toba Tek Singh")*

Based on Saadat Hasan Manto's short story "Toba Tek Singh", Gulzar's Urdu poem of the same name, rendered in English and with the same title by Dr. Anisur Rahman (Rahman 2001), creates a new ground for what Manto had referred to as 'no man's land' in the end. In the poem, Gulzar endeavours to totalize a cultural narrative schema in explaining the heart-rending Partition experience that makes its tremors felt in the human hearts of the Indian sub-continent to date. As a microcosm of the partitioned reality, the poem lampoons the absurd division and the crude exchange of property and men in the wake of Partition. However, the large-scale upheavals of confused creation and dismantling is neither central to Manto's story, nor to Gulzar's poem. "Toba Tek Singh" is indeed the idea of a profound space, both, in the story as well as in the poem, where insanity, which is actually the protagonist Bishan Singh's hyper-sanity, is misread by the clinically sane. Bishan finds final and true asylum neither in India, nor in Pakistan, but in a 'no man's land', occupied by none. Here his sense of belonging is best obtained and realized since this (im)possible space is free from politico-territorial claim.

The protagonist Bishan Singh is an everyman of the Partition experience and his hometown Toba Tek Singh, wherever he may rightfully re-create it, is his breathing space as well as the space to bury his sighs fraught with the pathos of that unforgettable Partition in 1947. From there he can freely swear at both the nations alike, and curse freely in lunatic fits with his much memorable, ironic though gibberish line –"Uppar di gurrgurr di moong daal di laltein di hinustantepakistan di durrfithemoonh."

In the short story, set a little over a couple of years after Partition, the old and harmless lunatic Bishan Singh poses a serious problem that nuances the policies pertaining to the exchange of lunatics – a decision that was mutually agreed upon by the two Nations. The delirious lunatic who is supposed to be sent to India in the process, refuses to budge at the Wagah border and comes up with the searching question – "Where is Toba Tek Singh?" He queries about his hometown and though deranged in mind, he is anchored to the mooring of his belongingness and the space he could call his own. Keeping in synchrony with the theme of insanity, the narrator in the story reports that everyone calls the main character "Toba Tek Singh", i.e. by the name of his hometown (though in the whole course of the story we never actually hear anyone doing so). And the narrator himself refers to him as 'Bishan Singh' / 'Bashan Singh' (in certain editions). Thus, the readers are drawn into the mad-house, entangled with the pitfalls and are left confused as to what to consider – Toba Tek Singh, the man, or Toba Tek Singh, the sense of a space / locale? 'Toba Tek Singh', simply put, is a superimposition of the two that also creates a new space of anguish that one's Partition-traumatized psyche can call his/her own. Realism abounds in the horseplay between various lunatics and new philosophical meanings are crafted of the post-Partition political scenario.

There are possibilities of reading Manto's "Toba Tek Singh" as an experience of the phenomenal sublime, experienced only through some kind of inspired insanity which we find in Manto's protagonist. For example Gulzar's poeticization of Manto's "Toba Tek Singh" sublimates insanity from the textual into the experiential and takes Bishan Singh, Manto's protagonist, beyond the confinements of discourse and the textual contours of the imagined into the realm of the (im)possible. Like Slavoj Žižek, resonating other epistemic engagements on the ideal of the sublime, Gulzar too, in Žižek's manner, conceives it as "a positive material object elevated to the status of the impossible thing" (Žižek 2008: 77). The sublime is thus understood as an experience that is haunted by the supplement of impossibility. It becomes an experience which falls beyond the symbolic order of being and existence, never fully comprehended, but provoking the desire of comprehension. The empirical limits of the being of the sublime subject dissolves as the sublime possesses two continuous and simultaneous states of being – the ordinary and the ethereal-mystical – the everyday, and the occasional. The experience of the sublime rests in the interstices of both, half revealed and half concealed. The same pattern recurs in Gulzar's perception of 'Toba Tek Singh'. Bishan Singh, the spectral personification of the anxiety of homelessness and lack of identity, sublimates beyond the historical and the lived real. Gulzar decontextualizes Bishan Singh deliberately to uphold the paradox of the very idea of any preconceived 'context'. Bishan Singh, alias Toba Tek Singh, refuses to belong to any context of political dictum and is able to achieve sublimity by embracing this miraculous death, which, for the onlookers, is an altogether un-pre-supposed supplement of (im)possibility.

Every lunatic in Manto's story is yearning for a space that is un-striated and embodies an essence of unconditional ontic freedom, a territory void of the political agenda of the two countries. In trying to find such a space, one of the lunatics climbed up a tree and resolved never to come down as he would go to neither Pakistan nor India. The situation reminds us of Calvino's Baron in *The Baron in the Trees* (1977), who decides to spend his life not on land but in the organic and floral order. He climbs up a tree and never comes down, living his life in branches. Rejecting the life of decorum and sophistication that is deeply reliant on the performative of nobility; the Baron seeks and consolidates his free space in the natural. This lunatic, in Manto's short story, dubs his *Trishanku* situation ('in medias res', swinging between heaven and earth) as his free space for himself, much like Calvino's Baron. Simultaneously, he echoes what Bishan does in the end and Gulzar well re-iterates this in his lines too. Yet another lunatic, a Muslim named Mohammad Ali, declared himself to be Mohammad Ali Jinnah, the-then Prime Minister of Pakistan, and in reply, a Sikh lunatic proclaimed himself to be Master Tara Singh, who refused Jinnah's private concessions. Thus, in a 'tit-for-tat' gesture to fight the post-Partition psychological trauma accruing from rifts, blood, gore and displacement, a new space is created where Politicians and self-styled Gods are invoked and juxtaposed as being equally deceptive, diplomatic and manipulative. Hell breaks loose and the co-equation of the political satire on India and Pakistan strikes the core of the monumental idiocy of Partition. Bishan gives a sudden scream and lies flat facing the ground which belongs to neither India nor Pakistan. He considers this no man's land to be his hometown, his sublime haven.

The story ends with Singh's daughter travelling back to the asylum one last time to place a sign on the no man's land where Bishan / Toba died, labelling that unnamed patch of land "Toba Tek Singh is here!" As for Gulzar's art, unlike the other strains in his 'Footprints on Zero Line', where Partition memory is high-strung with emotions and cravings for what can be brought back no more, his assertive poetic lines about 'Toba Tek Singh' rather firmly reaffirm the existence of the land / space that Manto had given to Bishan Singh when he was seen at the end of the story. Gulzar confidently begins saying –

I've to go and meet Toba Tek Singh's Bishan at Wagah,

I'm told he still stands on his swollen feet

Where Manto had left him …

The name of the actual locale Toba Tek Singh in Pakistan's 'Punjab' province has a historical significance. *Toba* in Punjabi means 'pond' and 'Tek Singh' is a Sikh religious figure after whom the place is named. Legend has it that Tek Singh served water and provided shelter to the weary and thirsty travellers irrespective of caste or creed when they passed by a particular small pond. The place got its name thus, and later, the British developed it into a canal system and many agriculturist Punjabis moved in there. But the non-identification of that particular place just years after the Partition may have been politically motivated and no one is eager to re-visit the pathos of Partition and identify it again, nor give it a certainty as to where in India the canal begins and where in Pakistan it ends. This exposure to anxiety is perhaps the present psychological space that the place called 'Toba Tek Singh' is symbolical of. Yet, Gulzar believes it is there, for it is really there, that locale of angst, in every heart that has to bear the numbing brunt of Partition. He is confident that Bishan's 'no man's land', even if it could not be located on Partition maps as Toba Tek Singh, must be there in essence, since that is where Bishan fell to live and die with the spirit and sense of belonging to 'One Nation'. He embodies the stretch of land that lies like him between the two Nations and becomes co-equable to his long lost Toba Tek Singh which he finds (and founds) there. He becomes Toba Tek Singh. No wonder Gulzar is confident that he will find the protagonist where Manto had left him, since, ironically enough, the Partition will remain, and so will the 'no man's land', Bishan and Toba Tek Singh.

Since between locales and personae comes History with its attendant conundrum, it would be relevant to revisit Manto's own perplexity which echoes the disjuncture in the mind of millions:

> I found it impossible to decide which of the two countries was now my homeland— India or Pakistan. Who was responsible for the blood which was being mercilessly shed every day? ... When we were colonial subjects, we could dream of freedom, but now that we were free, what would our dreams be? Were we even free? Thousands of Hindus and Muslims were dying all around us. Why were they dying? All these questions had different answers: the Indian answer, the Pakistani answer, the British answer. Every question had an answer, but when you tried to look for the truth, none of those answers was any help.
>
> *(Nair 2011: 179)*

And then Manto takes a walk through the lanes of Lahore in the newly independent Pakistan, a city made strange by the incredible hiatus of turmoil. With his characteristic irony, he sketches the general decay and degradation of a once glorious city:

> A little ahead I came to a familiar chowk, but the statue I had known was missing. I asked a man where it had gone.
>
> 'It went,' he said.
>
> 'On its own?' I asked.
>
> He laughed: 'No, they took it.'
>
> 'Who?'
>
> 'Those who owned it.'
>
> I thought to myself, even statues were now refugees. There might come a day when corpses would also be dug up and moved across the border.
>
> *(Patel 2014: 67)*

The "swollen feet" on which Gulzar's Bishan stands is the outcome of the post-Partition Everyman's never-ending and anxious and traumatic standing spree even

66 Tuhin Sanyal

prior to the Partition, perhaps sceptical about the idea of "two nations in the main". It clearly suggests this Everyman's previous anxiety for the approaching Partition, which, he knew, was inevitable. In real life, at the asylum, that Bishan never slept and never sat for fifteen years is reportedly true, and his apparently lunatic but actually super-conscious sense of belonging, and condemnation of the 'two-nations' theory, resurface in an oblique way as Gulzar portrays the sanity of the insane. Even though Toba Tek Singh or 'Bishan' / 'Bashan' insanely mutters the seemingly gibberish "Opad di gudgud di moong di dal di laltain" in sheer desperation against lunatic political times, it is actually a form of protest and resistance. His confinement in the asylum is less stringent than his being confined between the very ideas of two separate Nations, the whimsical preparations of which spanned over forty years with a handful of selfish politicians decisively contributing to the ill-fate of millions.

As death, distress and disquietude heighten the pathetic related to the Partition, Gulzar has agenda enough on hand, for he says,

> I've to locate that mad fellow
>
> Who used to speak up from a branch high above:
>
> He's god
>
> He alone has to decide – whose village to whose side.

Gulzar clearly identifies the madness of the inmates, equates it aslant with the coarse political madness that stood in favour of two nations, and addresses the plight of the homeless. He re-iterates the incident when 'Bashan'/ 'Bishan' in Manto's story had repeatedly questioned another mad man who feigned to be God, that of the two countries in which country Toba Tek Singh (Bishan's hometown) actually was. The whole aspect of the idea of nationality is beautifully reiterated thus by Gulzar, by re-visiting the conversational space and the camar-aderie between the lunatics, which is seemingly saner than those of the con-troversial spaces of antagonism between architects of the ill-fates of the two nations. Diplomatic manipulations, misleading, betrayal etc. were common from bureaucrats and politicians, and Gulzar simultaneously equivocates and identifies them too as lunatics "who used to speak up from a branch high above". Their space too is not at all differentiated from any asylum, only in their cases, their separate asylums are more dishonest and corrupt, and reminds the post-Partition generation as to how Nehru and Jinnah had both played the roles of soi-disant pseudo-gods in the blistering history shared by the two nations. If Bishan's 'Toba Tek Singh' cannot be found, it cannot be found in the cases of Nehru and Jinnah as well. Toba Tek Singh, the sublime locale for Bishan, is lopsided in the cases of politicians, for they shall never understand the essence and sublimity of Toba Tek Singh, the locale, as 'Bishan' would. 'Bishan' and 'Toba Tek Singh' stand for each other and are interchangeable, but such can never be the case with power-mongers who ravish their motherlands with a 'Zero Line'.

Translating trauma into sublime **67**

When I met Dr. Anisur Rahman at a Seminar on translation at Salesian College, Sonada, Darjeeling, back in 2010, he had opined over a cup of evening tea that in a bid to inform about the present post-Partition situation and about the essence called "Toba Tek Singh", Gulzar, as if in a prophetic bid, warns the lunatic inmates of both the countries and the lunatic, fundamentalist political systems alike, that:

There are some more – left still

Who are being divided, made into pieces –

There are some more Partitions to be done

That Partition was only the first one.

Here, like Jacques Lacan (see Changing Minds n.d.), Gulzar puts the subjective 'self' at the centre, where it is alienated from its own history, formed in and through otherness, and is inserted into an external symbolic network. "Toba Tek Singh" becomes a 'faction' (fact + fiction), or even a paradoxical (mis)conception, born of a misrecognition that masks a fractured and unconscious desire of the Antithetical New for reunification with the Old Primary. Thus, in viewing 'Toba Tek Singh', Gulzar, quite in the Lacanian vein, adheres to and upholds:

- the de-centring of the subject
- the loss and impossibility of unified psychic life
- the primacy of signifier over what is signified in the unconscious
- the fragile and precarious relationship with the 'Other'.

In this, it may be said that the characters and their identities get dislocated, blurred and superimposed elsewhere simultaneously. The old primary space is superseded by the cruel antithetical new, because the post-Partition predicament remains fraught with distress equally for everyone. The familiar is defamiliarized and vice versa, as it is in the case of 'Bishan' / 'Bashan' or 'Toba Tek Singh'. The post-Partition readers naturally ask themselves the paradoxical question: "'Toba Tek Singh' – more *place* than person, or more *person* than place?" As for meeting *"Toba Tek Singh's Bishan at Wagah"* (the no man's land), the Wagah border itself becomes a new and antithetical Toba Tek Singh, and only there can the old primary 'Bishan' be met.

Finally, Gulzar rattles off the names of characters that Bishan and his friend knew, and endeavours to report what happened to them (once he reaches the locale Toba Tek Singh and the persona of 'Bishan') thus:

His friend Afzal has to be informed –

Lahna Singh, Wadhwa Singh, Bheen Amrit

Had arrived here butchered –

Their heads were looted with the luggage on the way behind.

68 Tuhin Sanyal

and that the unfed girl (much allusive of the sordid predicament of the post-Partition, cross-border daughters and perhaps Bishan's own daughter)

> who grew one finger every twelve months,
>
> Now shortens one phalanx each year.

With these lines Gulzar intends to heighten the pathos in the very essence of Toba Tek Singh (both locale and persona) by presenting human beings who actually belonging to nowhere, yet some are butchered and others in excruciating pain accruing from the Partition. In utter despair he flings a scathing sarcasm on the dividedness of the people and politicians on either side of the border, saying:

> It's to be told that all the mad ones haven't yet reached their destinations
>
> There are many on that side
>
> And many on this.

Gulzar has shown his 'courage of hopelessness' (Žižek 2017: 97) in his search for Toba Tek Singh, and, like the postmodern existentialist Žižek, he too perhaps wants to say that what he advocates is not the process of democratic self-purification by means of which we get "rid of the dirty water (abuses of democracy) without losing the healthy baby (authentic democracy and human resource)". The "task is rather to trans-value the (politically determined) values themselves," because the "critique of the content legitimized by formal democracy should be radicalized into a critique of the form itself". The "dirty water" of a political system that compels millions to bear the brunt of wanton, arbitrary decisions must be cleared out to look for radical ways of reformation (Žižek 2017: 97).

Thus, the sublime essence of the real 'Bishan' or the true 'Toba Tek Singh' can hardly be ascertained or realized in this post-Partition political scenario which actually translates to everything unconstructive, inconclusive, remains blurred, and is resignedly dubbed as largely gibberish. So, 'Toba Tek Singh' and / or 'Bishan' / 'Bashan', in a bid to revolt, " ... beckons ... (the poet) often to say:"Opad di gudgud di moong di dal di laltain di Hindustan te Pakistan di dur fiteymunh."

Works Cited

Calvino, Italo. *The Baron in the Trees*. New York: Harcourt, 1977.

Changing Minds, Lacanian Psychoanalysis. Changing Minds, n.d. Retrieved from http://changingminds.org/disciplines/psychoanalysis/articles/lacanian_psychoanalysis.htm on 10 August 2018.

Gulzar. On "Toba Tak Singh", Dead Poet Society, n.d. Retrieved from http://mainshairtunahi.tumblr.com/post/74494221752/gulzar-on-toba-tak-singh on 10 August 2018.

Manto, Saadat Hasan. "Toba Tek Singh". In *My Name is Radha: The Essential Manto*. Trans. Muhammad Umar Memon. New Delhi: Penguin Random House, 2015. Nair, Neeti.

Changing Homelands: Hindu Politics and the Partition of India. Cambridge, MA: Harvard University Press, 2011.

Patel, Aakar (ed.), *Why I Write: Essays by Saadat Hasan Manto*. Chennai: Tranquebar Press, 2014.

Rahman, Anisur (trans.) "Toba Tek Singh" by Gulzar, in *Translating Partition*, ed. Attia Hosain et al. New Delhi: Katha, 2001.Retrieved from http://mainshairtunahi.tumblr.com/post/74494221752/gulzar-on-toba-tak-singh on 10 August 2018.

Žižek, Slavoj. *Sublime Object of Ideology*, London: Verso, 2008.

Žižek, Slavoj. *The Courage of Hopelessness: Chronicles of a Year of Acting Dangerously*, London: Penguin Allen Lane, 2017.

PART II

Memory and mnemonic: of homeland and homelessness

6

POLITICS OF MEMORY AND THE MYTH OF HOMELESSNESS

Intizar Husain's *Basti*

Mitarik Barma

The title of Intizar Husain's novel, *Basti*, refers to a place where a group of people live; a settlement. As this suggests, the novel revolves around issues of settlement and home. 'Home' here also bears the greater connotation of homeland, for the novel's protagonist, Zakir, who lives in Rupnagar in India until the Partition in 1947. Following Partition, he leaves India to settle down in Pakistan, his new homeland. The novel chronicles the last few months of 1971 in Pakistan, before the separation of Bangladesh. Bangladesh, then East Pakistan, also housed relatives of many people living in Pakistan and therefore this second Partition brings in issues of homelessness, immigration and national identity of individuals. The novel shows how the essence of homelessness in the refugee diaspora of the newly formed Nations is related to their diasporic displacement.

Gautam Premnath in his article "Remembering Fanon, Decolonizing Diaspora" states that R. Radhakrishnan

> defines diasporic location as the space of the hyphen that tries to co-ordinate, within an evolving relationship, the identity politics of one's place of origin with that of one's present home... with my diasporic displacement there is a 'now' and 'then' to my life, underwritten by a 'here' and 'there.'
>
> *(Premnath 2000: 61)*

Premnath goes on to argue how Radhakrishnan's position in an American university led him to present his "diasporic displacement as the enabling condition for his considerations of postcoloniality" (ibid.). While spatio-temporal dislocation may act as a way to cosmopolitanism for some, it is much more difficult to justify such displacement to oneself, especially when it is related to Nation-formation and requires the acceptance of a new nation–identity for individuals. Politically defined national boundaries might not necessarily align with culturally defined selfhood,

74 Mitarik Barma

and when national identity is in conflict with one's cultural identity it leads to the same kind of uprooted, homeless feeling that Zakir in the narrative deals with. Zakir's constant remembrance of his childhood in the days of political turmoil in Pakistan shows how his childhood memories become a mode of escape for him since he is emotionally not at 'home' in the new country. The name of the place in India where Zakir's childhood was spent, that is Rupnagar, immediately suggests a place of fantasy – 'roop' meaning beauty, or forms, and 'nagar' meaning city. Rupnagar for Zakir is a city of forms, of beauty to which he no longer has access. Muhammad Umar Memon notes in his introduction to Frances W. Pritchett's 1995 translation of the novel;

> The ostensible purpose of the prolonged flashback is to acquaint the reader with Zakir's past. But it is not there merely to evoke a childhood idyll, as some have already assumed. After all, the childhood is recalled through the eyes of an adult Zakir, who both meditates and transforms its events, assigning them a value and importance based on his experiences in the present. The process of remembrance itself is triggered moreover, by specific events in the present. The purpose of the idyll is thus to bring into form some fundamental psychological traits of Zakir's personality – traits which will later provide the rationale for his conduct and responses to events in the present.
>
> *(Memon 1995: n.p.)*

While it is true that the idyllic representation of Zakir's childhood functions as a literary device for Zakir's psychological exposition, Umar Memon's claim that Rupnagar is pure fiction can also be argued against. It might be true that Rupnagar quite possibly does not have a real-life equivalent outside of the narrative space. However, questioning the fecundity of Rupnagar in the narrative would require us to accept almost the entire narrative as a mere fantasy, which is detached from Zakir's reality. It would invalidate Surendar's letter in chapter 6 of the novel and Zakir's yearning for Sabirah as well. Treating the entire narrative as a purely fictitious allegory would also downplay the realities involving the real-life Partition which the novel is trying to address.

The novel deals with a diasporic nostalgia at the moment when national identity of individuals is at crisis. Stuart Hall in regard to diasporic nostalgia notes in his article, "Cultural Identity and Diaspora":

> Who has not known, at this moment, the surge of an overwhelming nostalgia for lost origins, for 'times past'? And yet, this 'return to the beginning' is like the imaginary in Lacan – it can neither be fulfilled nor required, and hence is the beginning of the symbolic, of representation, the infinitely renewable source of desire, memory, myth, search, discovery – in short, the reservoir of our cinematic narratives.
>
> *(Hall 2000: 120)*

The formation of Zakir's symbolic narrative is consistent in his remembrance of the past. His profligate use of Hindu myths and iconographies in his narrative shows how he still emotionally relates to the land he left in India, even though he never tries to physically get back to that land. His vision of India is a synthesis of his memories of the past and his imagination of the current scenario. Despite his desire for Sabirah, his childhood love, we do not see Zakir writing a letter to her. In chapter 6 of the novel, we see Zakir's friend Irfan commenting after reading Surindar's letter where Sabirah is mentioned, "Yar, I thought that Sabirah was a figment of your nostalgic imagination. But she really exists" (Husain 1995: chapter 6). Zakir replies, "Yes, Yar! I want to go and see her one time; before – " (ibid.). Zakir is interrupted by clamours outside and Zakir's mother informs him that a war has broken out. Zakir's remembrance is interrupted by political conflicts of the present. His possible union with Sabirah is therefore fraught with political tension accompanied by his own issues of identity. While Zakir is characterized by a certain kind of inaction on his part, his childhood love is spatio-temporally dislocated through effects of Partition and this distance is emphasized with the conflict between India and Pakistan. Sabirah therefore, like Rupnagar, attains a symbolic form for Zakir and is posited only in memory, marked by a distance which he is afraid to overcome. Rupnagar for Zakir symbolizes an idyllic state to which he cannot return and Sabirah is given the same kind of symbolic treatment in his imagination. Interestingly enough, Sabirah, unlike her other relatives, did not leave India and therefore is now symbolic of the otherness that Zakir has to overcome. Zakir's leaving Rupnagar and India makes him doubly removed from that symbolic land of his childhood and his childhood love. To quote Hall, "The boundaries of difference are continually repositioned in relation to different points of reference" (Hall 2000: 114). Here the difference is more of a political nature than cultural. The politics of difference is employed with the politics of nationhood where religion has been used as a point of difference. As Hall has noted, cultural identity

> is a matter of 'becoming' as well as 'being'. It belongs to the future as much as to the past. It is not something which already exists, transcending place, time, history, culture. Cultural identities come from somewhere, have histories. But like everything which is historical, they undergo constant transformation. Far from being grounded in mere 'recovery' of the past, which is waiting to be found, and which when found, will secure our sense of ourselves into eternity, identities are the names we give to the different ways we are positioned by, and position ourselves within, the narratives of the past.
>
> *(Hall 2000: 112)*

If identities are constructed in such a way that they become emplaced in the past, they also become limited by individual cultural histories which also have a spatial nature. Therefore, it was harder for immigrants in newly formed Pakistan to accept a new national identity. They still carried the cultural history of a pre-Partitioned land. Post-Partition India and Indian culture to them was the political other, but

76 Mitarik Barma

such political otherness had been enforced by a nationalism which for the immigrants was not likely to be as natural, since they lacked a shared cultural history in the new homeland. Moreover, religious undercurrents played a vital role in the politics of India–Pakistan Partition, while linguistic and cultural otherness led to the formation of Bangladesh. Zakir's continual employment of Hindu myths or his visions of mythical Hindu figures attest to the cultural influence of his past. The effect of the enforced otherness can also be seen in case of his peers who are both proud and spiteful of the WAPDA House in Lahore, which is alluded as a pseudo-Taj Mahal in the novel (Husain 1995: chapter 7 (first half)). Since religion played an important role in India-Pakistan Partition politics, the novel shows that as a result of the political otherization, Taj Mahal, a product of the Mughal Civilization becomes the object of hatred. It is turned into an icon that defines and marks the other. Otherization for refugee diaspora, when taken to an extreme, is likely to raise issues of identity where the individuals never feel truly at 'home'.

Kathleen R. Arnold notes in the introduction to her book, *Homelessness, Citizineship and Identity: The Uncanniness of Late Modernity*:

> Rather than simply being a problem of poverty, homelessness is symptomatic of the uprootedness of the nation-state. The formation of national identity does not entail the construction of an ideal citizen, but normative criteria based on economic, gender and racial status, allowing some to be "at home" and politically uprooting others… The lack of a home signals an asymmetrical power dynamic: homeless individuals are not merely inconvenienced by their homelessness but culturally stigmatised and politically disenfranchised.
>
> *(Arnold 2004: 3)*

While politically Zakir is not truly homeless, culturally he is not truly at home. During the sound of explosions in chapter 6 of the novel, the various lanes of the city rise up in Zakir's imagination whereas in chapter 7 he fantasizes about a Hindu king (and he identifies himself with the king) and his meeting with Lord Shiva, where Lord Shiva replies to him that peace is not something that can be attained in the ocean of existence. Here Zakir's inability to be peaceful in the new land portends not only the turbulent political and military situation but also his inability to let go off the cultural past which is now part of the political other. In chapter 8, Zakir thinks about the city ruined by war:

> 'Then where does this smoke come from?' From where? From inside me? But where am I myself? Here, or there? There in the ruined city? And the ruined city? But I myself am the ruined city. 'It's as if my heart is the city of Delhi.'
>
> *(Husain 1995: chapter 8)*

While Zakir observes the political turmoil in Pakistan, his fantasies run around Delhi. The novel therefore suggests that his internalization of Rupnagar's culture and history is so strong that it is even more difficult for him to accept the new politics of otherization. As a Professor of History, he has greater awareness of the shared cultural background of the two countries. Not being a religious jingoist, otherization based on religion is something he cannot easily accept either. In chapter 9, regarding Irfan's statement on his desire for Sabirah, he thinks: "Between her and me time and space have both interposed themselves. They've allied themselves against us. How much time has passed since we walked on the same land, since a single sky spread over both our heads" (Husain 1995: chapter 9).

Here again the distance is perceived both as geographical and temporal. Zakir's desire is thus thwarted by both time and space, where the lack of a shared space is particularly highlighted. Zakir's desire here is being interceded by the political otherness he is having difficulty coping with. He is struggling against the political binary of self and other, where exclusion of the other is part of the politics. Arnold notes in reference to such polarization of political identity in case of citizenship:

> Citizenship in itself represents many things: exclusion and inclusion, a norm of political identity, and territorial belonging. A political identity that is defined by ethnicity or other rigidly exclusive determinants takes all of those factors to the extreme where, for example, exclusion and inclusion means friend and enemy, national identity signifies purity, and territory is an extension of this identity. In this way political identity becomes polarised and the Other a contaminant that must be purified, a dehumanized object of hatred. This polarization involves a collective unconscious in which primitive emotion become reticent during political and economic crises.
>
> *(Arnold 2004: 135–136)*

This characteristic binarism of identity politics is apparent in Zakir's friend Salamat's behaviour in chapter 8 where he calls Zakir and Irfan "imperialist stooges" (Husain 1995: chapter 8). As the novel shows, such binary politics based on hatred impairs self-formation. Self-aware subjects are likely to be wary of such impairment in their identities. In chapter 10, for example, Afzal tells Zakir:

> 'Yar, it happens sometimes that a man, finding others disgusting – well, some morning he discovers that his own face has changed. For the last couple of days I've somehow been fearful that I too might – that my face might – ?'
>
> *(Husain 1995: chapter 10)*

Here it seems that Afzal is aware of the fact that forming his own identity against such binary of self/other is detrimental for his own moral development since this binary formation is fuelled by politics of hatred. Forming one's own identity against such political binary also makes it unstable since political ideologies are dependent upon multiple socio-cultural and economic factors and as such are not necessarily fixed.

78 Mitarik Barma

Eventually such politically motivated self-formation where the political motivation is enforced by state-apparatus leads to a kind of effacement of individual identity and leads to a homogenization of collective self. This effect of politically enforced identity formation is noted by Zakir in chapter 5, when he gets stuck in a rally:

> People walk along in the spell of posters and slogans, ignorant of the handwriting on the wall. As though they're oblivious. Do they walk? Who? Seeing a man pass by him, he hesitated. Several people passed nearby, before him and behind him. He couldn't see their faces clearly, for it was dusk and the streetlight was some distance away. Is it because of the lack of light, or because in the dusk faces usually look strange, or are their faces really like that? Again, someone passed by him. But this time either his eyes failed him, or the man walked very fast, for he couldn't see the man's face at all …
>
> A man is recognized by his walk. Every man, every creature. But they're walking as though they've lost their identities.
>
> *(Husain 1995: chapter 5)*

Upon noticing how identities under political influence are being homogenized, Zakir starts examining his own walk and therefore is able to retain his internal alterity till the end of the narrative. Arnold notes in her discussions on homelessness: "Just as life in the city can be compartmentalized and segregated, on a national level, the binarism of self and other is manifested geographically. Land is an extension of the political self (national identity) … " (Arnold 2004: 137).

When in chapter 11 of Husain's novel, Zakir sees the bunch of keys to their home in Rupnagar, his mother tells him: "'Yes, son, they're a trust from your forefathers. You should keep them carefully.'" But at the same time she reminds him, "'Son, these are the keys of a house to which you no longer have any right'" (Husain 1995: chapter 11). And Zakir thinks:

> The keys of that house, and of that land. The keys of Rupnagar. The keys are here with me, and there a whole time is locked up, a time that has passed. But time doesn't pass! It keeps passing, but it doesn't pass. It keeps hovering around. And houses never stay empty. When those who lived in them go away, the time lives on in the houses.
>
> *(Husain 1995: chapter 11)*

Arnold notes that, "Paradoxically, stability, order and sovereignty are gained through force – exclusion, displacement, prejudice – that is violence" (Arnold 2004: 138). Following Samuel Weber's notion of home, self-determination and violence, she notes how violence is an "imposition of a certain alterity upon the self and others" (Arnold 2004: 138). Since violence can also be defined in terms of infringement on property, one can see how in *Basti*, Husain makes use of Zakir's feelings of homelessness in order to portray that political and ideological violence affects both the self and the other. Exclusion of India from Pakistan therefore gains the greater significance of exclusion of the self from other. Owing to such politics of exclusion, Rupnagar to Zakir is always excluded spatially and temporally and represents a problematic space that he is unable to let go off. On the other hand, in such politics of ideologies, there remains the tendency to efface identity of the other altogether through modifications of history. Ted Svensson, for example, notes that Yoginder Sikand in a visit to a Sufi shrine in East Punjab noticed how the Muslim Pir of that shrine is now accepted as someone belonging to the Hindus and Sikhs only (Svensson 2013: 74). Since Muslims seldom visit that shrine in post-Partition India, and do not live in that area either, the religious history of that shrine is being obfuscated. Husain's narrative does not display this kind of historical revision, rather Zakir's internalization of Hindu myths and his subsequent fantasies of Hindu legends where he would face them shows an attempt towards religious syncretism against one's differential religious identity. At the same time, even in chapter 1 where Zakir is recollecting his idyllic childhood in a time when Hindus and Muslims lived as peaceful neighbours, we find Bi Amma scolding Zakir:

> "Son! Why were you born in our house? You should've been born in some Hindu's house! Your father is always invoking the names of God and the Prophet – he doesn't realize that his son has taken to Hindu stories!"
>
> *(Husain 1995: chapter 1 (first half))*

Husain's narrative therefore also tries to show how individual sense of religious affiliation undercuts attempts of religious syncretism at the grassroots level. It explores the fissures separating the individual from the social, the familial from the political. Arnold in her discussion concludes that home is a continuously evolving paradigm of space and notes: "A politics that embraced lived, daily experience as realistic would allow for greater inclusion, more flexibility in the political process, an expanded notion of home and ultimately, a sort of political homelessness" (Arnold 2004: 161).

She argues that, only through destabilization of home would one be able to feel at home and the rootlessness of cosmopolitanism is actually created by Nation-states. As part of refugee diaspora, Zakir's narrative in the novel reflects similar feelings of rootlessness as observed in the political homelessness of cosmopolitan culture. Since Zakir literally means 'one who remembers', his memory of the past is not only filled with nostalgic reverence for the past but becomes a true unfolding of the emotional history of the people of two newly formed Nations. Svensson notes regarding issues of migration and identity that

> two things that intensely affected the experience of partition both at the state and individual level were the violence that accompanied the division and the ensuing uncertainty regarding what marked out and circumscribed identity. An indicator of the prevailing ambiguity, as regards the space and identity of the new states, was that the borders were not finalised until a few days after dominion status was formally effected ... another vestige of the suspense at

80 Mitarik Barma

play in the migration and territorial division is that the authorities in East Pakistan did not register the number of people that crossed the Indo-Pakistan border until April 1950 ... The latter should be seen as a consequence of the absence, before October 1952, of a demand on those crossing the border between India and East Pakistan to verify their nationality with visas and passports.

(Svensson 2013: 76)

He further notes:

When refugees could, they settled in towns where they were able to join kin and fellow caste members ... In a setting where the nation was represented as a vessel for everyone independent of kinship, caste and birthplace, these attributes did not dissolve or abate in significance.

(Svensson 2013: 78)

Enforced nationalism does not necessarily eradicate politics of caste, kinship and birthplace, nor does it remove economic and gendered divisions.[1] Husain's novel primarily deals with the male protagonist Zakir's problematics of semi-diasporic identity formation and a narrative point of view from female perspective is almost entirely absent.

Readers of this novel, however, would not fail to see how Sabirah is metamorphosed into a symbol for Zakir's idyllic past. In the first chapter of the novel when Zakir as a boy is playing with Sabirah, they enact the making of graves and Sabirah tells Zakir, "Zakir, make me a grave too" (Husain 1995: chapter 1 (first half)). Despite his retention of amorous feelings for Sabirah, Zakir fails to act on those feelings during the political turmoil of 1971. She becomes a part of his buried memories of the past, adding to the symbolic significance of grave-digging as children. Alternatively, Sabirah's not wanting to embrace Pakistan as her new homeland makes her the political other. In her religion and ties of kinship to people in Pakistan and East Pakistan, however, she occupies a position of alterity in the territory of the other. It should also be noted that Sabirah in newly formed India does not live at Rupnagar either. Therefore, she essentially disavows identities of exclusion (which Zakir was trying to accept) by excluding herself from geopolitical territorialities. This does not imply that Sabirah's decision is necessarily a politically conscious one, rather it shows how both as a woman and as someone with possibly poor ties with relatives, she does not feel the need to embrace a national identity that is politically enforced and mitigated by religious difference. Her actions may have no impact in the greater politics of the production of other identity but simultaneously she is placing herself in a position of alterity which Zakir could not do. As a Muslim woman in a Nation-state where Hindus form the majority, she is a subaltern and typical of that kind of marginal emplacement, we do not find much of her voice in the post-Partition narrative. Her narrative existence is limited in Zakir's recollection and Surendar's letter – both of whom are males. Therefore, borrowing Spivak's phrase, it can be said that we do not encounter "the testimony of the women's voice-consciousness" (Spivak 1985: 122) beyond what is presented to us through an essentially masculine narrative point of view. In the second half of chapter 1 when Surendar and Zakir walk together and come to Meerut Gate, before Khirki bazar, the road is bifurcated towards Hindu and Muslim neighbourhoods, "At this fork both hesitated, looked at each other in silence, and set out on their different roads – " (Husain 1995: chapter 1 (second half)). Earlier in the narrative it has also been stated: "After Bi Amma's passing, and the departure from Rupnagar, it was as though he had all at once grown up, as though his childhood had been left behind in Rupnagar" (Husain 1995: chapter 1 (second half)).

Since in Zakir's recollection these events gain significance in retrospect, the fork between Surinder and Zakir's neighbourhood becomes a premonition for Partition. On the other hand, in chapter 5, when Zakir says that he has written two letters to Surendar and is yet to receive any reply, Irfan tells him to write to Sabirah directly. However, we see that instead of embracing Irfan's suggestion right away, Zakir drifts into his solitary remembrance, emphasizing his inability to act. Later in chapter 10, when Surendar states in his letter that Sabirah has broken into tears after hearing about Zakir's letters, Zakir fails to comprehend how his letters can be linked with Sabirah's emotional breakdown. Surindar's letter states:

> "During those days when the worst news kept coming from Dhaka, I always found her calm. But today she burst into tears. I didn't understand. But it made me sad to see her. My friend! May I say one thing? Don't take it amiss. You're a cruel person, or perhaps now that you're in Pakistan you've become so."
>
> *(Husain 1995: chapter 10)*

As is insinuated in Surendar's letter, regardless of Sabirah's opposition to immigration to Pakistan or East Pakistan, quite possibly she retains her feelings for Zakir (although in Zakir's narrative it is never clear how such developments might have occurred in the past) as she might have held her identity in terms of pre-Partition memories as Zakir did. But for Zakir, who finds in her a symbolic significance of a past that is inaccessible to him, it is impossible to understand her emotional state after hearing about him. He wonders: "When she heard about my letters she burst into tears! Why? Am I cruel? On what grounds?" (Husain 1995: chapter 10).

Zakir's inability to understand Sabirah might be interpreted as his own denial of the alterity embedded in the pre-Partition past, which he is trying to keep away to construct his present identity in the new homeland. In chapter 6 of the novel Surendar states in his letter: "Zakir, this Sabirah of yours seems less like a girl than like a historical relic! ... your Sabirah. A silent melancholy girl, staying on alone in the whole of India" (Husain 1995: chapter 6).

Surendar's statement regarding Sabirah being a historical relic gains ironic significance in the narrative since that is precisely how Zakir treats Sabirah. According to Surendar, Sabirah has punished herself for staying back in India by leaving Rupnagar. Rupnagar has lost its meaning for her. Surendar himself is unable to

82 Mitarik Barma

trace back his childhood as he is conscious of the void that persists in the absence of the 'other'. As he states in his letter in chapter 6:

> And sometimes I feel that in my childhood I must have offended some holy man, and he cursed me: 'Son, your native land will no longer let you see her.' So the town of Vyaspur doesn't let me see her. When I go there, the town seems to ask, 'Where is the other?' And when I can't find an answer, she closes her door against me.
>
> *(Husain 1995: chapter 6)*

Surendar's childhood memories are therefore marked by the absence of the other in the present. At the same time, it is noticeable how Zakir's attempt to think about Sabirah is always interrupted by interventions of the reality at present. For example, at the end of chapter 6, when Zakir starts to think about Sabirah, his thinking is interrupted by the sound of droning noise made by Indian planes. Similarly, both in chapters 9 and 10, his thoughts of Sabirah are interrupted by knockings at the door. It is not until the end of chapter 11, when the conflict between India and Pakistan is over and Shiraz (the place where Zakir and his friend would meet on a regular basis) is completely at ruins that Zakir is able to make the decision to write a letter to Sabirah. It can thus be said that only when the clamour of the outside world has subsided Zakir is able to face his internal complexities and suppressed emotions. If Sabirah is for Zakir a relic of history, then reconciliation with that past is possible only when the present has been destroyed. Afzal's final statement, "This is the time for a sign – " (Husain 1995: chapter 11) is therefore symbolic of a new beginning, where following the catastrophe of the war, national identity of Pakistan is liable to reconstruction. At the end of chapter 9, Afzal suggests of creating an idyllic Pakistan and states, "In beautiful Pakistan there will be only beautiful people" (Husain 1995: chapter 9). Even at this point in the narrative Afzal is trying to place himself in the altar of a prophet. However, near the end of chapter 11, sitting before the ruins of Shiraz, he finally accepts that he is not eligible for such moral high ground and as the narrative goes, "Afzal stood for a while. Then he sat down, then he said slowly, 'Yar, we weren't virtuous either.' He fell silent, and looked at them both. 'We're cruel. We too.'" (Husain 1995: chapter 11).

Here Afzal's realization is not clearly traced out, but it is symbolic of understanding the cultural violence of exclusion that pervades even the conceived utopia of Pakistan and culminates in the rupture and subsequent formation of Bangladesh. Afzal's assurance against Irfan's despair and bitterness at the end of the narrative that it is times like these when a sign can be seen therefore suggests the possibility of a historical reconstruction of national identity, where political development would be positive.

In this regard, one would also notice that Husain's narrator, despite being a professor of history, refrains from providing us with a detailed, pedagogic reconstruction of history. Zakir never tries to provide a larger historical narrative with great details. As Deepesh Chakrabarty notes in the article "Postcoloniality and the Artifice of History: Who Speaks for 'Indian' Pasts?":

So long as one operates within the discourse of 'history' produced at the institutional site of the university, it is not possible simply to walk out of the deep collusion between 'history' and the modernizing narratives of citizenship, bourgeois public and private and the nation state. 'History' as a knowledge system is firmly embedded in institutional practices that invoke the nation state at every step – witness the organization and politics of teaching, recruitment, promotions, and publication in history departments, politics that survive the occasional brave and heroic attempts by individual historians to liberate 'history' from the metanarratives of nation state.

(Chakrabarty 1992: 19)

For Chakrabarty, academic history with its themes of nation states and citizenship defer the possibility of a history where the word is imagined as "radically heterogenous." Husain's narrative subverts such politics of homogenized historical narrativizations through Zakir's dream-like narration. While Zakir is observant of the politics of Partition, he is also a person in whom the confluence of Hindu and Islamic culture can be seen. His narrative is largely personal and only brings in the Partition narratives in disjointed segments. Moreover, his largely symbolic narrative effaces intricate personal details to guide the readers towards a greater understanding of the subjective experience of immigrants during the 1971. As Umar Memon notes:

If 1947 divided the South Asian subcontinent on the basis of religion, 1971 left no doubt that religion itself had proved an insufficiently strong bond to keep people united. Such estrangement could be explained only by the weakening of the individual and national moral sensibility. Society had not been regenerated or renewed. The loss of memory, the loss of collective identity, spelled disaster and even death – a death which didn't come soft-footed or unannounced, but was preceded by a state of moral turpitude in which a nation's conscience darkened and lost all power of distinction between right and wrong, good and evil.

(Memon 1995: n.p.)

Husain's novel has not only been able to bring out the state of moral confusion in the newly formed Pakistan but has also been able to portray how nationalism in the new nation state affected every individual differently. Zakir's friends, for example, do not have the same worldview as him and yet their meetings in Shiraz and the interactions there would show how on an individual level there was always an attempt to cope with the situation to bring progress in Pakistan. It is true that there is an undercurrent of religious sentiments in the novel and Umar Memon identifies Zakir's worldview to be a Shiite one. Nevertheless, religion is not the foreground in the narration. Rather, Zakir's identity formation around religious myths suggests a religious syncretism and cultural plurality. The attempted religious and cultural syncretism in Zakir's character and his final decision to connect with Sabirah across the border symbolizes a greater need for communication and emotional exchange with the political other. The novel thus should not be treated as only the story of an individual's emotional journey or a narrative of Partition but can also be interpreted as a subversion of the politics of border.

Note

1 As Anita Inder Singh notes in *The Partition of India*, "a person may identify himself as a Hindu, Muslim, Sikh, Christian or whatever. Merely by doing so he does not create a social, religious or political problem. The problem arises when a unified religious, political, social or economic consciousness is assumed, usually without evidence" (Singh 2008: 7).

Works Cited

Arnold, Kathleen R. *Homelessness, Citizenship, and Identity: The Uncanniness of Late Modernity*. Ed. Thomas M. Wilson. New York: State University Press of New York, 2004.

Chakrabarty, Dipesh. "Postcoloniality and the Artifice of History: Who Speaks for 'Indian' Pasts?" *Representations* 37 (1992): 1–26. Retrieved from http://www.jstor.org/stable/2928652. Accessed on 11 May 2019.

Hall, Stuart. "Cultural Identity and Diaspora." *Contemporary Postcolonial Theory: A Reader.* Ed. Padmini Mongia. New Delhi: Oxford University Press, 2000, pp. 110–121.

Husain, Intizar. *Basti*. Trans. from the Urdu by Frances W. Pritchett, 1995. http://www.columbia.edu/itc/mealac/pritchett/00litlinks/basti/index.html. Accessed on 18 August 2018.

Memon, Umar." Introduction" to *Basti*, by Intizar Husain. Trans. Frances W. Pritchett, 1995. http://www.columbia.edu/itc/mealac/pritchett/00litlinks/basti/index.html. Accessed on 18 August 2018.

Premnath, Gautam. "Remembering Fanon, Decolonizing Diaspora." *Postcolonial Theory and Criticism*. Ed. Laura Chrisman and Benita Parry. Cambridge: D.S. Brewer, 2000, pp. 57–74.

Singh, Anita Inder. *The Partition of India*. New Delhi: National Book Trust, India, 2008.

Spivak, Gayatri Chakravorty. "Can the Subaltern Speak? Speculations on Widow Sacrifice." *Wedge* 7(8) (Winter/Spring/Winter/Spring1985): 120–130.

Svensson, Ted. *Production of Postcolonial India and Pakistan: Meanings of Partition*. Ed. Jenny Edkins. Oxford: Routledge, 2013.

7

REDRAWING THE BORDERS OF NOSTALGIA

A reading of Ritwik Ghatak's selected short stories

Somasree Sarkar

> Any work of art is the artist's subjective approximation of the reality around him. It is a sort of reaction set in motion by the creative impulse of the human unconscious.
> *(Ritwik Ghatak,* Cinema and I)

> The struggle of man against power is the struggle of memory against forgetting.
> *(Milan Kundera,* The Book of Laughter and Forgetting)

In his engagingly erudite essay titled "Cinema and the Subjective Factor", Ghatak re-considers the relationship between the aesthetic and the material. The aesthetic to him isn't a sovereign discursive paradigm that is independent of reality. Instead, the real and the material are often complemented by the imagined order of the aesthetic. As such, the artist is often discursively determined by his/her art; it is the aesthetic essence which overrules his/ her ontological essence of being. Ghatak observes "As civilisation progresses, Prometheus becomes Aeschylus; the Titans give place to Shaw-like supermen, magic is transformed into art" (Ghatak 1987: 62).

The cultural and the consequent ideal of the aesthetic, which in Theodor Adorno's opinion, possesses an 'irrevocable autonomy' (Adorno 2002: 1) influences the material-real; it can essentially transcend its determinant material modes of production and influence, often override the material. As such, the aesthetic generates a second life to the real; it becomes "afterimages of empirical life in so far as they help the latter to what is denied them outside their own sphere and thereby free it from that to which they are condemned by reified external experience" (Adorno 2002: 4). The after-life that the aesthetic and art has, derives its essence from the material.

The material inevitably involves the subjective, the being and becoming of the subject is inextricably associated with the material disposition of the self. Barbara Bender points out: "It is through our experience and understanding that we engage

86 Somasree Sarkar

with the materiality of the world. These encounters are subjective, predicated on our *being in* and learning *how to go on* in the world" (Bender and Winer 2001: 4).

As such, material truths are not just hermeneutic entrapments which systematize a structure and valorize the collective; it is also relevant as an irreducibility that is pre-conditional and as such, foundational to any considerations of singularity. The singular subject is often associated with the material-social, where both, human and the non-human, the socio-cultural and the spatial influence the contingent ontic essence of being.

The spatial is an integral aspect of the material and as Lefebvre points out, it is "not a pre-existing void, endowed with formal properties alone" (Lefebvre 1991: 170). Instead, as Lefebvre argues, the spatial has a relational and an 'immediate relationship' with the body or the living subject. John J. Su observes that the spatial has been relevant in any considerations pertaining to the ontological essence of the self since antiquity and the "idea that the individuals are profoundly influenced by their place of birth" (Su 2005: 23) have been nurtured by philosophers like Aristotle and Herodotus. As such, the spatial doesn't merely signify the geo-political; it is equally relevant within the considerations of the material.

The Partition of India had affected not just the ethical and the juridico-political; it was also significant in its re-formulation of the spatial. The Radcliffe line had displaced multitudes and within a very short span of time, had turned these erstwhile residents into refugees. The refugees were encumbered into a climate of loss, where the spectral reminiscence of homeland lingered as a foreknowledge and which sustained as a point of reference, validated in contrast with the present state of being of the displaced migrant. In other words, the 'then' of home would consistently haunt the 'now' that was dystopic and disjointed, in form of a memory that would volatize the spatial and the temporal and refuse a distinction between the two. Negotiating and resolving the tension between the now and then, the old and the new, the home and exile becomes the characteristic essence of the displaced consciousness.

The constant strife to fit into the new, to build a home away from home, to embrace, to adapt and adopt, find place in the fertile oeuvre of Partition works of the writer and film-maker, Ritwik Ghatak. His stories and films based on Partition of India voice his personal ache and angst as a refugee. His works are disturbingly realistic and are deeply emotional that zoom into the torn and disheveled lives of refugees in Calcutta and its suburban areas. Ghatak says,

> Tagore once said – "art has to be beautiful, but, before that, it has to be truthful'". Now what is truth? There is no eternal truth. Every artist has to learn private truth through a painful private process. And that is what he has to convey.
>
> *(Ghatak 1987: 75)*

For Ghatak, the private experience of an artist shapes the artist's expression that finds place in his work of art. In other words, it is the material consciousness of the artist that influences and shapes his artistic or aesthetic sensibility. Ghatak abides by this belief of his as his works of art, both films and writings, reflect the anxiety of his age. His own material consciousness of displacement and the experiential reality of homelessness are captured in his literary and visual modes of representation.

The irrevocable rupture and the consequent displacement had deeply affected Ghatak and his literary representations are often burdened with a consciousness of loss that valorize an idyllic essence of home which is a remembered truth. The memories of the past intrude the present to create a liminal space for the immigrants. They dwell at the threshold, confused, anxious, with the uncertainty, with feeble hope of assimilating into the broader space with the majority. The existence in the liminal space breeds nostalgia and the longing for the past, the home lost. The term 'nostalgia' was coined and popularized by Johannes Hofer, the Swiss physician in 1688. Its early connotation has been in medical term as its origin bears reference to a disease of homesickness. It refers to a pathological condition of severe longing for home. 'Nostalgia', however, has gradually broken ties from its early association with psycho-pathology. Alastair Bonnett observes, "the pathological paradigm was giving way, by the end of the nineteenth century, to a broader conception of nostalgia's power. It became connected to the sentimentalization of the past, to common place feelings of loss, yearning and attachment" (Bonnett 2010: 5). Nostalgia, surpassing the realm of pathology, had transgressed into the realm of social. With spatial dislocation at the turn of the twentieth century, nostalgia among the dislocated communities had become a shared phenomenon.

'Nostalgia' expresses the shared loss and pain of a community, hence it is ubiquitously public and personal. It at once embodies the memories of past of many and also the personal pangs of each, yearning for yesterday. The yearning for the old, the pervasive sense of loss, results in disorientation with the present and it also suggests "the past is emerging as a site of shared and continuous rupture, in a society that has come to be characterized by uncertainty" (Bonnett 2010: 20). The profound sense of loss and the ambiguity in the process of cultural assimilation among thousands of uprooted expatriates, add to the uncertainty.

Memory emerges as a defense strategy to the culture of change and dislocation and the consequent climate of uncertainty that pervades the Modern age. Memory is that alternative discursive paradigm that can contradict the homo-hegemonic discourses of power and can essentially validate a counter-narrative, setting up a mythic spatial-temporal that stands in sharp contrast to the empirically authentic spatial-temporal real. The real is already grounded and discursively stable, while the remembered is unreliable but equally authentic.

This opposing disposition in the immediate aftermath of Partition complicates the web of the social structure. Partition is the cause of disarrayed lives of many and the nostalgia bred is the pain for the past, both among the direct victims and the victims who suffer out of the chaos due to mass influx in their recognized space of home. The pain is not restricted to the loss of home in another land, but is also for the loss of settlement, loss of friends and family, loss of community living with considerable solidarity. The present proliferates under nostalgia that paradoxically is opposed to present and is also seen to be an impediment to the future. But, nostalgia has been the living experience within the new space of partitioned India. Memory has the mobility to flout the temporal norms and to travel in time, displacing an individual temporarily in psychological space, while remaining grounded in geographical space. The mobility of memory evokes the 'algia' that in turn may lead to a state of mourning. This mourning is constructed upon a loss that the subject doesn't want to replace and the mourning subject is a formulated agency who is preoccupied with the idealization of absence. Vijay Mishra observes,

> The condition of mourning is after all predicated upon a loss that the subject (such as Goethe's Werther) does not want to replace because to do so would taint the purity of the object lost. The subject turns away from reality and clings on to the object of mourning even when reason dictates that the object can no longer be grasped,
>
> *(Mishra 2007: 9)*

The idealization of absence and the persistence of mourning has often been a characteristic response of the displaced subject to the loss of the familiar that was a result of Partition. The mourning is captured in the heart wrenching lamenting query of a bereaved old man in Ghatak's *Meghe Dhaka Tara*: "Repair? Will you be able to repair my heart – will you? So that I can enjoy Wordsworth again? That Swan and Shadows float double!" The heart of the old man is damaged beyond recovery. His deep-rooted nostalgia has shattered him irrevocably. Nostalgia, perhaps for him is the source of pain and pleasure, his reason for being shattered, as well as the reason for his existence. Nostalgia is never dismissed, rather by nurturing nostalgia one derives masochistic pleasure. It is damaging on one hand, but it is also the life-pursuing force.

Ghatak's short stories, "Sarak" ("The Road", 2018b) and "Sfatikpatra" ("The Crystal Goblet", 2018a), exemplify the hues of nostalgia and the pain of longing that the estranged self experiences in the fractured and fragmented purview of Partition. "Sarak" ("The Road") is a narrative that captures the confusion of being uprooted. It pans into the life of Hindus, forced to migrate to the western part of Bengal (part of present India) and also focuses on the life of Muslims on the western side of the border that is part of geographically renewed India. With Partition, the familiar space for Muslims in the western part of Bengal was abruptly defamiliarized by heaping upon them the identity of non-Indian who must be forced to cross the borders to East Pakistan. The story presents the misery of loss of home both within and outside the space of the familiar. It is a depiction of the gradual transformation of the familiar into the unfamiliar and the estrangement of the subject within a gradually impinging milieu of dystopia. The deprivation of the familiar and the realization of hostility leads to the view of the past as better than the present that in turn creates nostalgia. This is termed the 'poverty of the present requirement' where "the intentional object of nostalgia is necessarily a past regarded as preferable to the present" (Howard 2012: 643). Nostalgia primarily involves a negative evaluation of the present in relation to the past. It also idealizes the past, negating all the deficiencies,

Redrawing the borders of nostalgia **89**

evoking a tranquil image of an idyllic bliss. The memories triggered by nostalgia may not cover a wide range of past experiences as they are restricted to the memories of brighter past, deliberately overlooking the grey. Linda Hutcheon reflects on nostalgia:

> The simple, pure, ordered, easy, beautiful, or harmonious past is constructed (and then experienced emotionally) in conjunction with the present – which, in turn, is constructed, complicated, contaminated, anarchic, difficult, ugly, and confrontational. Nostalgic distance sanitizes as it selects, making the past feel complete, stable, coherent, safe …
>
> *(Hutcheon 2000: 195)*

Nostalgia is a feeling that is evoked "when two different temporal moments, past and present, come together … and, often, carry considerable emotional weight" (Hutcheon 2000: 94). The feeling of longing erupts from a feeling of lack and the lacuna in the present is fulfilled by transporting to the past by the vehicle of monochromatic images retrieved from memories that now gradually seem to fade away. The realization of loss and the inability to regain those ideally constructed past days leads to nostalgic mourning. Mourning comes after a trauma, trauma after a death. It is the death of the past. The fragments of memories conjure the mourning, ensuring that the past is dead, never to return. Within a Derridean understanding, mourning "consists always in attempting to ontologize remains, to make them present, in the first place to by identifying the bodily remains and by localizing the dead" (Derrida 1994: 9). Here, the memories of the past (dead) embody the physical remains, realization of which instigates one to mourn.

The phantom of memories haunts the present, the haunting assumes more importance than the present being, as the narrator of the story, "The Road", recalls: "My dear Israel used to live in one of the rooms belonging to this slum" (Ghatak 2018b: 200). Israel subsequently appears as a chaotic wreck after the loss of his abode and his son, Emdad. Israel mourns, "It was all over for him last night you know. Emdad died of cholera at the Park Circus refugee camp last night" (Ghatak 2018b: 202). Emdad is now only a scrap of the past, a memory, a specter of 'hauntology'. A similar situation is echoed in "The Crystal Goblet", where a woman wails for the impending death of her son from cholera as the narrator visits refugee slums in Delhi. This story gives a similar picture of Partition refugees on the north-western borders of India. The narrator narrates the woman's hapless condition:

> She was groaning and saying something. I could catch only some of her slurred words – "Meramunna, meralaal". She was sitting with her feet apart and pulling at her hair; her mouth was dripping with saliva. A beautiful child, gasping and on the point of death lay in front of her.
>
> *(Ghatak 2018a: 158–159)*

The pathetic experience of death of sons bind Israel and the woman with the same thread of trauma. The ghost of their sons' memories pervade their cursed world of

90 Somasree Sarkar

silence. The memories haunt the living experience, they become specters of hauntology. Martin Hagglund, in his exploration of hauntology argues,

> Derrida's aim is to formulate a general 'hauntology', in contrast to 'ontology' that thinks being in terms of self-identical presence. What is important about the figure of specter, then, is that it cannot be fully present: it has no being in itself but marks a relation to what is no longer or not yet.
>
> *(Hagglund 2008: 82)*

Their dead sons no longer have any physical presence, but they are part of the presence as figments of past, as memories. The sons are present in their absence.

The hauntology is intensified with the poignant song, that conjures the memories of the lost idyllic home: "You boat of my soul, driven by desire! / Go to the country where lives the radiant beauty!" (Ghatak 2018b: 203). The country left is the one with "radiant beauty", compounding the pain and making the longing even more intense and heart-wrenching. The country now is the home for unrest, hatred, hunger and poverty. The radiance is lost by the arbitrary division of the motherland that was one, but now broken into pieces, only to add to the misery of majority. The old man's petition to the Government to procure his belongings in "The Crystal Goblet" is a pointer towards the politics involved in Partition. The political leaders did not divulge away from lying in order to make people believe about the positive consequence of the Radcliffe line. The man makes a list of his belongings, "a cot, two buffaloes, one plough, clothes, other movables" (Ghatak 2018a: 164) to get them back "in the land of (his) Hindu brothers" (Ghatak 2018a: 165) as promised to him. When he learns from the narrator about the impossibility of the fulfillment of his expectation to regain his possessions and to meet Panditji, he infuriates with blazing eyes and cries with "terror-soaked voice":

> Who's the enemy … the enemy? I'll crack open his skull, finish him off, once I identify him. I'm sure I will … I'll find him out one day and that day … Yes, I'll live to see that day, without doubt.
>
> *(Ghatak 2018a: 166)*

The question, "who's the enemy?" must be pondered upon. The question lies at the heart of the narrative. The leaders have justified that the Hindus and Muslims are enemies of each other. But, after being transported to the land of their 'brothers', they meet with no justice. Yet, Israel says, "But I know there is no justice in this place. That is why I am leaving for Pakistan" (Ghatak 2018b: 203–204), the place of hope, the place of new dawn. The cycle of hope and desire continues among millions who seek for acceptance and abode in the new land of their 'brothers'. As "The Road" ends with the vibrating sound of march of millions, marching towards the promised land of their 'brothers': "Goom, goom, goom, goom, goom, goom, goom, goom. The pulsating throb of millions on the march!" (Ghatak 2018b: 214)

Works Cited

Adorno, Theodor W. *Aesthetic Theory*. Trans. Robert Hullot. New York: Continuum, 2002.

Bender, Barbara and Margot Winer (ed.). *Contested Landscapes: Movement, Exile and Place*. Oxford: Berg, 2001.

Bonnett, Alastair. *Left in the Past: Radicalism and the Politics of Nostalgia*. New York: The Continuum International Publishing Group, 2010.

Derrida, Jacques. *Specters of Marx: The State of the Debt, the Work of Mourning and the New International*. Trans. Peggy Kamuf. New York: Routledge, 1994.

Ghatak, Ritwik. *Cinema and I*. Calcutta: Rupa & Co., 1987.

Ghatak, Ritwik. *Meghe Dhaka Tara*. Trans. Sudeshna Chakrabarty as *The Trauma and the Triumph: Gender and Partition in Eastern India*. Ed. Jasodhara Bagchi and Subhoranjan Dasgupta. Kolkata: Stree, 2003.

Ghatak, Ritwik. "The Crystal Goblet." *Ritwik Ghatak Stories*. Trans. Rani Ray. New Delhi: Niyogi Books, 2018a. 156–167.

Ghatak, Ritwik. "The Road." *Ritwik Ghatak Stories*. Trans. Rani Ray. New Delhi: Niyogi Books, 2018b. 199–214.

Hagglund, Martin. *Radical Atheism: Derrida and the Time of Life*. Stanford, CA: Stanford University Press, 2008.

Howard, Scott Alexander. "Nostalgia." *Oxford Journals* 72. 4 (2012): 641–650.

Hutcheon, Linda. "Irony, Nostalgia, and the Postmodern." *Methods for the Study of Literature as Cultural Memory*. Ed. R. Vervliet. Amsterdam: Rodopi, 2000. 189–207.

Kundera, Milan. *The Book of Laughter and Forgetting*. Trans. Aaron Asher. London:Faber & Faber, 1996.

Lefebvre, Henry. *The Production of Space*. trans. Donald Nicholson Smith. Oxford: Basil Blackwell, 1991.

Mishra, Vijay. *The Literature of the Indian Diaspora: Theorizing the Diasporic Imaginary*. London: Routledge, 2007.

Su, John J. *Ethics and Nostalgia in the Contemporary Novel*. Cambridge: Cambridge University Press, 2005.

8

MEMORY OF HOME AND THE IMPOSSIBILITY OF RETURN

Reading Jibanananda Das's "I Shall Return to This Bengal" and "I Have Seen Bengal's Face"

Madhuparna Mitra Guha and Rupayan Mukherjee

> In every stranger's face I searched
> The maps to my home.
>
> *(Faiz Ahmad Faiz, "Dil-e-man, musaafir-e-man")*

In James Joyce's *küntslerroman*, *Portrait of the Artist as a Young Man*, Stephen Dedalus, the growing artist in a troubled history of the immediate, experiences the need to transcend the politically appropriative limits of the age and seek the possibilities of asserting a liminal identity that is transpolitical. Stephen realizes that the material realities of a politically turbulent Ireland, which is engaged in an endeavor to authenticate Irishness by excluding colonial English as the malicious influence on 'Ireland's hope' (Joyce 2000: 194), appropriates the identity and agency of the individual Irish subject, who in turn, is striving to explore the artistic sensibility in him. Stephen's continuous attempts of negotiation between the political and the aesthetic, the times and the timeless, the immanent real and the transcendental ideal, ends with his epiphanic realization that silence, cunningness and exile are the possible traits to be inculcated to ensure a sovereignty to his art and artistic sensitivity.

The aesthetic has often been ambiguous in its tryst with reality, wherein it is both confounded in the real and it also has the possibility to unmake the real, it is both relevant in history and yet it enables the historically grounded subject to unburden the nightmare of history. This is the element of supplement that the aesthetic has, wherein it can both be absorbed in the immanent and can extend beyond the finitudes of immanence. Gayatri Spivak defines the 'supplement' in her preface to Derrida's *Of Grammatology* as a 'playful dissemination' (Derrida 1974: lxvi) which can extend beyond the hermeneutic contours of interpretation. The supplement, in Derridean terms, is an excess which is not just relevant as a substitute but is also functional in its redemptive appeal to the deficiency of the present. The wistful economy of supplement that the aesthetic has, is relevant in the way it seeks to unmake the inferno of the real and actual and instead provokes the possibility of seeking other truths and contemplating other realities which are ahistoric and atemporal.

Jibanananda Das, whom Buddhadev Basu described as the most solitary and sovereign Bengali poet, and who has often been inarguably considered to be the precursor of Modernism in Bengali poetry, was deeply reliant on the autonomy that the poetico-aesthetic cherishes in being a trans-socio-political discourse. Das, in his book, *Kobitar Kotha*, writes that poetry instead of advocating a social or epistemic vitality and usefulness, nourishes an "incomprehensible, unfamiliar surplus" (Das 2013: 9) that is an offspring of the poetic imaginary and the constituent sovereignty of essence that the imaginary embodies or internalizes in thought and experience. For Jibanananda, the poetic and the poet is sacrosanct in their independency and sovereignty from the collective, where philosophy, politics, society and religion all cease to exist, and even in their existence, they are ontologically distinct from their essence in praxis. In other words, the poesis of the imaginary ontologically subverts the praxis of the immanent (Das 2013: 9).

The historical cataclysm of Partition in the Indian subcontinent marked a moment of departure and rupture, not just within the fabric of collective history but also in the collective experience and perception of history and historical consciousness, continuously perturbing the immanent. A continuous saga of displacement and shifting identities, of unmaking and (re-)making citizenship, of violence and recuperation, the epoch of Partition promoted and consolidated an immediate reality of the outside which was always-already in a state of perpetual flux. This is the intrinsic essence of estrangement that haunts the Partition-afflicted consciousness of the subject, wherein the troubled socio-political milieu disengages the subject from the apriori conceived, stably perceived convictions of space and habitus. The displaced subject, engulfed by the dystopia of space, is subjected to an ontological disorientation. The historical catastrophe of Partition involves not just a violation of the subject and the constituent body and mind of the subject; it is also a tragedy of violated spaces. This space, in turn, is intertwined with the ontic self and the ontological sensibility of the subject, with the inter-related 'other' or outside being elementary in formulating the sense of being in the subject. Henri Lefebvre points out that spaces are not just perceived and conceived but also lived, with the subject often apprehending, interpreting and evolving his state of being in co-relation with the dynamics of space (Lefebvre 1991: 371). Simmel, anticipating Lefebvre, in his essay "The Metropolis and the Mental Life", writes: "all the most banal externalities of life finally are connected with the ultimate decisions concerning the meaning and style of life" (Simmel 1969: 51).

The spatial is thus instrumental in determining, moulding and constituting the being of the subject, for identities are contingent with spatial paradigms. This is best experienced when one takes into account the predicament of exile, which Edward Said describes as "the perilous state of non-belonging" (Said 2000: 187). In Said's opinion, exile dissociates the self from the familiar contours of homeland and topos. The exiled is beckoned by constant remembrances of homeland, which tempts him/her with a desire of return and yet it is imbibed within the economy of the impossible. Said observes, "No return to the past is without irony, or without a sense that a full return, or repatriation, is impossible" (Said 2000: 29).

Returning sustains its impossibility for the exiled self in the sense that homelands are not just constituted in atemporal ideologues of space but they are temporal renderings of space. To be more precise, spatial perceptions are not necessarily independent of temporal conjectures, rather homes are time-bound. They are located in a past that is remembered and experienced, that is shared and lived. Hence, although the returning migrant can reconcile with the displaced space, reconciliation with the displaced time is an impossibility. It is only with an 'imagined' home that the displaced subject can reconcile, which, to use Rushdie's words, are "broken mirrors, some of whose fragments have been irretrievably lost" (Rushdie 1991: 11).

The complementary poems "I Shall Return to This Bengal" and "I Have Seen Bengal's Face" by Jibanananda Das are specimen poetic endeavors which can be read as the displaced subject's longing for a lost homeland, explored within the logos of the imagined. The poems elaborate an uncontaminated sacrosanct ideal of Bengal, rich in its bounty of nature. This chapter will substantiate how Das's Bengal, through the transubstantiated poetics of the imagined, universalizes an ideal of the homeland that is acultural, ahistoric and atemporal. The chapter shall further implicate how the poet's faith in the sovereignty of the aesthetic enables him to surpass the immediacy of displacement and the impending doom of the dehumanized politicos.

The two poems in discussion were a part of the 1957 collection, *Rupashi Bangla*, which was a collection of 62 sonnets, all of them published posthumously. Believed to have been written around the mid-1930s, these poems cherish a mythic, transcendental ethos of Bengal and remonstrate Bengal (Das's homeland) by placing it not just within the economy of the natural and the familiar but also the surplus of historico-mythical and the imagined. The spatial is conceived in the familiar, i.e. within the geological, political, cultural and natural contours of the space but with the intervention of the poetic consciousness, the spatial paradigm of Bengal transcends the systematic and hermeneutic categorical imperatives of the immediate and instead conceives the space in a 'mythic time', a kairos that doesn't necessarily contradict, yet nevertheless refutes to limit its possibilities within the governed and structured schematic of the chronos.

The poem "I Have Seen Bengal's Face" can serve as a perfect instance of Das's transubstantiated poetics where the natural life and condition of a primordial Bengal cohabits the literary space with the fictive and the historicized. In Das's ideal of Bengal, the mythic and the natural are intertwined, so much so, that the poet cherishes an ecstasy of satiation as he reflects that the Banyan, the Tamal, the Hijal, the Cactus and the Doyel, all of which are an inseparable and comprehensive part of rural Bengal, have remained timeless and eternal in their appeal, mesmerizing both the poet and the merchant Chand Saudagar, the adamant patriarch in the Manasha-mangalkabya, who refuses worship to Manasha, the ethnic goddess. Das's reference to Chand Saudagar introduces the imagined and the fictive within his ideal of Bengal and, what is more, they are simultaneous co-habitants with the mnemonics of the natural life of Bengal. The split between the real and the imagined, the natural and the fictive is jeopardized and Das refuses to valorize or prioritize one over the other, cherishing a liminal spatial experience, where the natural becomes the missing link that can enable a continuity between the ficto-factual mythic and the temporal now, transinfusing the local 'now' into the mythic/historic-cultural 'then'. What is more, Das consistently folds the natural into the mythic as he imagines the natural flora and fauna of Bengal to be the *ghungru* of Behula, the daughter-in-law of Chand Sauda-gar, dancing before Lord Indra at Amaravati. Behula is the suffering heroine in Manasamangalkabya, who is married to Lakhindar but loses her husband to a fatal snake bite on her nuptial night. She consequently sets out in her quest to redeem the curse that Manasa, the snake goddess, had inflicted on the family. She sails across Gangur and finally reaching Amaravati, redeems the curse with her dance and wins back the life of her deceased husband Lakhindar.

The tentative period during which the poem was composed (the 1930s) was an epoch that was anticipating the political devastation called Partition. Bengal had previously experienced the tremors of Partition in 1905, with Lord Curzon, the then viceroy, putting forward the controversial proposal of dividing the province of Bengal in terms of religious majorities. In his speech at Dacca, Curzon put forward his notorious plan of 'bifurcating Bengal' (as he preferred to call it), facading the communal overtones with the mask of good governance. Curzon declared:

> which must give to the people of these districts, by reason of their numerical strength and their superior culture, the preponderating voice in the province so created, which would invest the Mahomedans in Eastern Bengal with a unity which they have not enjoyed since the days of the old Musulman Viceroys and Kings…Is it not transparent, Gentlemen, that you must be the head and heart of any such new organism, instead of the extremities, and do you really mean to be so blind to your own future as to repudiate the offer?
>
> *(Curzon n.d.: 303)*

The implementation of the bifurcation policy had both immediate and long-lasting implications. Surendranath Banerjea, a staunch and vehement opposer of the Viceroy, records the immediate aftermath of the bifurcation resolution, which was passed on July 19, 1905. Banerjea writes:

> We felt that we had been insulted, humiliated and tricked. We felt that the whole of our future was at stake, and that it was a deliberate blow aimed at the growing solidarity and self-consciousness of the Bengali-speaking population. Originally intended to meet administrative requirements, we felt that it had drawn to itself a political flavour and complexion, and if allowed to be passed, it would be fatal to our political progress and that close union between the Hindus and Mahomedans upon which the prospect of Indian advancement so largely depended.
>
> *(Banerjea 1963: 173)*

The latent implications of the policy were, however, far-reaching, carrying the germs of communalism, which would manifest chronically in systematic outbreaks of riots and epidemics of violence. M.R.A. Baig, in his rigorously researched essay *The Partition of Bengal and Its Aftermath,* points out that the Anti-Partition movement, which evolved as a reaction to the bifurcation policy that Curzon implemented in Bengal, was constantly haunted by the inescapable shadow of separation. Referring to the Shivaji festival, which was held as a part of the Anti-Partition campaign in Calcutta from June 4 to June 8, 1906, Baig draws our attention to the fundamental disarray that the cult of Shivaji had with the purpose of the event. In his words: "Shivaji, in any case, would have been a strange patron saint to preside over Hindu–Muslim integration. In fact, there was no integration; and the Muslim participation in the movement was the minimum" (Baig 1969: 118).

The period between 1905 and 1947 was a time of systematic outbreaks of communal riots in Bengal. The riots in Rajshahi, Kumilla, Jamalpur, Calcutta at regular intervals all substantiate the growing religious hostilities which would ultimately pave the way for the culmination of the two Nation theory. If these socio-historical instances of mass violence were not directly responsible for rupture and birth of a new Nation, they were functional in justifying the speculations of the fruition of a two Nation theory. Joya Chatterji rightly points out that the validity of the 1947 draft of Partition put forward by the Radcliffe commission was inarguably accepted by the Bengali society, especially the middle class bhadroloks (Chatterji 1994: 220–222). The debates and arguments pertained to the schematics of distribution of the provinces and the ensuing agitations were often directed not at the legitimacy or validity of Partition, but at the manner in which the proposal of Partition was to be executed, i.e. the logistics of the divide.

Jibanananda Das survives in this epoch that is passively, and at times, actively preparing for the line that will rupture a 2,000-year-old civilization. He would be one of those migrants who would arrive at Calcutta from Barishal, which, courtesy of the Radcliffe line, has now become a part of Bangladesh, formerly East Pakistan. His vision of a timeless Bengal, thus isn't, in all possibilities, a fanciful poetic indulgence. Rather, as this chapter is trying to argue, it is an attempt to idealize the sacrosanct essence of Bengal in the paradigm of aesthetic, where, irrespective of the contaminated immanent, it can preserve its sovereignty.

Das's poetic world in "I Have Seen Bengal's Face" blurs the real and the imagined, juxtaposing the natural real and the historic-mythic, which isn't completely dissociated from history but is a part of the *unreliable history*. It is the element of unreliability that ascertains the legend of Chand Saudagar its mythicality. The folkloric traits that the legend has is self-referential in itself, in its autonomy it doesn't need the real to validate itself and thus can survive as a possible impossibility, much the way a myth does. Yet, in its considerable influence on the non-modern rural society of Bengal, the myth has historical implications. It has shaped the cultural, religious and social life of Bengal and thus has somehow sneaked into the sanctified economy of history. Jibanananda's attempt to intertwine the natural with the historic-mythic by making them the impersonated companions of myth (the floral beauty which Chand Saudagar and Behula appreciates in their voyages, the empathizing Nature which is compared by Das to Behula's ghungur) is but a definitive attempt to mythologize the habitus of Bengal. Das extends the ideal of the myth to substantiate not just the already existent myths in the cultural repertoire of Bengal; rather he seeks to mythologize the natural simultaneously. Roland Barthes argues that myths aren't historically and culturally stable timeless discourses of the primordial, rather he illustrates the contingency of myths and argues that myths are continuously shaped, moulded and appropriated by time. For him, Myth is a "semiological system" (Barthes 1972: 110), where "objects will become speech, if they mean something" (109). The floral and faunal natural in the poem no longer 'mean' (signify) the geographical and ecological essence of Bengal, it invokes the transcendental ethos of Bengal and takes the spatial locale of Bengal beyond the contours of the immediate and the immanent.

It is to this timeless Bengal that the poet wishes to return and his second poem in question, "I Shall Return to This Bengal" is a poetic experience steeped in the jouissance of return. This return lingers as a perpetual impossibility within the poetic speculation and the repeated use of the word 'hoyto' (perhaps) explores that threshold which is folded and unfolded within the dynamics of the possible and the impossible. Das's poem evokes his desire to return to his mythic Bengal, the Bengal that is suggestive and evocative and not spatially or geo-politically defined and determined. In doing so, Das problematizes the semiotics of remembrance and memory, where the signifier and signified do not necessarily function within the hermeneutics of referent and referred, but opens up the possibility of the formulation of a poetic chora, where the referred can be a referent in itself. For instance, the crow of dawn, the Dhanshiri river, the season of harvest, do not merely sustain as referential signifiers transcribing an ecopoetic image of Bengal; rather they are imperatives that signify an unchangeable idealized essence of Bengal. It is in the chronotopic renderings of the spatial paradigm of Bengal and in the sacrosanct ritual of recurrence of the natural that the poet seeks the possibilities of reincarnation.

Das's consequent urge to return as the *shankhyachil* or *shalik* are desires which apparently resemble wistful fancies but they are also symptomatic of the poet's urge to transcend the human condition. The human, to the poet, is not a fertile impregnated subject of possibility, he is rather one who is constantly subjected to the turmoils and turbulences of the immediate real. The human subject is almost always a politico-social subject whose being is contingent within the epoch of history. Nietzsche explores this human condition which is burdened by the historical consciousness as he observes:

> Man [...] resists the great and ever greater weight of the past: this oppresses him and bends him sideways, it encumbers his gait like an invisible and sinister burden which, for the sake of appearances, he may deny at times and which in intercourse with his equals he is all too pleased to deny: to excite their envy.
>
> *(Nietzsche 1980: 9)*

98 M.M. Guha and R. Mukherjee

Hence, it is the historical consciousness of man that constantly subjects him to a consciousness of the 'now' and in his consciousness of the present, the human subject also co-habits the discursive limits of history. The past never exists without the present and yet there is a temporal split that enables the historically conscious subject to distinguish now from then, the immediate from the happened. The consciousness of the ambiguity that the present is spilt from the past and is yet helplessly dependent on it, i.e. the way the past sustains as a double to the present, shaping and formulating it, makes the historical subject conscious of the night-marish burden of history, who sees that ungoverned imagination of the past is an impossibility, since the temporal now has, to a great extent, tyrannized the past in forms of the remnants of history which lives in the now. Walter Benjamin rightly observes, "Are we not touched by the same breath of air which was among that which came before?" (Benjamin n.d.: ii)

Jibanananda is conscious of this inescapability of the immediate and the histor-ical, both of which are dominantly functional in contextualizing Man's reality to a 'now' that is politically conditioned. Jibanananda's 'now', as has been argued before, is the impending doom of Partition that is lurking on the horizon of Bengal. With the socio-political unrest and the climate of communal disharmony threatening his familiar space of homeland, Das realizes the need to unburden his historico-temporal consciousness. He is aware that his human identity will not allow him to; for the human is a historically conscious subject inhabiting the poli-tically stable commune of the 'bios' (Agamben 1995: 1). Hence, Das rejects the human form of consciousness and subjectivity for the other non-human forms, all of which are an integral component of the natural and organic life, which Agam-ben calls the 'zoe' (1). The 'zoe' is a 'bare life' which is ahistoric and apolitical, free from the burden of the immediate in its obliviousness of the spatio-temporal. Nietzsche argues that the animal/natural is unconditionally happy owing to its lack of historical consciousness and Jibanananda, almost resonating Nietzsche, expresses his desire to return as the *shankhyachil, shaalik*, the crow or the swan, all of which are emblematic of the natural order of existence and a bare life.

The jouissance of return for the poet is conceptualized within a framework of the imaginary, which is liable in a threshold of impossibility, for it is an imagined, timeless Bengal that Das evokes within the semiotics of the poetic. Žižek defines the imaginary not as fanciful conjectures of the mind but as the state in which one identifies with the image that is likeable to oneself with the image representing what one intends to be (Žižek 1989: 105). Das's image of Bengal is the Bengal he idealizes and which he intends to preserve, it is the timeless pastoral nature that he determines as the essence of Bengal. This timeless is, however, not completely dissociated from the real, for the essence of Bengal that Jibanananda develops and sublimates is founded within the natural praxis of the real; the seasonal cycle, the flora and fauna, the natural resources of Bengal are all forms and not ideas. Žižek, in the aftermath of Anderson's seminal, often misinterpreted proclamation that Nation is an "imagined political community" (Anderson 2006: 6), revises the paradigm of the spatial reality called 'the Nation' by claiming that not all of it is imagined. Instead, he claims that there is "remainder of some real" (Žižek 1993: 202), which is functional in designing and conceiving the Nation as a space. The natural life of Bengal exists as a remainder of real in Jibanananda's poetic imaginary, it is a residual truth that is beyond the epochs and liminalities of time and history. Returning to this ideal, transfixed paradigm of Bengal is an impossibility, which is not impossible in the sense of being absurd but which is, to use Hamacher's phrase, impossible as a "non-actualised possibility" (Hamacher 2005: 38). The non-actual can never dissociate itself from the sacrosanct economy of possibility, as something that hasn't arrived yet but has the probability of coming and it is in this dynamics of a speculative reincarnation that Jibanananda cherishes his jouissance of return. The impending historical reality of Partition, with all its catastrophic undeniable nightmarish influences on the spatial real of Bengal, fails to de-sanctify the jouissance of return that survives as a liminal possibility in the self referential paradigm of the aesthetic. No wonder then, these two poems were the everyday companions of the muktijoddhyas of 1971, who, in Liberation camps, would often cherish the visions of a timeless, pastoral Bengal, free from the clutches of dominion of East Pakistan.

Works Cited

Agamben, Giorgio. *Homo Sacer: Sovereign Power and Bare Life*. Trans. Daniel Heller-Roazen. Stanford, CA: Stanford University Press, 1995.

Anderson, Benedict. *Imagined Communities: Reflections on the Origin and Spread of Nationalism*, London: Verso, 2006.

Baig, M.R.A. "The Partition of Bengal and Its Aftermath". *The Indian Journal of Political Science*, Vol. 30, No. 02, April–June1969, pp.103–129. JSTOR, https://www.jstor.org/stable/41854318?read-now=1&refreqid=excelsior%3A214bde1aefbc41940a77424671a0d94f&seq=6#page_scan_tab_contents. Accessed on 1 September 2018.

Banerjea, S.N. *A Nation in Making*. Oxford: Oxford University Press, 1963.

Barthes, Roland. *Mythologies*. Trans. Annette Lavers. New York: The Noonday Press, 1972.

Benjamin, Walter. "On the Concept of History". Trans. Dennis Redmond. Retrieved from https://www.marxists.org/reference/archive/benjamin/1940/history.htm. Accessed on 9 September 2018.

Basu, Buddhadev. "Banalata Sen, Jibanananda Das". In *Jibanananda Das: Bikash Prothishar Itibritta*. Ed. Debiprasad Bandyapadhyay. Calcutta: Dey's Publishing, 2007.

Chatterji, Joya. *Bengal Divided: Hindu Communalism and Partition, 1932–1947*. Cambridge: Cambridge University Press, 1994.

Curzon, Lord. *Speeches by Lord Curzon of Kedleston, Viceroy and Governor General of India Vol. III*, Calcutta: Office of the Superintendent of Government. Retrieved from https://archive.org/details/in.ernet.dli.2015.51502/page/n315/mode/2up. Accessed on 1 September 2018.

Das, Jibanananda. *Kobitar Kotha*. Kolkata: New Script, 2013.

Das, Jibanananda. *Kobita Samagra*. Kolkata: Bhabishyat, 2015.

Derrida, Jacques. *Of Grammatology*. Trans. Gayatri Chakravorty Spivak. London: Johns Hopkins University Press, 1974.

Faiz, Ahmed Faiz. "Dil-e-man, musafir-e-man". Trans. Madhuparna Mitra Guha. Retrieved from https://www.rekhta.org/nazms/dil-e-man-musaafir-e-man-mire-dil-mire-musaafir-faiz-ahmad-faiz-nazms. Accessed on 9 September 2018.

Hamacher, Werner. "'Now': Walter Benjamin on Historical Time." In *Walter Benjamin and History*. Ed. Andrew Benjamin. London: Continuum, 2005.

Joyce, James. *Portrait of the Artist as a Young Man*. Oxford: Oxford University Press, 2000.

Lefebvre, Henri. *The Production of Space*. Trans. Donald Nicholson-Smith. Oxford: Blackwell, 1991.

Nietzsche, Friedrich. *The Advantages and Disadvantages of History*. Trans. Peter Preuss. Cambridge: Hackett Publishing Company, 1980.

Rushdie, Salman. *Imaginary Homelands: Essays and Criticism 1981–1991*. London: Granta Books, 1991.

Said, Edward. *Reflections on Exile and Other Essays*. New York: Granta, 2000.

Simmel, Georg. "The Metropolis and Mental Life". In *Classic Essays on the Culture of Cities*. Ed. Richard Sennett. New York: Appleton-Century-Crofts, 1969.

Zizek, Slavoj. *The Sublime Object of Ideology*. London: Verso, 1989.

Zizek, Slavoj. *Tarrying with the Negative: Kant, Hegel and the Critique of Ideology*. Durham, NC: Duke University Press, 1993.

9

TRACING ERASURE AND RE-MAPPING THE MEMORY LANE

Partition movies of Ritwik Ghatak

Rajadipta Roy

> This partition of Bengal gave a serious jerking to our political and economic life … The whole economic structure of this country is shattered owing to this part i.e. the partition of Bengal. Never did I reconcile myself to the event of this partition. And I expressed my viewpoint in those three pictures. Against my intention, the films *Meghe Dhaka Tara, Komal Gandhar* and *Subarnarekha* formed my trilogy. When I started *Meghe Dhaka Tara*, I never spoke of political unification. Even now I don't think of it because history will not alter and I won't venture to do this impossible task. The cultural segregation caused by politics and economics was a thing to which I never reconciled myself as I always thought in terms of cultural integration. This very theme of cultural integration forms the theme in all the three films.[1]

I

Ritwik's indeterminate political position of remaining at once eloquent and silent on the question of Partition is distinctly identified in the abundance of inevitably counter-responding arguments compiled in any of the noteworthy editions on his works. The prevalent ambivalence in attitude faced by the general readership regarding Ghatak's positionality is well evinced in the editorial maneuvers of clubbing together agonizingly disparate readings of Iraban Basu Ray and Tapadhir Bhattacharya even in a latest publication edited by Mukhopadhyay on Ritwik, titled *Ritwikcharcha: A Bengali Collection of Essays on Ritwik* (2017: 78–108). Ritwik's creative urgency as an artist is unquestionably configured by his involved response to the event of Bengal's Partition which was in simultaneity with Indian Independence, and yet, his tactical refusal to talk on the subject in trouble-free terms in the majority of his films is a glaring reality. Ashis Nandy attempts a socio–psychological pathology of this creative binary of intention/un-intention in Ritwik, along with some other heavyweight intellectuals of the Indian post-colony, who had been artistically operational in the historical wake of the Partition and comes up with a convincing exegesis. While writing an incisive foreword to the book *Mapmaking: Partition Stories from Two Bengals* (2011), Nandy makes a very interesting observation on the famous Urdu writer Saadat Hassan Manto's unassuming refusal to talk on the one most traumatic moment in the geopolitics of the Indian subcontinent – the Partition of India and Pakistan in two separate independent states back in the year 1947.

What followed the otherwise glorious moment of independence for the two young sovereign siblings coming out of a 200-year-long colonial rule are irrational carnages, mass murders, rapes and lootings, with seemingly interminable waves of migrating people becoming rootless forever in the name of religion. The Partition of India is indeed still the most haunting of all its national experiences which has been tackled with ambiguity both in memory and forgetting over the years in literature and cinemas likewise. The geography of South Asia had never before witnessed such a holocaust and politically forced exodus of homeless people in its entire history. Among many other historians and sociologists working densely on Indian Partition, Tan and Kudaisya examine the issue closely, especially in relation to Bengal, and they come up with telling statistics.

> In view of the prolonged conditions of insecurity, an estimated 1,575,000 people left East Bengal in 1950 to seek refuge in India. The following year another 187,000 refugees came, and the figure of incoming refugees stood at 200,000 during 1952. This influx continued throughout the 1950s and even beyond, with 76,000 persons coming to India in 1953, 1.18 *lakhs* in 1954 and 2.40 *lakhs* in 1955.
>
> (Tan and Kudaisya 2002: 146)

Perry Anderson identifies the event of Partition in the subcontinent as a motivated ploy of the elitist power politics as it was "imposed from above, deliberately circumventing any expression of a democratic will" (2012: 73–74). Anderson's immediate rejoinder after a few lines is also very befitting in imagining the massive historical largesse and import of the specific situation when he unequivocally explains: "[The] number of those uprooted, fleeing to lands they never knew, was anywhere from twelve to eighteen million: the largest avalanche of refugees in history" (74). All taken into account, it is impossible to grip the fact that Manto, being an extraordinarily sensitive writer of marginal lives, denied talking, as informed by Nandy, on the Partition and its trauma. The reason, at once simple and yet tremendously challenging and problematic in itself, is researched and represented by Nandy in following words:

> Manto identified the day with the division of British India into two countries and the carnage that marked it ... Why did the earlier generation not speak out? One answer could be that the violence of 1946–48 brought out the worst in us. Those of us who saw it tried to forget what we saw; our imagination of

Tracing erasure and re-mapping memory lane **103**

evil failed to cope with it. Manto was not the only one to whom Independence came packaged in genocide, necrophilia, ethnic cleansing, massive uprooting and the collapse of a moral universe.

(Nandy 2011: xi)

Understandably, it is the insane nature of the whole event unleashing beyond the capacities of normal imagination that drove people like Manto to negotiate trauma with silence. The name of the multitalented Bengali filmmaker Ritwik Ghatak may also be linked with that of Manto, for trying to tackle the trauma of Partition with a problematic silence, for reasons to be decoded hereafter. But this silence and refusal of a generation of people physically surviving the trauma is distinct and dissimilar from the silence and refusal of the later generations to address the trauma of such an imperious moment in history. While the former is a syndrome, triggered by the heavy weight of memory, the latter can well be read as a product of anti-memory. Nandy rightly identifies and demarcates between the generically different natures of the silences and exhorts:

Evidently, the expensively educated, cultivated, urbane South Asians were the ones who were blinded by the dazzle of two brand new states and the scope that the new dispensation gave to their contesting models of social engineering. They banished the memories of Partition and with that, they felt, they had banished the genocidal fury and exterminatory fantasies that had devastated large parts of British India. Silence became their main psychological defence. It ensured that the new states in the region would conduct their affairs on the ruins of the past, armed not with self awareness but with fragile defensive shield of anti-memories.

(Nandy 2011: xii)

Ritwik Ghatak, like Manto, survived the trauma physically but psychologically, the culture shock was never overcome by Ghatak. As such, the entire oeuvre of his cinematic aesthetics, whether re-created by mnemonic movements or characterized by aphasia, is built, engendered and ontologically determined by this single fact of Partition and its trauma. What is interesting to note in this context, however, is that Partition persists as a spectral after-thought in his cinema. His films, unlike his popular non-cinematic statements, do not overtly emphasize his resentment of contemporary real-politics and the historical menace called Partition. Instead, the attempt to read his film narratives, especially the popularly identified Partition trilogy compromising of *Meghe Dhaka Tara* (Cloud Capped Star, 1960), *Komal Gandhar* (E-Flat, 1961) and *Subarnarekha* (The Golden Line, 1962) as simple Partition narratives is instantly unsettled. It is for the reason that Ghatak is found persistently coming up with different strategies to un-address, sometimes almost to the level of a refusal, in tackling with, the memory, post-memory or any explicit reading of the event of Partition through his creations. This unsettling paranoia between the man, as an extremely aware ideological activist, and the artist, compelled from within by an extremely sensitive creativity, leads to an inevitable aporia

104 Rajadipta Roy

in Ghatak's understanding and expression of the trauma of the big event in his films. There is hardly any doubt that Partition and its massive implications are the constituents of Ghatak's essential creative oeuvre, though the event finds indirect treatments in most of his film narratives, leaving aside the one important exception of *Komal Gandhar* (E-Flat) in 1961. Ghatak himself seems to be well aware of this aporia in his creative imagination, as he makes a very rational reply on the bearing of the refugee issue in his films during the course of one interview:

> It doesn't affect me directly. It does in a broader sense, in an indirect way, in a subliminal way. Film-making is a question you know, of your subconscious, your feeling of reality. I have tackled the refugee 'problem', as you have used the term, not as a refugee problem. To me it was the division of a culture and I was shocked. During the Partition period I hated these pretentious people who clamoured about our independence, our freedom. You kids are finished, you have not seen that Bengal of mine. I just kept on watching what was happening, how the behaviour pattern was changing due to this great betrayal of national liberation. And I probably gave vent to what I felt. Today I am not happy, and whatever I have seen unconsciously or consciously comes out in my films. My films may have been ridden with expressive slogan-mongering or they may be remote. But the cardinal point remains: that I am frustrated with what I see all around me, I am tired of it.
>
> *(Ghatak 1987: 80)*

Ghatak's political awareness makes him read the event of Partition from the general historical position of an ideologue, denying it any spatio-temporal immediacy. This broader perspective of the event as the historical "division of a culture" might be responsible in bringing a textual ambiguity to his treatment of the theme of Partition in the films in discourse. Nandy is specifically doubtful of this implicit treatment of the theme as a creative strategy by Ghatak and suspects a traumatized silence in the director. He identifies a case of "cultivated aphasia, not negligence" in this unnerving refusal to talk of the socio-political menace in a direct manner in the film narratives of Ghatak and discovers that Ritwik Ghatak,

> [Who] made a series of brilliant films on the subject but, when it came to writing on his films, he seemed convinced that he was exploring class conflicts, production relations and other such lofty left-Hegelian themes. Fortunately, his emotions and artistic self were more analytic than his reason. They defied his piteous ideological repertoire to produce some of the finest psychological documentation of the Partition. His self-destruction through alcoholism, like that of Manto, could itself be read as a statement – as a belated psychosomatic effect of the trauma of Partition violence and as an introjections of the larger self-destruction he had seen around him. I cannot but suspect that his intellectualisation was a defence. Like Manto, he wanted to talk but also did not.
>
> *(Nandy 2011: xiv)*

Yet, the fact remains straight enough to be appreciated from even a simple reading that Ghatak's whole creative imagination was involuntarily shaped by the very disturbing memory of the Partition. It is a memory that he sometimes refused to talk of directly and sometimes chose to evoke voluntarily through nondescript images and undertones even at the risk of being spurious at moments in relation to the final thematic movement of certain films. None other than Satyajit Ray was aware of this subtle mnemonic manipulations of Ghatak while refusing, negotiating, addressing or exhibiting his pathological engagement with the issue of Partition and detects the same engagement as the fundamental component of Ghatak's imagination in his significant preface to Ghatak's book *Cinema and I*.

> Thematically, Ritwik's lifelong obsession was with the tragedy of partition. He himself hailed from what was once East Bengal where he had deep roots. It is rarely that a director dwells so single mindedly on the same theme. It only serves to underline the depth of his feeling for the subject.
>
> *(Ghatak 1987: 12)*

II

For an argument supposed to deal with the impulsion of a notorious political event like that of the Partition on the culture-space of Indian films, Ritwik Ghatak's take on the subject matter with his routinely accepted trilogy on Partition proves nothing less than a jigsaw puzzle. Due to his utterly problematic mnemonic movements put into praxis of the three films, differing heavily in degree and kinds with each other, Ghatak has ever proved to be a hard customer to fit straight into the globally marketable brand of Partition narratives. The trope of memory, configured by the central crisis of displacement and the eventual yearning of his protagonists for the place, feeling, culture or person left forever, is undeniably crucial to his cinematic texts. But the fact that makes Ghatak's position as a chronicler of the situation immensely slippery is his paranoia of politics fissuring out of the collision between his idea of big history and small history. Ghatak's public image, his social commitment and his overt assertion of leftist ideology in almost all his works and statements voluntarily negotiate with the event in broad historical terms. As a result, the crisis of rootlessness dealt with in *Meghe Dhaka Tara* and *Subarnarekha* take a back seat eventually and are adequately sidelined by the larger focus cast on problems pertaining to class, caste and gender.

On the flip side of this crucial negotiation, we come across the other prominent aspects of Ghatak's creativity. Every piece of history is broken into small molecular bits by the ever-restless artist in him. The sensitive artistic self of Ghatak consequently struggles to find inevitable solace for and solution to the existential crisis of an individual in the mythic-historical metaphors of his films. *Komal Gandhar* documents his utterly private appreciation of this enormous public event of Partition, forged on the destiny of the migrated people against the will of the majority resulting in mindless holocausts and wasteful exodus of millions forever losing their home and heritage. It might well be surmised that public issues of larger historical significance play the key role in the tragic climates and environs of *Meghe Dhaka Tara* and *Subarnarekha*, where the general historical pathology of a person's crisis is foregrounded against the backdrop of a rootless present. In both these films, as well as in *Komal Gandhar*, the issue of a culture shift in the lives of the refugee protagonists is highlighted by recurrent references to a perpetual loss. Their private and not public use of the local dialect of the eastern part of Bengal within the intimate space of family conversations is a definite cue to such a loss. The loss is desperately being tackled with both in memory and in experience on the part of the chief protagonists in the two films other than that of the *Komal Gandhar* through amnesia. It seems that Ghatak's ultra-left ideological take on history forcefully induces an economically stratified pattern of reading in general terms on the specifics of a politically engineered historical situation. Consequently, the maladies of the refugee protagonists busy in relocating their lives in the newly settled colonies achieve broad-scale universality applicable to the experiences of any lower-middle-class community at any point of history. It is a universality that denies them their specificity of experience spawned particularly from the situations in post-Partition Bengal.

On a diametrically opposite note, the reshaping of the private world of Anasuya, the female protagonist in *Komal Gandhar*, is made theatrically telling and intensely urgent in the movie by creating the nuances of a lost selfhood among the rootless people. Anasuya and Bhrigu, the central protagonists of *Komal Gandhar*, are perhaps the only young people among a cohort of Ghatak's characters who let the issue of Partition and its harrowing memory occupy the central position in their lives. They, unlike others, talk of it most explicitly without double meanings. This explicit address to memory is in stark contrast to the negotiation of the trauma implicitly portrayed in the other two films of the unintended Partition series. In support of this claim, a scene in *Meghe Dhaka Tara* might be mentioned where an old father is shown wallowing in nostalgia while alluding to a long and lush stretch of paddy field, reminiscent of his *desher bari*, or the homeland, lost forever to him. The pathos of the loss is dispelled when his gesture of hunger is treated as a source of fun and humour by his grown-up daughter and son. Neeta and her elder brother, the protagonists of *Meghe Dhaka Tara*, laugh at the expense of their father's cultural invocation of his involuntary memory and dilute it to the level of a reminiscence. But, that mood is rather cruelly debunked and sidelined by the comic expressions of the actor Bijon Bhattacharya, portraying the father to the siblings, making gestures while eating under the heavy pressure of poverty and hunger. For the young protagonists in the film, not the loss but the immediate existential requirement of economic as well as cultural adjustments and relocation are more important issues in the backdrop of the post-Partition Bengal.

The result of such mutually opposite treatments offered to the identical crisis of the refugee people, for whom Partition is the root of all the evils, is in itself a unique one that adequately problematizes Ghatak's take on such a historically specific event. Given the kind of historical reading that one might amass after almost 75 long years of the event, it would not perhaps be a superfluous claim to assert that in *Meghe Dhaka Tara* and *Subarnarekha*, Ghatak voluntarily remained silent over the issue of Partition leaving aside one or two passing thematic or visual references made to the historical situation of post-Partition Bengal in the 1950s. If this silence is a tactical one and a metaphor of forgetting, then the creative schizophrenia of his private and public selves resolves finally into a touching and very sensitive tale of finding solace down the memory lane of the "Partitioned self" in *Komal Gandhar*. As a Partition narrative, *Komal Gandhar* attempts to queue up the past memory of the protagonists inevitably with their collective future, perhaps with compromises, but definitely with more positive determinations of living a life to its fullest. Repetitive memory tracking in *Komal Gandhar* with many verbal and visual references culturally tries to do away with the tiring and tedious upshots of a historical disjunct in the destiny of Bengal.

In order to achieve his coveted end to disseminate a feeling of the trauma of Partition to his audience back in the year 1960 with their fresh moments of collective memory, Ghatak effectively explores the interstices of myth and history in the movie. The objective correlative functioning between the affected memory-scape of the characters in the movie and that of collective unconscious of the mass watching it is the key point to render subjective specificity to the overarching theme of Partition in *Komal Gandhar*. Partha Chatterjee pays attention to this immediate point of communication between the individual memory refashioning on the part of the director and its target collective trope kept in the milieu of the time and briskly suggests that Ghatak, "achieved these artistic counterpoints and obligations quite instinctively. His cinema for all its swift cross-currents of ideas seemed created wholly out of the moment rather than carefully pondered over a period of time" (Chatterjee 2002: 64).

It would perhaps not be inappropriate to mention that earlier, while pondering on Ghatak's previous movie *Nagarik* (The Citizen, 1952–1953), Chatterjee unequivocally clarified that in Ghatak's film narratives, more often than not "history has become memory and memory history" (Chatterjee 2002: 60). This tactic of replacing or replenishing history with a multilayered idea of memory allows Ghatak to erase the much spectacular issues of the crude realities of riots and genocides, normally associated with the phenomenon of Partition. Erasure of direct violence crucially marks a fine point of departure for his narrative strategy from the iconic approach put into praxis by his Punjabi counterparts in the Indian film fraternity. Ghatak rather is more engaged with the cultural aspect of the trauma than with its immediate political import. This absence of explicit documentation of the moment in unequivocal terms might be a possible reason for Nandy to find Ghatak's voice on the matter at best as a silent one. To fashion out an idea of a cultural past in its imaginary entirety in the memory is necessarily the object of Ghatak as the current absence of such an entirety configures the idioms of Partition and an irreparable loss in the minds of Bhrigu and Anasuya in *Komal Gandhar*. Chatterjee explains this idiomatic transfiguration of the trauma of Partition in the aesthetic imagination of Ghatak and concludes: "The Partition never figures directly in Ritwik Ghatak's films; rather it is a riveting memory image of a cataclysmic event that had far reaching consequences" (Chatterjee 2002: 59).

In *Subarnarekha* on the other hand, a film made one year after *Komal Gandhar*, Ghatak reverts back to his initial stance of talking big issues of relatively universal nature than remaining engrossed with the sole issue of Partition. Partition and its aftermath definitely draw the backdrop to the cinema-scape. But the questions of caste, gender and the self-conceited prudery of the *bhadralok* or the middle-class gentility preclude adequately the kind of attention that an event like Partition demands to share even against as vast a panorama of mythic treatment as it is found in *Subarnarekha*.

Under the pretext of treating a complicated brother–sister relationship, Ghatak portrays Ishwar as the patriarch who protects and almost owns his sister Sita's individuality in the movie. Sita grows up despite the stereotyped parenting man-euvers lavished by Ishwar on her and goes against his will to marry her childhood love Abhiram, overlooking their difference in caste. Ishwar's shock comes as a dual blow as Sita asserts herself against his patronizingly dictating will and at the same time puts his patriarchal caste-conscious hegemony into jeopardy. The film *Sub-arnarekha* deliberately maps out Ishwar and Sita's existential trip from the refugee camp in 'Naba Jiban Colony' first to the scenic setting in Chhatimpur on the bank of the river Subarnarekha around Chhotanagpur. Next, they meet again in the slums of Kolkata and finally Ishwar moves from Kolkata with Sita's child back to the serenity of the hills in Chhatimpur on the river Subarnarekha. Dramatic twists in the plot land Ishwar somewhat incoherently as a solicitor to the widowed Sita's pov-erty-stricken slum quarters, a shock that compels her to commit suicide producing perhaps the most brilliantly built tragic effect ever in the history of Indian films. The disintegration of the society due to multiple politico-historical fallouts takes the shape of the most ethically tensed moment in Ghatak's treatment. The artistically loaded moral impetus of this moment occupies the focus of the human drama and relegates the immediate historical implication of Partition in the narrative of *Subarnarekha*. The immensity of an event called Partition of a country is compromised to the universality of the existential crisis emanating from the complex thematic matrix of gender, caste and commerce in the movie. The Partition of India and its ramifications indeed intensify the crisis of existence in the film. But, the issue of the 'social individual' in relation to his or her society is given a universality that refuses to attribute the sole onus of the crisis on the shoulders of an explicit event like Partition. Paul Willemen, as quoted in Bhaskar Sarkar's *Mourning the Nation: Indian Cinema in the Wake of Partition*, reads the ambiguous stance of Ghatak quite perceptively and insists,

> The drama and the analytical presentation of socio-historical processes fit so closely together that it is impossible to say whether the environment is there to explain the characters and their drama, or whether the characters were selec-ted/ constructed as exemplary and necessary to convey an analysis of the social. In effect, the question becomes irrelevant: people are presented as living in and determined by history, superseding the false oppositions between the subjective and the social, between the individual and society, as idealist philo-sophies tend to put it. Ghatak ... depict(s) social existence, nothing less.
>
> *(Sarkar 2010: 213)*

III

Although being sufficiently preoccupied with the irreconcilable trauma of Partition for his entire life, the roles ascribed to memory in Ghatak's films remain problematic. The urgency of relocation of the refugees, as it is treated in his themes, calls more for an act of forgetting than memorizing the actualities associated with the historical situation. In a nutshell, scrutiny of his unintentional Partition trilogy brings forward many maneuvers made aesthetically by Ghatak, the artist, in dealing with the memory of this single incident of exponential importance that considerably rattled Ghatak, the man, in actuality. However unbelievable it might sound from the outset, Ghatak's voluntary attempts to forget the actual event and its gruesome fallouts are more prominent in the treatment and mobility of the themes chosen by the artist in films like *Meghe Dhaka Tara* or *Subarnarekha*. Conversely, *Komal Gandhar*, coincidentally made in 1961 in between the two films mentioned above, deals relatively in more explicit metaphors with the immediate trauma and tragedy of the specific historical event of the Partition. Indians on a larger scale have not been able to cope with the aftermath and the trauma of the event even after 70-odd years of their much-celebrated independence. But for Bengal and Punjab, the provinces which had to bear the entire heat and brunt of Partition, the cultural effect of the event as it is addressed in the sphere of literature, art or film to date is different in almost every respect. Punjab has recorded its moments in narrations across genres in the culture sphere, whereas an allegation of unsettling silence over the experiences of Partition and imminent mass slaughters in the sphere of Bengali films has earned possibly the status of the commonplace. Ghatak, ironically, chronicles both these attitudes of addressing and taciturnity, involuntarily though, in his lavishly acclaimed Partition trilogy. He strides upright down the memory lane of such experiences in *Komal Gandhar*, but refuses to do the same in *Subarnarekha*, where the larger issues of caste and gender neatly overshadow the sense of immediacy of a specific but huge historical event like Partition, which is pushed to the background and is made almost silent as the larger historical issues of universal connotation across time and space are prioritized in Ghatak's most popularly celebrated film *Meghe Dhaka Tara*. It is remembered in its corporeal actuality and is repeatedly enacted out through the scenes of dramas played by the theater troop of Bhrigu, the Protagonist, in *Komal Gandhar*, which works up the abysmally traumatic memories associated with the specific moments of Partition in the film. In *Subarnarekha*, Ghatak strategically chooses to forget the essentials of the event yet again as the passing references dissolve into the existential stupor of Ishwar Chakraborty, busy in relocating his and his sister's life. The immense finality of ongoing events in the lives of the individuals evolves to be more important than the trauma of rootlessness caused by Partition in the narrative.

This famous trilogy, if read with an exasperating vantage point of ethical close reading, takes shape both as an actual exemplar and a historical denial at once. A reading ironically guarded with the callous certitude of a chronicler that happily meddles up the real sensitive person in Ghatak with the more intellectually objectified and therefore distanced artistic self of the filmmaker will definitely land one on a more problematic zone when these films are asked to be treated out and out as real specimens of Partition narratives. The cue that Ghatak himself offers to this complex relationship between his own position as an individual in relation to Partition and that of his artistic treatment of the theme of Partition in his Partition narratives is also no less confounding and ambiguous. The ambiguity seems to be imperative owing to the implosive nature of his imagination. In an article entitled "Cinema and the Subjective Factor", Ghatak quotes a statement of Joseph Campbell, the famous structuralist myth-critic, and tries to justify his 'schizophrenia':

> The two fundamental types of mind are complementary: The tough-minded, representing the inert, reactionary; and the tender-minded, the living progressive impulse – respectively, attachment to the local and timely and the impulse to the timeless universal. In human history the two have faced each other in dialogue since the beginning, and the effect has been that actual progress and process from lesser to greater horizons, simple to complex organisations, slight to rich patterns of art work which is civilization in its flowering in time there is a deep psychological cleavage separating the tough-minded 'honest hunters' from tender-minded 'shamans'.
>
> *(Ghatak 1987: 60)*

After this, Ghatak crucially elaborates the process of artistic expression and talks on the creative procedure of a sensitive mind in translating his/her thoughts laden with the immediacy of a firsthand experience into an objectified and universalized idiom of art. He detects an awareness of the ineradicable dialectic between the subjective and the objective selves of the artist/poet. He expounds,

> It follows that all art is subjective. Any work of art is the artist's subjective approximation of the reality around him. It is a sort of reaction set in motion by the creative impulse of the human unconscious. The entire history of human civilization shows a peculiar phenomenon ... there are always two types of minds operating through the length and breadth of human history: the 'tough' and the 'tender-minded'. The tough-minded are always the 'honest-hunters'. It does not matter whether they hunt for mammoth, dollars, pelts or working hypotheses. The tender-minded ones are the 'shamans', the rishis and the poets, the seers and the singers, the possessed and the inspired of this world.
>
> It is the second kind of men who are eminently the vessels or vehicles of that force of the unconscious and through whom and whose creations become manifest the images and symbols of that dark deep. Objectivization of this essentially subjective element is the task allotted to such men. And thus, the dialectics is born: the interplay of the subjective and the objective.
>
> *(Ghatak 1987: 61–62)*

Now, in this long excuse given in the guise of an artist's discourse on the process of creation, one may trace the latent logic of Ghatak's not personal but artistic application of the ambiguous tactic laden with the binary of acceptance/denial in dealing with the subject of Partition. Nandy's allegation of an uncompromising negotiation with the mnemonic activity of erasure, or amnesia, and Sibaji Bandyopadhyay's insistence on understanding the very tissue of Ghatak's imagination as essentially configured on the traces of a lifelong memory of a *nirbaas*, or a refugee (2008: 283–284) are then not at loggerheads any longer if we explain an artist's take on history as ridden with the so-called duality as proposed by Ghatak himself in the above quotation. Ghatak's elaborate explanation of his own creative process helps to locate at best an indeterminate creative position for him inescapably negotiating between his voluntary and involuntary patches of memory (Whitehead 2009: 104) concerned with the event of Partition. An acute consciousness of a politico–cultural betrayal associated with the event of Partition might sometimes have made him silent and sometimes eloquent on the issue in his film narratives. But a steady historical commitment to the issues of the refugee lives engaged with the myriad crises of relocation, empowerment, gender, class, caste and personal memories do configure the creative aesthetic of Ghatak uninhibitedly. His reluctance at direct documentation confining the effect of the historical event only within a moment possibly produce ambiguities at times; but his involvement with the subject of Partition is unquestionable as it is evident from the reading of any of his films, greater or lesser in scheme or scope.

Note

1 Ghatak expressed this extremely useful view in a statement made in "Ritwik on Ritwik: An Interview", published in the1975 annual issue of the Kolkata-based film magazine *Chitrabikshan* (pp. 57–58).

Works Cited

Anderson, Perry. *The Indian Ideology*. Gurgaon: Three Essays Collective, 2012.

Bandyopadhyay, Sibaji. *Alibabar Guptadhan: Prabandha Sangkalan*. Kolkata: Gangchil, 2008.

Chatterjee, Partha. "The Films of Ritwik Ghatak and the Partition." In *Pangs of Partition: The Human Dimension, Volume II*. Ed. S. Settar and Indira B. Gupta. New Delhi: Manohar, 2002.

Ghatak, Ritwik. "Ritwik on Ritwik: An Interview". In *Chitrabikshan*, Annual Number, ed. Anil Sen, Calcutta, 1975, pp. 57–58.

Ghatak, Ritwik. *Cinema and I*. Kolkata: Ritwik Memorial Trust, 1987.

Mukhopadhyay, Chandi, Ed. *Ritwikcharcha: A Bengali Collection of Essays on Ritwik*. Kolkata: Prativash, 2017.

Nandy, Ashis. "The Days of the Hayena: Foreword". In *Mapmaking: Partition Stories from Two Bengals*. Ed. Debjani Sengupta. New Delhi: Amaryllis, 2011.

Sarkar, Bhaskar. *Mourning the Nation: Indian Cinema in the Wake of Partition*. New Delhi: Orient Blackswan, 2010.

Tan, Tai Yong and Gyanesh Kudaisya. *The Aftermath of Partition in South Asia*. London: Routledge, 2002.

Whitehead, Anne. *Memory: The New Critical Idiom*. London and New York: Routledge, 2009.

10

FROM HOME TO HOMELAND

Negotiating memory and displacement in Dibyendu Palit's "Alam's Own House"

Rupayan Mukherjee and Kritika Nepal

In his seminal essay, "Imaginary Homelands", Salman Rushdie observes that the ideals of home for the displaced subject are never confined and limited to the sacrosanct spatial paradigm called home. Instead, the consideration of home often extends beyond the finitudes of the domestic to include the nostalgic evocations of a past which survives in 'fragments', the mnemonics which do not necessarily allude and authenticate the limited and confined architectural habitus called home. The remembered home, Rushdie claims, sublimates into a more fertile province called homeland, where the remembered is complemented with the surplus of imagined, where the topological is complemented by the displaced (Rushdie 1991: 10). It is this fantasy of excess that is characteristic of homeland, which, in the words of Vijay Mishra, tends to occupy a "surplus meaning" (2007: 3). Home thus extends within the consciousness of past in the essence of a beyondness; it is the cloud of remembrance which becomes home, as Rushdie observes: "the past is a home, albeit a lost home in a lost city in the mists of lost time" (1991: 9).

For the displaced subject, the remembered is also often a problematic juxtaposition of nostalgia and trauma. The memory of home that sublimates into a greater paradigm called homeland is often poised within a chequered and contradictory economy, where the urge to mourn and remember the lost homeland is counterbalanced by the ensuing trauma which the loss of homeland evokes. Hence, trauma for the displaced subject becomes the correlative of home and homeland and conceives a predicament of mourning to which the displaced self is subjected to. Vijay Mishra observes, "The traumatic moment may be seen as crystallizing that loss, as a sign around which memory gives itself to the past" (Mishra 2007: 8). With the persistence of trauma, survives the disjunctured self of the displaced subject which, along with its being in the spatio-temporal, is also conditioned by the loss. Hence, the displaced subject owes its agency to a moment in past, its quest of home and homeland is a quintessential quest of loss. Home, thus exists for a subject, not in now but in the outside of now. It is in a state of disjointness and displacement that a subject can conceive his/her home.

Developing Victor Burgin's conviction of the two-dimensional authenticities of urban spaces – the geographical and the representational and in coherence with post-modern geographies, James Donald substantiates that spaces are not just geographical realities; they are imaginatively conceived truths which are spatio-temporally governed and yet not limited to space and time. Instead, as fictive truths, spaces are often sanctified as ideals, thereby fermenting the perceived space into a trans-material ideal of conceived space. Fog, citing Lefebvre, argues that this idealization of space occurs in the lethal zone of "language, signs and abstractions" (Donald 1970: 13). This abstracted ideal of space becomes the constant companion of the spatial subject and for the displaced subject, it is this ideal of abstraction which becomes the lost homeland. The abstraction is a living absence, never really managing to escape the sensibility and consciousness of loss which is constantly fed and sustained by the lost abstraction of home. This abstraction called the home and homeland become the *elene vitale* for the displaced self, it is the sustaining fulcrum to the agency of the displaced subject. Vijay Mishra points out, "There is no immediate cure for the condition because the loss remains abstract; it is not compensated for by happiness in the new nation-state and is therefore internalized as the absence of ego itself" (2007: 10).

The Partition of the Indian subcontinent prompted an epoch of history which was founded on the prerogatives of displacement. Multitudes were subjected to spatial shifts, fracturing the homeland from the sovereign state to which they subsequently owed their citizenship. Ritu Menon and Kamla Bhasin observe: "By the time the migrations were finally over, about eight million people had crossed the newly-created boundaries of Punjab and Bengal, carrying with them memories of a kind of violence … unmatched in scale, brutality and intensity" (Menon 1993: 3).

The ideal of citizenship in these newly founded Nations were thus haunted by the irreproachable gap that existed between the persona of the citizen and the displaced self, pining for a lost homeland. The displaced subject is a political subject in an alien, defamiliarized space, which isn't necessarily his homeland, thereby initiating a conflict between, to use Agamben's phrase, 'nativity' and 'Nationality' (1995: 131).

This is the longstanding implication of Indian Partition, whereby the displaced subject is rendered in a state of perpetual mourning for a loss. The loss can be reconciled with, only within the fictive possibility of the impossible. To cherish this possibility is, however, as has been argued before, to engage in the nostalgic invocations of a trauma. Hence, every possibility of reconciliation with the loss is also an invocation of the moment of trauma, the moment of rupture which, is resubjectified and restructured by the remembering subject with every practice of remembrance (Rauch 1998: 113). It is this constant ramifications of remembrance which brings the absent in relevance within the topos of memory and thereby provokes the essence of mourning in the displaced subject. Mourning is thus consolidated by the performatives of memory, where the very act of remembrance

114 Rupayan Mukherjee and Kritika Nepal

ushers the remembering subject into a liminal state of mourning. This mourning deeply consolidates the ideal of the lost homeland, one which is as much conceived as it is perceived. Vijay Mishra, citing Derrida at length, classifies this state of mourning, that the displaced subject is often subjected to, as "true mourning" (Mishra 2007: 8), which is a conscious valorization of absence.

The chapter seeks to illustrate the impossibility of reconciliation between the displaced subject and the lost homeland and the consequent persistence of mourning in the displaced consciousness by referring to Dibyendu Palit's short story "Alam's Own House". Palit's short story explores the paradigm of return from diverse perspectives and subsequently seeks to substantiate return as an empty performative, which the displaced subject can only rehearse, thereby cherishing only a possibility of return, a return which ultimately remains unmaterialized. In other words, returning in the story is conceived as an endeavor without essence, where the telos of the desired return is never arrived at, consequently prompting an ennui of dystopia in the displaced subject.

Alam is the chief character in the story; a once resident of Calcutta, now living in Bangladesh. The story is shaped by the two epochs of displacement which occurred in the Indian subcontinent, one following the Partition of India in 1947 and the other during the Bangladesh war of Liberation in 1971. The politico-cultural world that Alam inhabits is founded on the politics of exclusion and inclusion, divided by narrow domestic walls which segregate the 'us' from 'them'. This systematic division, however, as the story explores, isn't necessarily limited to the juridico-political, to which it owes its origin historically. Instead, the political lines of rupture have produced long-standing effects on the cultural, social and personal, subjugating and conditioning the subject and creating the climate of xenophobia for the religio-political other. Alam's father, a practicing physician in Calcutta, sensing the unfamiliar communalism which starts haunting the metropolis in the aftermath of Partition of 1947 observes: "There were two Partitions – one political, the other in the mind. Mountbatten had not put his signature to the second. Earlier, the same stethoscope would be used on Ram and Jamal. But those days were past" (Palit 2011: 58).

Partition, which had 'cracked'[1] one Nation into two on the basis of religion, is a crucial juncture in the politico-humane history of the subcontinent. It is the juridico-political moment when the private and sanctified imperative of religion is officially politicized. It is also the epiphanic moment when the sovereign acknowledges religion as a political and not personal practice, thus contemplating or envisioning communities that are founded on the principles of homogeneity. Jean-Luc Nancy argues that the sovereign subject in a community always exists in a relationality, where the absolute sovereignty of the singular isn't necessarily eclipsed by the collective or commune and yet the individual constantly derives his/her consciousness through a mediation of the community, i.e. in retrospect with the limits of the community. Community thus lingers as the unavoidable spectre in the individual's consciousness of being and becoming. Nancy writes:

> This consciousness – or this communication – is ecstasy: which is to say that such a consciousness is never mine, but to the contrary, I only have it in and through the community … it is clear consciousness at the extremity of its clarity, where consciousness of self turns out to be outside the self of consciousness.
>
> *(1991: 19)*

The principles of religious exclusivism which has been evoked by the Radcliffe line dissipates into the social communities and the familiar spaces, affecting the microcosmic relationship between the physician and his patient. Alam's father thus experiences a dwindling fortune, as he is no longer the doctor for all but has now become the doctor of "Jamals and Karims" (Palit 2011: 58). The outside, the commune, now makes him conscious of his otherness in the unfamiliar familiar, for he is now a 'Muslim' doctor, with his religious identity magnified in the aftermath of Partition. Almost under coercive circumstances of appropriative violence, Alam's father emigrates to East Pakistan, exchanging his house for Anantashekhar Sanyal's house in Dacca.

Alam returns to Calcutta to participate in a Friendship Committee Seminar and while driving expectantly back to his childhood home from the airport recollects this estranged past. Calcutta appears to him unfamiliar, which is but an essential prerogative of a metropolitan space, which to use Georg Simmel's phrase is subject to "swift and continuous shift" (1969: 1). Simmel argues that the modern man is so inextricably fashioned and nurtured within this ferment of change that he is perpetually in a state of 'blasé'. Simmel defines blasé as an "indifference towards the distinction between things", wherein "the meaning and the value of distinctions between things, and therewith of the things themselves, are experienced as meaningless" (14). However, Alam, our returning native, is a displaced subject. Unlike the metropolitan subject, he is susceptible to change and the miniatures of change constantly subject him to a reconciliation with the lived space that is still fertile in his memory. Hence, within the materiality of return, the displaced agency of Alam realizes that although the names of places are still fresh and habitual signifiers registered in his memory, seducing him to cherish the ideal of homeland (C.I.T. Road, Maniktala, Narkeldanga), the signifieds have changed. Calcutta, his homeland, has changed.

This is precisely the point from which Alam's estrangement begins and soon condenses into a dystopia. Alam reaches his house to find it architecturally unchanged but soon realizes the extended boundaries of home; those surpluses and mnemonics which sublimate home in memory into a volatile fertile locale called homeland, have altered. Hence, the kathalichampa tree, which has once been an integral component of the house, has now been replaced by a sweet shop. Inside the house, Alam also notices the absence of his great-grandfather's oil painting, which in the words of the omniscient narrator, was "that piece of history (which) had effortlessly sailed into Alam's mind as he scattered the loose dry soil at Baba's grave in a Dhaka cemetery" (Palit 2011: 64). The absence of those tokens of past which have so long sanctified Alam's home in the fissures of memory, compels Alam to subject his consciousness into the ritual of unlearning and thus Alam's reconciliation with the impossibility of return begins.

These little subjections to change and consequent reconciliations are undoubtedly disturbing for the displaced subject, pushing him into an optimality of apprehension, where the subject is continuously haunted by the spectre of change. However, Alam's greatest apprehension, since the beginning of return, has been his possibility of reconciling with Raka, his beloved.

Raka is as central to Alam's consciousness as his home is. The story, through a critical analysis of Alam's relationship with Raka, attempts to explore the dynamics of human relationships in a political world, where the macrocosmic paradigm of the political latently infiltrates into the microcosmic filial and fraternal bondings. Alam's relationship with Raka emerges as a point of departure in the story. Their relationship evolves against the greater political reality of Partition and its consequent evolution of homogeneous communities founded on religious similarities. Alam doesn't accompany his family to Bangladesh, owing to his impending final year M.A. examination and is treated as a member of the Anantashekhar household, who had exchanged their house in Dacca with Alam's father. Alam thus starts living in the house with Anantashekhar's family and the house starts evolving as a site of resistance, a sanctified microcosm which is insulated from the ideologies of the macrocosmic. The dramatic description of Alam and Raka standing side by side on their roof, witnessing the decadent city parched in the flames of riot, seems to indulge the final possibilities of resistance that the sanctified vision of a human world can offer to the political. It is the finitude of the private in an overpowering political world, whose influence the personal cannot ignore for long.

Alam succumbs to the political and eventually migrates to Dacca, yet nurtures the possibility of returning to this contested 'home', which he has secretly cherished as not merely a nostalgia-evoking habitus, but also as a space which has the possibility to subvert and surpass the social spectrum of ideology. The sanctity of the house for Alam doesn't just rest in being an archive and repertoire of his childhood and youth; for him it is also the space which has, to an extent, managed to resist the dominant xenophobic tendencies in the politicos. It has lingered in Alam's memory as a promise and a possibility of reconciliation between a Hindu woman and a Muslim man, an Indian and a Pakistani-turned-Bangladeshi.

Alam soon realizes the impossibility of reconciling in that interstice called house, which he has so long conjectured to be occupying a paradigm beyond the 'us' and 'them', free from the principles of a community constructed on the politics of inclusion and exclusion. His return perpetuates a dystopia in the consciousness of Alam, for he experiences the change, not just in the realm of the visible socio-empirical but also in the intimate personal. The family of Anantashekhar appear strangers to him, while it is the absence of Raka which provides Alam the confirmation that the house has been derided of its transpolitical possibility. The politicos and its binaries of black and white, friend and enemy, the familiar and the strange have now crept into the house. Reflecting the greater homogeneous design of the sovereign Nation which Partition has promoted, it is now a space where differences remain unaccommodated and the politico-national 'other' is a perpetual stranger. Anantashekhar thus declares to the returning Alam: "But water and oil can never mix" (Palit 2011: 67).

This is the point where the relevance of Partition and the burden of history becomes an imposing, immanent and persistent reality, succumbing and appropriating the spatial 'now' with the memories of a historical 'then'. This historical can never be undermined as unreal; rather, much of it is consolidated by the experiences of the lived which the subject in history can never transcend. However, this fateful and faithful surrender of the individual to the historical annihilates the possibilities of redemption from the nightmarish burden of history. What is more, it appropriates the striving agencies of deviant subjects who are trying to negotiate with the historical and the lived and aspiring for an alternative understanding of the politico-socio-cultural reality.

Hence, Raka fails to transcend the limits of her lived experience as a refugee, displaced by the shadow lines segregating between the 'us' and 'them', the friend and foe. She is not completely unacquainted or unconscious of the ideologues of transcendence that seems to be the overpowering drives of agency formulation in case of Alam. However, her visions of transcendence fail to overpower the material truths of the lived. The essence of transcendence is more relevant to her in its non-actuality as she confesses to Alam in the letter which she leaves for him,

> "I questioned myself and realized I had asked you to come here precisely because I knew you never would … Something holds me back – somewhere, I am hurting! I don't know what it is. We had to change our addresses – this wall dispossessed us and many others too, before us."
>
> *(Palit 2011: 71)*

These final words of Raka compel Alam to reconcile with the continuity of immanence, a historical burden which he realizes he can never shed. The sovereign twin Nations formulated by Partition and divided on the basis of religion, have, in the long run, managed to penetrate into the more sanctified dictums of the personal. It has conditioned the human subject to identify the religious 'other' as its enemy and has conjectured the sister nation as the antagonist, against which it must seek to define its subjectivity and idioms of citizenship. The possibility of transcendence and the urge to redeem this binary opposition of limits which Alam as the deviant subject has so long cherished in his ideal of return is denied by the milieu of immanence. Alam's return to his home is thus an impossibility, for he is now the 'essential enemy' who in the words of Umberto Eco is "an obstacle" (Eco 2012: 8) against which the sovereign Nation state fashions its symbolic and ideological order. He can never be at home in the homeland which has evolved into a foreign country. At best, he can only survive as the stranger whom Derrida describes as a "being in question" (Dufourmantelle and Derrida 2000: 3), an irreducible agency who can neither be included nor be appropriated. Herein survives the relevance of Alam's dystopia, unmaking the stereotypic tendencies that the Nation embodies, with its trailing fragrances of a possibility which is denied but which fails to wither.

Note

1 Bapsi Sidhwa's novel *The Ice-candy Man* was initially titled *Cracking India* and the word 'cracked' has been used as an allusion to the novel.

Works Cited

Agamben, Giorgio. *Homo Sacer: Sovereign Power and Bare Life*, Trans. Daniel Heller-Roazen, Stanford, CA: Stanford University Press, 1995.

Donald, James. *Imagining the Modern City*. Minnesota: University of Minnesota Press, 1970.

Dufourmantelle, Anne and Jacques Derrida. *Of Hospitality*. Trans. Rachel Bowlby, Stanford, CA: Stanford University Press, 2000.

Eco, Umberto. *Inventing the Enemy and Other Occasional Writings*. Trans. Richard Dixon, Boston, MA: Houghton Mifflin Harcourt, 2012.

Menon , Ritu and Kamla Bhasin. "Recovery, Rupture, Resistance: Indian State and Abduction of Women during Partition." *Economic and Political Weekly*, 24 April1993: WS 2–11.

Mishra, Vijay. *The Literature of the Indian Diaspora: Theorizing the Diasporic Imaginary*. London: Routledge, 2007.

Nancy, Jean-Luc. *The Inoperative Community*. Trans. and ed. Peter Connor, Minneapolis: University of Minnesota Press, 1991.

Palit, Dibyendu. "Alam's Own House." Trans. Debjani Sengupta. In *MapMaking: Partition Stories from Two Bengals*. Ed. Debjani Sengupta, New Delhi: Amaryllis, 2011. 49–72.

Rauch, Angelika. "Post-Traumatic Hermeneutics: Melancholia in the Wake of Trauma." *Diacritics*, 28. 4 (1998): 111–120.

Rushdie, Salman. *Imaginary Homelands: Essays and Criticism 1981–1991*. London: Granta Books, 1991.

Simmel, Georg. "The Metropolis and Mental Life". In *Classic Essays on the Culture of Cities*. Ed. Richard Sennett, New York: Appleton-Century-Crofts, 1969.

PART III

Body politics: the woman in question

11

DECENTRIFICATION AND GENDERED PERSPECTIVES IN PARTITION NARRATIVES

An analysis of *Garm Hava*

Soumik Hazra and Shubham Dey

> Vafaon ke badle jafa kar rahe hain
> Main kya kar raha huun, vo kya kar rahe hain?
> [Fidelity begets cruelty,
> What are you and I doing here?]
>
> <div align="right">(<i>Hafeez Jalandhari, Popular Urdu Ghazal</i>)</div>

The spatial and the ontological are often involved in a dialectical relationship, where one is framed, constituted and formulated by the other. Spaces, as Edward Soja points out, are not dead and inert, constrained to a mere landscape or arena that contains the Anthropocene (1989: 10). Rather, they are affected by the intrusions of the self and they in turn regulate the ontological essence of the subject. The hermeneutics of the spatial involves an ethics of familiarisation and it is invoked within the sanctified considerations of intimacy that the self posits in relation with the outside that can be arguably considered as spatial.

Gaston Bachelard's consideration of the spatial locates the foundations of ontological essence in the sacrosanct paradigm of home. The intimate paradigm of home, for Bachelard, is "our first universe, a real cosmos in every sense of the world" and a "vital space" (Bachelard 1969: 4) where memory and imagination infuse to produce a subjective sensibility that is both organic and striated. In other words, home is a space that both precedes the ontological being and is contingent with it. Home is the intimate spatial, embodying the ambiguities of abstraction and reality, inheritance and evolution. Bachelard's understanding of home echoes Henry Lefebvre's "lived space" (Lefebvre 1991: 362), where not the abstract conceptualisation of the spatial but also the materiality of the lived are harmonised to conjure a paradigm that is contingent and precedent with the cogito or growing self.

The Partition of India created a rupture that was manifested in not just the birth of a macrocosmic bios–politikos, it also affected the sacrosanct paradigms of intimacy like home. The Radcliffe line and its aftermath was characterised by displacement, homelessness and exile where the self was ushered, coerced and conditioned into an essence of homelessness. Home, as Bachelard proposes, is associated with the primary consciousness of the self, "a primitiveness which belongs to all" (1969: 4). The moment of homelessness thus is also the moment of disenfranchisement where the foundations of agency are robbed from the self. Partition and its ensuing displacement hence was not just a catastrophe that was characterised by a material dislocation of (dis)membered and (dis)enfranchised bodies, leading to the genesis of the refugee. It was also an epistemic and ontic violation where the residual sense of being that is fundamental to the cogito was derided. The plenitudes of hope, faith, justice, ethics, morality, which are otherwise rendered to the self by the sacrosanct climate of home and the familial, increasingly proved obsolete in the changing milieu of estrangement. The centred matrix of consciousness, consolidated on the intimate epistemes of the familiar, was increasingly dislodged by the evolving milieu of alienation and estrangement.

Released in 1973, fresh after the 25th anniversary of Indian independence and the independence of Bangladesh from East Pakistan in 1971, *Garm Hava* can be read as an introspective stance for the Nation itself to look back at the earlier traumas of Partition. In the natal Nation state, the concept of citizenship was equated with religious affinity, debunking the myth of secularism and looking down upon religious minorities as downright suspicious. The presence of the refugees, or in this case, potential refugees, i.e. the religious minorities, to re-contextualise Giorgio Agamben, became discomforting to the modern Nation state. They problematised the illusion of the sovereign structure by disrupting the chain between Nation and nationality, man and citizen (Agamben 1998). The modern Nation state presupposes an undisputed shift from man to citizen where "man is the immediate vanishing ground (who must never come to light as such) of the citizen" (63). Refugee stands as the nuance that jeopardises such easy equating strategies and puts "the originary fiction of modern sovereignty under crisis" (64). "Nativity" and "Nationality" at odds, the refugee is the aporia underlying any considerations of sovereignty. *Garm Hava*, the text in question, deals with the problematic consideration of the refugee, as an affluent Muslim family in Agra refuse to migrate to Pakistan in the wake of 1947. For them, the 'sense of home' lies in their ancestral birth place, which produces a particular sense of ownership resisting any sort of permanent displacement to find a new home.

Garm Hava, based on an unpublished short story by Ismat Chughtai, deals with the Mirza family of Agra and their trials and tribulations after the Partition of India. The film opens with the declaration of the 'Independence of India, 1947' in a voice-over with montages of still photographs of the declaration of independence and the formation of India and Pakistan, shots of Gandhi, Nehru and Muhammad Ali Jinnah, coupled with celebrations of independent Nations. The montage then abruptly changes track and focuses on photographs of guns and swords, with the successive photographs depicting real-life refugees and their journeys in carts and trains across the border with shots of refugee camps. The montage ends with the

Decentrification, gendered perspectives **123**

sound of three gunshots in the background as a portrait of Mahatma Gandhi is displayed on the screen, as if reminding the audience of the ensuing chaos (or the titular scorching winds which uprooted green livelihoods) that took place soon after the death of the proverbial Father of the Nation. The death of the Father is also the significant annihilation of the centre that is otherwise a pre-cultural truth and Jacques Lacan points out that the "Father is a proper name … interested in the order of the world" (Lacan 1987: 88–89). The foundations of order dismantled, the subsequent social-political and cultural milieu is haunted by the spectres of dystopia and estrangement. The patricide generates a suspension of the familial-ethical and invokes a decentred politicos where the erstwhile is non-functional and the self must negotiate with an altered ethical approach towards the outside which in turn doesn't come under the considerations of the pre-determined and the regulative. It is also the epiphanic act that provokes the progenesis of blinded children who now have to reconcile with the unprecedented that falls beyond the traditional acquired symbolic order and the familiar. The death of the Father renders the pre-discursive modules of subjectivity as redundant and demands the genesis of a new ideal of being. The fulcrum of "We", which is "the common belonging of one I to everyone" (Sartre 1992: 130) is dismantled and the self must now, in absence of the Father, act in exclusion and as a bare subject. This is the probable genesis of anxiety whereby the self must now be responsible for "my I" (ibid.). This anxiety in turn renders the exterior unfamiliar which is now no longer comprehensible through the dysfunctional poetics of sense making that the pre-subjective has so long rendered to the self. The haunting anxiety of the estranged self, who is now ushered into the estranged world, has no referential in the 'we', which in turn is dysfunctional in the culture and order of inversion.

As such, Salim Mirza, one of the principal characters in the film, fails to arrive at any plausible response in context of the disruptive outbreaks of communal violence and genocide. The immediacy of the situation and its violent disposition doesn't discomfort him, for such enactments of violence are not unfamiliar occurrences within his experiential paradigm of lived reality. Instead, what perplexes him is the absolute failure of the self to reconcile with its communal other and the consequent expulsion of the other from the familiar habitus of the self. As Muslims start migrating to Pakistan (including Salim's sister) Salim introspects to the Tonga-wallah about the uncanny aftermath of displacement that is subsequent to the incidents of riots. With the annihilation of the paternal, both at a symbolic and literal level, the former ethical paradigm has been obliterated. The new order valorises exclusion over negotiation which Salim's agency, still containing traces of the erstwhile, fails to respond to. Simultaneously, his considerations of the ethical as a pre-founded truth can't accommodate or appropriate the occurring. The occurring sustains as an occurrence that the self cannot reconcile with and it sustains as the perilous dystopia within an ethical sensibility that has been rendered redundant.

Salim is a misfit, not merely within the intimate ethical framework but also within the greater considerations of the political. His political orientation is deeply intertwined and often aligned with his ethical sensibility. Unlike his brother Halim,

124 Soumik Hazra and Shubham Dey

who is an affluent leader of the Muslim League and is apprehensive of the conditions of Indian Muslims, Salim is an ardent follower of Gandhi and is optimistic
that the conditions of the Indian Muslims will gradually improve. This inherent
ideological difference between brothers and kin is efficiently established in the very
opening episodes of the film and the narrative gradually unfolds along these lines.

Halim and Salim Mirza of Agra live with their respective families and their
mother in their lavish ancestral home (*haveli*), although the legal papers of ownership of the *haveli* is in Halim's name. Halim is a local politician who doesn't believe
in his own rousing political speeches, whereas Salim is a shoe manufacturer who
has inherited the leather factory from his father. Salim has a wife, Jamila, a daughter
and two sons: Bakr, who has a wife and a son of his own and helps his father with
the family business, and Sikandar, who throughout the course of the film becomes
a college graduate, embarks on a job search with his classmates, gets rejected and
consequently becomes disillusioned with the state of the Nation. Salim's daughter
Amina is in love with Halim's son, Kashim. However, Partition causes Halim to
move to Pakistan with his family under false pretences – while Salim, adamant in
his love for his hometown and his locality refuses to move. Later, Kashim comes
back to marry Amina, in an inspired act of rebellion against his father who
wanted to use his son's marriage as an opportunity to climb the social ladder. This
union, though, is interrupted by the newly formed nation state, as it is soon discovered that Kashim doesn't have the necessary papers and documents to stay in
his erstwhile motherland and is deported soon after. The state continues with a
series of private disruptions in the Mirza household which forms the crux of the
filmic narrative.

Throughout the narrative, binaries are posited in form of the mainstream collective and the marginal individual, the ever-engulfing tendencies of social fluidity
and the stasis of the self, the unfamiliar koinon and the sacrosanct idion. The
conflict between these apparently disparate, yet relational oppositionalities, provokes the essence of misfortune and anguish in the movie. The misfortune has its
premonition (almost in the classical Greek tragedy sense of the term) in the introductory sequence of Salim Mirza which is juxtaposed with the image of a moving
train. This sequence skilfully overlays the binaries which will operate within the
film – of the displaced (signified through the face of the crowds migrating through
the train, including Salim's elder sister) and the static – Salim himself, who is
introduced in a mid-shot with the tombs of Agra visible in the background,
thereby establishing the inherent rootedness with the space he inhabits. Simultaneously, Agra is represented as a heterotopia where the homogenic potencies and
tendencies of the post-Partition Hindu majority Nation state are negated by an
evocation of a heterogeneous plurality. This essence of heterogeneity is foregrounded both in terms of the monumental and the lived. The tombs of Agra that
serve as the backdrop to the corporeal prominence of the marginalised minority
subject draw reminiscences of the Islamic past that is an irreducible component of
the Nation where now the Muslim subject is a disenfranchised minority.

The disenfranchisement that Salim experiences, owes as much to his minority status as to his epistemic faith in the mainstream ideologues of the Nation state. Unlike his brother, who is imbibed in counter-hegemonic politics and embraces prologues and performatives which endeavour to speak for the minority, Salim is a believer of the Gandhian ideology of secularism. As such, he consciously avoids the calls of resistance against the state from his fellow union members. The character of Salim brings out the problematics of the minority in being a 'national subject' (Menon 2012: 93–94). The minority ought to perform his identity and Salim's refusal to do so locates him in the perilous terrain of non-belonging. He is neither here nor there. As the Muslim subject, he is almost an outcast in his own land where he has to prove his loyalty to ensure protection from the state. Simultaneously, this (un)conscious performative of the ideologues of the dominant majority by the self locates it in dissociation from the intimate community that has a greater material pertinence than the imagined community of the Nation. The counter-cultural milieu of the minority identifies Salim as an exception who can set the meta-narratives of resistance in jeopardy. This ambiguity locates Salim as the perfect outsider, a disenfranchised subject who belongs neither to the centre nor the periphery. The irreducible self sustains unappropriated beyond the binary obsessed ethico-political-cultural.

This is prevalent in the sequences where Salim and his son Bakr have to move from one moneylender to another in order to gather money to save their ancestral home because of their religious inclination. The minority subject is hypothesised to have a more optimistic future, if they migrate to Pakistan and become a refugee instead of holding on to the aspirations of being an 'ideal Indian citizen'. Menon points out that in the aftermath of Indian Partition, minorities were often considered as "potential immigrants" (2012: 89). The film immaculately captures such anxieties that the mainstream majority nurtured against the minority. As Salim Mirza and his son Bakr Mirza exhaust themselves in search of loans, they are often blatantly and at times slyly denied aid under the pretext that they are Muslims, potential immigrants and not ideal citizens, ready to emigrate at any time without clearing their debts. This notion of 'ideal citizen' therefore is brought into question by the film itself through these three sequences. The sequences appear in three major crisis points of the film – two involving Salim Mirza and one involving Sikandar. All the three sequences involve conversations with upper-class, Hindu, empowered male figures; in short, the ideal national citizens who are tactically positioned in the off-screen space. Primarily consisting of mid-shots of both Salim and Sikandar, these sequences posits Salim and Sikandar in direct address with the audience – almost creating a visual division between 'us' and 'them'. The sequences produce a disorienting mode for the audiences who are posited as the surrogate for the empowered and privileged citizens. Through the usage of direct address, the film forces the audience to take into consideration the discriminatory scrutiny that was unjustifiably inflicted on the minority subject in erstwhile India by the upper-caste (mostly Hindu) citizens. This mimetic occupancy of "positions of power" also allows the filmmaker Sathyu to make the audience evaluate their complicity with regards to the routine discriminations encountered by the minority subjects in daily lives (Menon 2012: 95). In the first of the three sequences, Salim Mirza is shown to be pleading for money in front of the banker, and in turn the spectators. This sequence expertly exposes the tension between the uneven power structure and brings out in foreground the hypocrisies of secular India. Interestingly, in all the three sequences, the undemocratic behaviour towards the minority subject can be read as a unanimous endeavour of the ideal citizens to demote the Mirzas (Muslim minorities) into refugees. However, the failure of the endeavour actually complicates the idealistic 'nation as a family' narrative. Therefore, the very presence of the Muslim subject, albeit male, exposes the tensions between birth and nation more vividly.

Considerably influenced by the Victorian construct of *angel in the house* and in line with it, colonial Indian society identified the woman as a preserver of the home and the hearth. As such, women in colonial India were ideologically and materially restricted to the sanctified home interior. This locational paradigm of women, constricted and sanctified, was influential in the identification of the feminine with the familiar (traditional). The spatial of home evolved as a distinct sacrosanct interior, sanctified from the contaminations of modernity and the woman was conceptualised as its (un)acknowledged custodian. Partha Chatterjee points out,

> Applying the inner/ outer distinction to the matter of concrete day-to-day living separates the living space into ghar and bahir, the home and the world. The world is the external, the domain of the material; the home represents one's inner spiritual self, one's true identity. The world is a treacherous terrain of the pursuit of material interests, where practical considerations reign supreme. It is also typically the domain of the male. The home in its essence must remain unaffected by the profane activities of the material world- and woman is its representation.
>
> *(Chatterjee 1993: 120)*

While the restriction of women to the contrived corridors of the interior had definite coercive patriarchal implications, it simultaneously valorised the feminine as an emblem of sanctity. Woman was the embodiment and the figuration of the intimate essence of the collective, both in consideration of the family and the community. Simultaneously, her perennial status of being an objectified subject within the patriarchal economy of desire, posited her in a state of ambiguity where she was disenfranchised in enfranchisement. Her agency absorbed and appropriated, the woman was reduced to an emblematic existence, both in honour and in shame. As such, in the post-Partition milieu haunting the subcontinent, where religious communities were engaged in an unconditional defamation of the other, women were identified as frequent targets. The marginality of women and their susceptibility to the ensuing violence owed as much to the consideration of desire as to defamation. The inflicted violence extended the limits of the bare subject to infringe upon the foundations of the material collective. In other words, the violation of the woman was synonymous with a violation of home, the arena which devises pre-discursive subjectivity, both of the individual and the collective.

Garm Hava explores this intricate relationship that the woman shares with home. Home isn't free from the rigours of patriarchy and is pre-governed by hierarchical considerations. At dinner, the men converse and reflect upon the prospects and adversities that a possible displacement is likely to bring. Women are mere accompaniments in the discourse. At best, they can only rebuke unauthorised intrusions which question the sombre inferences that the patriarch(s) make. Hence, Sikander's dissident voice that emerges in response to Halim Mirza's advocacies for an immigration to Pakistan is immediately censored by his mother with the prompt affirmation "Respect your elders" (*Garm Hava,* Sathyu). The ramblings of children and old women are in turn laughed at and dismissed. Thus, Dadi's urge to stay rooted in the house where her husband's bones lay buried withers initially before the sceptic strains of Halim Mirza and in due course, the constrains that the circumstantial material has in store. The house in the sinister aftermath of Partition ceases to exist in split or separation from the greater politico-juridical. Instead, discarding the considerations of lived and belonging, it is now reduced to the considerations of ownership. The intimacies that the individual has so long cherished with the spatial are irrelevant without the acknowledgement of the juridical. Women, as subjects mediated by and dependent upon patriarchal agents, lack their agency to claim rights of possession. As Vazira Zamindar points out:

> Women were not entitled to autonomous citizenship because Article 5 of the citizenship laws by which their "domicile" was vested in that of their father or husband. Because permits were issued to both individuals and households, women, often incorporated in households, moved between the two states without directly engaging contestations of citizenship.
>
> *(Zamindar 2007: 209)*

The status of women thus lingers as 'relational truth', even within the corridors of intimacy and familiarity of home. In the film, the ecstasy of home is enfolded within the greater striations of the juridico-political and the patriarchal where woman is often a relational and marginal identity. Simultaneously, the home is also an irreducible paradigm of self affirmation and is one of those sanctified premises where the unperformed agency of the feminine self lingers. To illustrate this further, the chapter will take into consideration the three principle female characters of the narrative – Daadi Amma, Amina and Jamila.

Daadi Amma has a unique relationship with her ancestral home – for her it is not just a space of accommodation but also a space which bears witness to the histories of the dead and the departed. The space of her ancestral home, as far as Daadi Amma is concerned, exists beyond the limits of the state and she is unable to comprehend the statist intervention in an intimate, private sphere. In one of the early sequences, where the family is contemplating displacement from their ancestral home due to the lack of required papers, she says almost adamantly, that the government can't take away her residence, they can talk to her if it is needed. This sequence brings into foreground Daadi's rejection of "the empiricist logic of the

128 Soumik Hazra and Shubham Dey

state's intervention" which is coupled with her equating the act of internal migration with a certain sense of betrayal with respect to her husband, who lived and died in the haveli (Menon 2012: 96). The inability of Daadi to reconcile with the statist laws of property possesion further asserts the loss of relevance of a figure like Daadi in the developmental narrative of the Nehruvian India.

However, when she is forced to leave her home, in the newly rented house, she insists on living in a room in the terrace from where she can get a view of the *haveli*. For Daadi, therefore, the notion of 'home' is an idea which can never get displaced as it is mostly shrouded in utopia – a place that doesn't have any real life precedent but is instead shrouded in memories and a misplaced sense of homogeneity. To further emphasise the point, the director M.S. Sathyu uses images of large iron rods planted over the top of the new house – a recurrent trope of the Indian New wave which toys with spatial configuration to bring home the themes of alienation and rootedness which becomes, ironically markers of displacement – resembling a cage which becomes an eerie symbol of the barbed wires of Partition. The director also tactically positions the camera over the caged structure to look down upon the remaining members of the Mirza household, who resembles prisoners with restricted movements, the gaze being indicative of the presence of Daadi who is unable to cope with this sudden transformation. Daadi's inability to negotiate with the temporal and spatial shifts comes into being more jarringly in her death bed where she insists on going to the *haveli* one last time on account of her ill health. She is carried through a palanquin and the soundscape is suddenly populated with wedding music. In a way, this sequence can be read as the literal return of the repressed for the frail matriarch as she enters the house and the soundscape inhabits voices from the distant past. The visual intercuts shots of her close-up with a generic pan across her family members while the voices keep on echoing conversations – somewhat incoherently. Sathyu's camera pans from one family member to the other – from her son, grandson, son-in-law, Mr. Ajmani, then holding to a sudden blank space with the haveli in the background – a space reminiscent of the displaced and the departed – indicative of a spectral presence and the impossibility of return. The pan ends abruptly, focusing on Dadi's close-up and she dies almost mechanically with the sound of the train (signalling the migration of another family member soon enough) invading the soundscape.

Daadi's relationship with the *haveli* points out the gendered concept of ownership and belonging. The dependence of a woman on the patriarchal structure makes her a citizen who is entirely dependent on 'patrilocal residence' and a 'movable property' who has no identity of her own (Menon 2012: 96). Thereby, Daadi's relationship with the residential space exists only with respect to her sons and husband and she ends up becoming a mere apparatus of the patriarchal structure, irrespective of the new social order. However, it is also in context of this patrilocal residence that Daadi is able to foreground her agency. The previously discussed sequence where the family is pondering upon the prospect of an imminent immigration to Pakistan witnesses Daadi's vehement unwillingness to evacuate the house. The potent resistance to the greater striations of patriarchy and the political do not materialise but indeed exist as possibilities, conquered in the real but unvanquished and irreducible as an urge. Home sustains not merely as a space where the feminine self is estranged, it is also a lived that the authentic self celebrates and cherishes in an unperformed ecstasy.

Amina, whom Jisha Menon reads as a "double of Daadi" (2012: 97), is an accessory and subsequently an excess in the patriarchal structure of the home. Her parents, following the tendencies and tradition of middle-class patriarchy, are eager to marry her off to a prospective husband. In the sequence where the family moves to a new but smaller house, she has to share a room with her brother Sikander, which she at first refuses to do. Her brother jokingly replies that it is Amina who is an excess in their house and it is not the house which is small. This sense of being a 'burden' can only be got rid of, within the Muslim patriarchal structure, when she gets married and starts a family of her own. In her introductory sequence, she is seen trying her wedding costume in the *haveli*'s courtyard and her father gives her money to buy extra bangles for her wedding. Her identity within this structure, therefore, is confined within the realms of marriage and domesticity, despite her ability to read and write. When she is left by Kashim, this identity crumbles and is shrouded by a sense of alienation which haunts her and displaces her within her own home. The second level of displacement takes place when another cousin, Shamshad, migrates to Pakistan with his family after prolonged courtship and promises of getting married. This second betrayal, occurring again within the intimate structure of kinship and family, precisely depicts the essence of being exiled at home. Amina's agency is an estranged agency and her estrangement is deeply materialised by the striated constructs of home and family.

To emphasise Amina's perpetual estrangement, the plot makes a dialectical progression, where she is both framed within the habitual reality of home and the unfamiliar proximities of the outside. While home has rendered her disenfranchised and dependent, the outside initially appears to be an arena of agency affirmation and consolidation. As she visits the greater remnants of history like the Tomb of Chisti and Taj Mahal with her wooing cousin Shamshad, the memory of her former lover Kashim slowly withers. History, in form of the spatial and the ritual (the legend about Saleem and Meherunnisa), enables her to reconcile with a selfhood that is not burdened by memory and that can instead contemplate a possible redemption from the material, which has so long haunted her in the trope of an inescapable alienation. Amina's initial reluctance and apathy towards Shamshad is a possible testimony of how the infringements of home and its material construct has weighed heavy on her agency formulation. She was more at home in her contemplations of spinsterhood than in envisioning the possibility of making a home with him. However, once away from home, Amina realises that there are more homes to be found – homes where the objectified and governed self can give way to an ungoverned expression of agency. As she tastes the forbidden fruit in form of stolen kisses in the corridors of Taj Mahal and enchanting lovemaking on a boat in the Yamuna river, Amina's desires make her consider an alternative essence of subjectivity, which is not a derived agency but is spontaneous and unmediated, acting and being at will.

As such, Amina destroys the letters from Kashim, which has so long nourished her conditioned agency. This annihilation of the mnemonic is significant as Amina's formulation of an ungoverned agency begins in an immediate proximity of this epiphanic act. The act symbolically transcribes the rejection of the matrix that has so long guided her essence of being, i.e. the spectre of an erstwhile love. The rues of subversion and the exertion of an authentic agency begin with the expulsion of memory, the trace that is likely to make the self encounter with the happened perils of objectification.

Significant, however, is the room. Amina's epiphany doesn't occur in the seductions of the outside but in the intimacies of home. Paradoxically, the rejection of memory and the ensuing act of annihilation of the matrix happens at home, i.e. within the precincts of the spatial that has so long estranged her. Very soon, Amina will return to this room. She is now a dejected self for whom the outside and its agent, Shamshad, have failed to be an exception. The paradigmatic relationship between woman and estrangement is foregrounded, yet again. It is in this milieu of alienation and estrangement that Amina faces the mirror where she now confronts an irredeemably objectified self whose possibilities of agency affirmation have withered and eroded. The room that had once granted her the seclusion for the epiphanic annihilation of memory now evokes it back in form of the spectral Shamshad, dressed in a wedding costume. With it return the last traces of selfhood which the perennial premise of objectification has denied Amina. Amina realises that even the most sanctified ecstasies which she had once mistakenly conceptualised as tropes and foundations of ungoverned subjectivities, were in reality, haunted by the inescapable nemesis of estrangement. The room and its valorised climate of seclusion and subsequent introspection bring back to Amina the choric, in form of dreams and voices, echoes and apparitions. Choric, as Julia Kristeva defines it, comprises a "nonexpressive totality" (Kristeva 1984: 25), which is characteristic of "rupture and articulations (rhythm), precedes evidence, verisimilitiude, spatiality and temporality" (26) and which is beyond the representing–represented binary. The choric sustains, only to efface with the departing spectre of Shamshad and Amina realises that not even the choric is free from the regulative purview of patriarchy and that her choric has been designed and regulated by Shamshaad, who has in his way, estranged her. As such, it constitutes an inauthentic experience of the feminine. In the scene to follow, she finally commits the act of suicide in her bridal outfit while the accompanying soundtrack stops abruptly. Here, taking cue from Freud, it can be said that her suicide is concurrent with the killing of an object with which she has identified herself in an intimate manner (Freud 1999: 13–33). Amina locates herself as an objectified subject and suicide becomes the only possible means through which the self can engage in an act of de-objectification. Simultaneously, suicide becomes the only possible attempt to reclaim a sacrosanct space and secure a room of her own, not just in terms of spatiality but also in consideration of the ontic. The reclamation of self through an annihilation of subject is the only resistance that the objectified self can offer. The very room that had granted the self a sanctified seclusion which could subsequently promote a departure from a governed essence of being now contains the irreducibly authentic self, resistant to the ever-pervading, repressive and estranging milieu of patriarchy.

Salim's wife, Jamila, however, is deprived of any sense of liberation in the narrative. As such, her engagement with home is significantly different from the preceding characters discussed, i.e. her mother-in-law and her daughter. Jamila has attuned herself to the constrictions of patriarchy and is subservient to the considerations of hierarchy. When Sikander raises his voice of dissidence against his uncle's consideration of immigrating to Pakistan, she steps in to preserve the hierarchy. Her occasional urges to re-unite with her kin at Pakistan are immediately negated by her increased performance to belong to the Mirza household. However for Jamila, this stance of belonging represents just another facet of the repressive authoritarian force of the nation-state, which once again invades her personal desires of re-uniting with her kin. Although the film ends with Salim's radical transformation into an embodiment of the state narrative of secularism and thereby into an ideal citizen: Jamila is denied the same rights, further asserting the fact that the minority woman has no discernible place in the national imaginary, where the gendered experience remains conservative and is not given a chance to emerge in the centre. This point is more emphasised if one reads the last sequence from Jamila's perspective. In the middle of their journey towards the railway station, Sikandar meets his old college friends who were protesting against scarcity of jobs and impending corruption. When Sikandar joins them with his father's approval, Jamila's frail voice is heard off-camera, protesting his actions, but to no avail. Towards the climax, when Salim decides to join his son, the audience finally encounters a hijab-clad Jamila, captured in a full-body profile, in the background and is ordered by Salim to return to their house again. She is handed over the keys of the house with a close-up focusing on the keys. This close-up suggests in a way the inability of Jamila to leave the house and her final submission to the authoritarian patriarchal structure yet again. She is held back to her world of entrapments, denying in the diegetic world any sense of subjectivity and closure.

However, these entrapments are foreknowledges to the feminine and herein lies the ambiguity that patrilocal reality of home shares with the woman. Jamila's feminine essence of being is deeply intersubjective and although one can clearly locate the ideological considerations that condition the feminine into a compromised essence of being, the suspension of the inter-subjective only posits the woman as an empty subject. Jamila's materiality of being is non-existent without her family and thus an extrication of the self from the regulatory other, only renders it maimed and de-ontologised. This is the problematic poise that home and family share with the feminine in the movie and this nuance is perfectly captured by the director through the apt use of melodrama. Christine Gledhill notes that melodrama as a narrative form allows women to get mobilized which in turn becomes representative of larger cultural values (Gledhill, quoted in Kapse 2017: 149). Furthermore, melodrama accentuates the shaping of dominant ideologies by exploiting realistic conventions and generates pathos through sequences of 'victimized racial suffering' (ibid.). Melodrama therefore, in a harmless fashion, as noted by Anupama Kapse, feminises and pushes boundaries of fantasy and pleasure to represent a larger social reality (ibid.). In other words, melodrama deals with the repressed desires of the individual and sudden eruption of violence from the repressed patriarchal structure which becomes the primary mode of expression of the peripheral subject. In a film like *Garm Hava*, where the violence is more layered and psychological, the traumas of separation and loss and the plights of the invisible female subject can only come across through fissures of melodrama, posited in due contrast with the prevalence of realism of the art films of that period (shooting in real life locations, the mise-en-scene reflecting the daily lives of the family). As such, the use of music, becomes an important tool for melodrama. To borrow from Thomas Elsaesser, melodrama can also be defined as putting *melos* (music) to drama (Elsaesser 1987: 46). This definition underlines melodrama as a musical modulation of narrative which depicts the emotional high and low. For instance, the impactful *qawali* in the courtship sequence between Shamshad and Amina makes a return in the suicide sequence of Amina – driving home a sense of emotional loss both for the character and the spectator. The mismatched use of music and image (also prevalent in Daadi's death scene) drives home the intensity of the visuals and accentuates the theme of female decentralisation – thereby making the formal structure of the film more sympathetic towards the female subject.

Works Cited

Agamben, Giorgio, *Homo Sacer: Sovereign Power and Bare life*. Trans. Daniel Heller-Roazen. Stanford, CA: Stanford University Press, 1998.

Bachelard, Gaston. *The Poetics of Space*. Trans. Maria Jolas. Boston, MA: Beacon Press, 1969.

Chatterjee, Partha. *The Nation and Its Fragments: Colonial and Postcolonial Histories*. Princeton, NJ: Princeton University Press, 1993.

Elsaesser, Thomas, "Tales of Sound and Fury: Observations on the Family Melodrama." In Christine Gledhill (ed.) *Home is Where the Heart is: Studies in Melodrama and the Woman's Film* (pp. 43–69). London: BFI Publishing, 1987.

Freud, S. " The Psychogenesis of a Case of Homosexuality in a Woman" (1920). In R. C. Lesser and E. Schoenberg (eds), *That Obscure Subject of Desire: Freud's Female Homosexual Revisited* (pp. 13–33). New York and London: Taylor & Francis/Routledge, 1999.

Gledhill, Christine, *Home is Where the Heart is: Studies in Melodrama and the Women's Film*. London: BFI Publications, 1987.

Jalandhari, Hafeez. "Vafaon ke badle jafa kar rahe hain". Retrieved from https://www. rekhta.org/couplets/vafaaon-ke-badle-jafaa-kar-rahe-hain-hafeez-jalandhari-couplets? gclid=CjwKCAiA4Y7yBRB8EiwADV1haXHvYIp9oB4dRUbw-d4805vq1AJDHk3xhp Bqe09T7uoeehZvWw45ZBoCLnwQAvD_BwE (accessed on 19 September 2018).

Kapse, Anupama, *Women in White: Femininity and Female Desire in the 1960s Bombay Melodrama*, 2017. Retrieved from http://www.academia.edu/34665666/Women_in_White_ Femininity_and_Female_Desire_in_the_1960s_Bombay_Melodrama.(accessed on 29 October 2018).

Kristeva, Julia. *Revolution in Poetic Language*. Trans. Margaret Waller. New York: Columbia University Press, 1984.

Decentrification, gendered perspectives **133**

Lacan, Jacques. "Introduction to the Names-of-the-Father Seminar." Trans. Jeffrey Mehlman, *October*, 40 (Spring1987), 81–95.

Lefebvre, Henry. *The Production of Space*. Trans. Donald Nicholson-Smith. Oxford: Blackwell, 1991.

Menon, Jisha, *The Performance of Nationalism*. Cambridge: Cambridge University Press, 2012.

Sathyu, M.S. *Garm Hava (film)*. Sponsored by Film Finance Corporation, 1973.

Sartre, Jean-Paul. *NoteBooks for an Ethics*. Trans. David Pellauer. Chicago: University of Chicago Press, 1992.

Soja, Edward. *Postmodern Geographies: The Reassertion of Space in Critical Social Theory*. London: Verso, 1989.

Zamindar, Vazira Fazila-Yacoobali. *The Long Partition and the Making of Modern South Asia: Refugees, Boundaries, Histories*. New York: Columbia University Press, 2007.

12

HONOUR, WOMAN'S BODY AND MARGINALISATION

A study of Amrita Pritam's *Pinjar*

Anisha Ghosh

> There is everything to forgive. You can't forgive me.
> If only somehow you could have been mine,
> What would not have been possible in the world?
>
> *(Agha Shahid Ali, "Farewell")*

In the discursive milieu of gender studies, the body has been considered as a site where social constructions of difference are inscribed by ways of subjecting it to several contesting regimes of power. The Partition of India is a horrible politico-historical fact that has been written large on female bodies through a history of violence. The female body, rarely a direct participant in the political tensions which snowballed into Partition, becomes the space where the history of Partition has left its impressions through violence.

The Partition of India in 1947 was a culmination of the two–Nation theory, which was motivated by the demand of a separate Nation state for the Muslim majority where they could practise their religion freely. Mass migrations led to unprecedented loss of property, life and most importantly, a lengthy period of trauma. The Partition generation experienced this looming sense of loss of one's home and loved ones, the precariousness of life in refugee camps and the attempts of making home away from home. They passed on their trauma to the succeeding generations whose experience of Partition is, however, not confined to one historical epoch; it is rather a lived reality for subsequent generations. In her study of Partition literature, Urvashi Butalia maintains that despite being a product of times when Partition of India was a historical reality of the past, it still haunts the post-Partition generation in its different manifes-tations. Be it the Sikh killings of 1980s, the Hindu–Muslim riots of Bhagalpur in 1989 or the 1992 communal violence (and the atmosphere of disquiet and distrust which followed it) perpetrated by the destruction of Babri Masjid in

Ayodhya, there are "partitions everywhere, communal tensions, religious fundamentalism, continuing divisions on the basis of religion" (Butalia 1998: 7).

In colonial India, women had never been incorporated in the performative of nationalism as active political agents and were denied political agency by the 19th-century nationalist resolution of the woman question, which relegated them into the sphere of domesticity, turning them into sacrosanct protectors of tradition. How did the Partition of the Nation then affect the lives of those who were never acknowledged to have played an active role in building it in the first place? By aligning women with tradition and the sacrosanct ideal of the feminine, women came to be invariably associated with the honour of their community and a soft target of honour crimes. Millions of women were raped, their bodies mutilated, on both sides of the border, mostly by men of the opposite community. Even now, Partition stories and memories are used as a pretext for any violence against one community by the aggressors of the other; the memories of killings, of rape and shame feed the honour-sensitive upholders of one religious code to reciprocate the hurt on the other, which evidently proves that Partition has not ended and will never be a closed chapter. It is this homogenic approach to Partition and its human dimensions that makes Amrita Pritam's novel *Pinjar* a remarkable text in Partition studies as it engages with not just the politico-historical catastrophe of a Nation but also the violation of a woman's body, her personality and her psyche.

Amrita Pritam is a major literary figure of Punjabi literature. During the six decades of her literary activity she has produced over 100 books of poetry, fiction, essays, biographies, a collection of songs and an autobiography, all of which have been translated into several Indian and foreign languages. Her most celebrated work, *Pinjar*, translated into English by another major Partition novelist Khushwant Singh under the title *The Skeleton and Other Stories*, takes us through the trauma of the catastrophe and the impacts of the new political developments of 1940s on the lives of women in Punjab. The novel focuses on different experiences of marginalization – gendered, social and religious. Here the trauma of Partition is complicated by the violence at physical as well as psychological level for women who were reduced not just to bodies but to skeletons,[1] ripped of flesh and blood.

Unlike the British poet Alfred Tennyson, who turns to poetic re-rendering of classical mythology and English medieval legend to shape the consciousness of his Nation, Amrita Pritam takes recourse to mythology to elucidate the subjection of women. The abduction of Pooro by Rashida is a re-enactment of *sitaharan* against the backdrop of Indian Partition. Just as Sita's abduction by Raavana was an honour crime, so is Pooro's abduction by Rashida. Both Pooro and Rashida are victims of the history of longstanding animosity between the two families: the Sahukars and the Shaikhs. The shame brought by a woman, abducted and defiled two generations ago, is avenged by the abduction of another woman. The man who avenges the misdeeds of the past in turn emerges as the saviour of the community by returning that mark of shame to the enemy clan. When Pooro manoeuvres her way out of confinement and reaches home with the hope of reuniting with her family, she experiences alienation in the form of rejection. Pooro is considered as defiled as

136 Anisha Ghosh

she has stayed with a Muslim man for 15 days. This rejection sets the course of Pooro's future. She is forced by circumstances to stay with Rashida.

The connection between women's bodies, their sexual purity and honour is one of the major tools of extending sexual control over women in the heterosexual matrix. As noted by Susan Brownmiller, sexual violence, even the threat of rape, creates a nexus of fear, shame and rejection which circumscribes women to their bodily existence. Sexual violence has little to do with the gratification of sexual desire or urges, rather it is the imposition of domination, stamping of authority, a mark of humiliation and sometimes annihilation of those who cannot retaliate (Brownmiller 1976: 312–326).

Partition perpetrated all kinds of ruptures – geographical, communal and psychological. Partition survivors would say that it was not a separation of land but of memories and lives. For women, however, this experience of Partition had another level – it was a dismembering of both the psyche as well as the body. Pooro's body becomes the object of conquest for the Shaikhs and a source of shame for her family, the Sahukars. Pooro's rejected body is conquered by Rashida through the institutionalised performatives of marriage. He even impregnates her against her wishes. When Rashida decides to move from Chhatto to Sakkar, it hardly makes any difference to Pooro as dislocation by now has become a way of life for her; she is already a dislocated subject, disowned by her familial bonds of kinship and community: "There was no reaction from her – after her parents had turned her away from their door, leaving the ancestral village did not seem so momentous. All said and done, what difference does it make? All villages were alike" (Pritam 2015: 24).

The rejection from her family instils in Pooro a feeling of perennial home-lessness. Her new refuge neither enriches nor dilutes her sense of non-belonging. Living with Rashida, carrying his child, are just bodily experiences for her. Despite the hospitality extended by the women of Rashida's family, Pooro continues to feel like "a stray calf in a strange herd of cows" (ibid.).

The moment of rupture in Pooro's life is dramatised by Pritam by the act of inscribing a new name – Hamida – on her arm as an attempt on Rashida's part to make a fresh start which is not possible without finalising her split from her past. Naming is indeed a strategy through which the 'other' is appropriated within the consciousness of self and Pooro's new name locates her within the performative milieu of a new identity. In her essay, "Performative Acts and Gender Constitution: An Essay in Phenomenology and Feminist Theory", Judith Butler writes that gender identity is an effect of the repetition of stylised bodily acts (Butler 1998: 519–520). This idea of 'doing' gender through body can be observed in Hamida's case as she 'does', or is made to 'do', her social identity through her body. Just as the choice of stylised bodily acts produce the effect that gender is never free but discursively regulated, for Pooro the choice of bodily performance of social identity is ever regulated by forces greater than her. Rashida's attempt to initiate a new course of social life for Pooro by inscribing her new name on the flesh creates a permanent partition of her female psyche. She can no longer be her old self 'Pooro', nor can her transformation into Hamida be negotiable:

The man tattooed on it the new name she had been given when she was married to Rashida. From that day "hamida" was not only inscribed on her skin in dark green letters but everyone began to call her by that name.

In her dreams, when she met her old friends and played in her parents' home, everyone still called her Pooro. At other times she was Hamida. It was a double life: Hamida by day and Pooro by night. In reality she was neither one nor the other, she was just a skeleton, without a shape or a name.

(Pritam 2015: 25)

These two irreconcilable identities make Pooro-Hamida the quintessentially homeless figure.

The rift in her psyche, the split in Pooro-Hamida's personality is best expressed through her feelings towards her newborn child. She starts loving the child as it is the only connection she has with her past, the child being her flesh and blood. But at the same time the baby is also a reminder of her present:

The boy tugged at his mother's breast. Hamida felt as if the boy was drawing the milk from her veins and was sucking it out with force, just as his father has used force to take her. All said and done he was his father's son, his father's flesh and blood and shaped like him. He had been planted inside her by force, nourished inside her womb against her will – and was now sucking the milk from her breasts, whether she liked it or not.

(Pritam 2015: 35)

This divided existence, her double life as Pooro and Hamida, the rift in her consciousness, her personality, the irreconcilable difference between the past and the present, contradictory feelings and conflicting emotions of Pooro-Hamida are but a metaphor of Partition.

Postmodernist thinkers have regarded subjectivity as fragmented and ruptured, denying the notion of a "stable coherent self" (Flax 1987: 624). Feminist theory and politics, in lieu with the trend, has taken a turn inwards and has questioned its own presumption of the woman as a stable subject. In this novel, the woman's body becomes the battleground not only of contesting identities and competing regimes of power, but also of conflicting emotions and unsettling memories. Amrita Pritam provides us with an insight into Pooro-Hamida's inner life through her dreams and memories by exploring her stream of consciousness as part of the narrative strategy. Pritam further establishes that loss of 'home' is not only a physical reality but also a psychological one.

Pooro-Hamida, despite having a family and a 'home', is haunted by a sense of homelessness which is characteristic of dislocation – forced or voluntary. It is through her relationship with several other marginalized women in the society that Pooro-Hamida even tries to cultivate a sense of belonging. First of these, her encounter is with Kammo, the 12-year-old from Chhatto whom she happens to meet by chance in Sakkar. Kammo is a marginalised entity in her family; she is a motherless, unloved child living with her aunt and hence is unwanted in that household. In Kammo, Pooro finds a link to her severed past and Kammo in turn, finds in Pooro, the mother she lost, the mother whom her aunt has never been able to replace. Both are liminal figures in their own way – while Kammo is unwanted in the family she lives with, to Pooro her new social identity and home are undesirable. Communal boundaries are too starkly drawn between the personal desires and wishes of these women – Kammo is barred by her aunt from visiting Pooro who is now Hamida, a Muslim woman. A woman's claims of the heart, her feelings and emotions always fail to compete with the powerful claims of religion. In this forceful separation between Kammo and Pooro, there is a re-enactment of the separation of Pooro from her own mother, again attributed to the claims of religion, society and the question of honour. As such, the greater considerations pertaining to the political decide what is sacred and what is defiled, consequently valorizing the social-religious idea of 'sacred' over the intimate personal.

The second marginalised woman whom Pooro-Hamida meets is Tara. Tara is a victim of patriarchy at both her husband's home as well as her paternal home. While her husband takes in another woman and forces her to become a prostitute not against the wishes of his own family, Tara's paternal family remains indifferent to her condition out of some misplaced sense of propriety. A woman, being the symbol of 'honour' in this society, is not allowed to walk away from an unhappy marriage, as dissolution of marriage will mar the name of her own family. After marriage the husband is the lord and master and can treat her in whatever way he wishes. This non-committal stance of Tara's parents, their non-participation in finding a solution to the condition of their daughter is a passive-aggressive form of persecution of the woman and is akin to the betrayal that Pooro experienced when her family disowned her on the grounds of social respectability. For Tara's in-laws, the marital harmony and verisimilitude are preserved as long as Tara is dependent on her husband for food and shelter, thus reducing the woman's existence to the level of the body. Tara's body is diseased as her soul is tormented. Other than Pooro, she is the only character to whose psyche and inner life we get direct access through Pritam's narrative. For Tara, the only way out of her misery is through death. This alarming episode becomes an eye-opener to Pooro, since for the first time she starts to appreciate Rashida, for, barring his one transgression, he has always been a kind husband to her. This is the first step in Pooro's journey towards reconciliation with her present reality.

The third important encounter which Pooro-Hamida has is with the madwoman. At a metaphorical level, the madwoman is all but a body and is limited to her corporeal essence of being; a social outcast, she lives in the margins of Sakkar and thrives on the charity of the people of the village. The madwoman's bulging baby bump reveals the most appalling side of humanity – how the cravings of flesh have not spared even a body without a sane mind to regulate its operations. When the madwoman dies in labour, Rashida and Pooro adopt the baby and care for it as their own child. Rashida cuts the umbilical cord by which the infant was attached to the corpse of his mother and Pooro nourishes the child on her own milk. In his acclaimed Partition short story "Toba Tek Singh", Saadat Hasan Manto writes about the exchange of asylum lunatics between India and Pakistan after Partition. There are heart-rending scenes at the asylum in Pakistan where bodies going berserk, without a healthy mind to take charge of them, are trying to come to terms with what Partition means. Bishan Singh's never-ending quest for his ancestral village Toba Tek Singh and his final demise at the 'no man's land' at Wagah border is one of the finest specimens of the trauma of Partition and its impact on the non-normatively functioning mind. In *Pinjar*, the village elders decide the religion of the progeny of the madwoman on the basis of the madwoman's Hindu connections, leading to the separation of the baby from Pooro; similar patterns of madness are replicated as that of the exchange of the asylum lunatics in Manto's short story.

Again the theme of separation and loss is enacted as the allegedly 'Hindu' baby is snatched away from its Muslim foster parents by the Hindu elders of the village. Religion gets the better of humanity once again; once again the claims of religion outdo the claims of motherhood. The baby too, like Kammo, has to be given up by Hamida. The scene in which Rashida is interrogated, compelled and threatened by the village elders to give up the Hindu baby for the sake of maintaining religious purity as well as for the sake of maintaining peace between the Hindus and Muslims of the village, reveals how patriarchal and religious interests regulate private emotions, how regimes of power determine the legitimacy of who should love whom and how. The returning of the nearly dead baby to Pooro and Rashida, however, is no act of selfless kindness on part of the village elders but a way to escape the guilt of causing the death of a helpless orphan.

Half-way through the text come the historical events of the Partition of India. Terrible realities of communal violence on both sides, massive loss of life and property, human relations of mutual love and kindness metamorphosing into inhuman hatred overnight have been documented graphically by Amrita Pritam. Pooro's abduction, an isolated instance of communal animosity, now becomes a way of settling scores between the two religious groups. Partition of the country on religious lines is written large on the bodies of its women as seen through Pooro's eyes. She witnesses hooligans parading a naked girl and dancing around her, she hears first-hand from the Hindu girl who escaped from the refugee camp about how girls have been abducted from the camps at nights and sexually exploited. After hearing about Laajo's disappearance from Ramchand, Pooro and Rashida investigate and find out that many Hindu women in Rattoval and several other such villages were forcefully made mistresses of Muslim men. Amrita Pritam, however, does not make a biased analysis of the realities of Partition as she reports similar incidents happening on both sides of the border.

While Pooro was abducted and taken away from her parental home and later had to move from her ancestral village, Ramchand's sister Laajo, who was married to Pooro's brother, was kept confined in her own house by Allah Ditta and his mother. She became a hostage in her own house, and hence as homeless as Pooro, or even more. Laajo's condition is a commentary on the nature of such feeling of homelessness and alienation which does not always have to originate from spatial dislocation. By rescuing Laajo and handing her over to her brother Ramchand and her husband who is Pooro's brother, Pooro attains the satisfaction of returning home. Both Pooro and Laajo are victims of cross-religious abduction at two different times. Laajo's abduction coincided with the time when religious views were more accommodative, as people from both sides and religions were accepting their women with open arms, without slightest consideration for defilement and purity – it was 1948 and people on both sides have been through a lot.

Pooro attains a heroic stature when towards the end of the novel she subverts her status of a victim of cross-religious abduction, the status of a pawn in the game of contesting male egos, by choosing her own reality, her own Nation. She rejects the idea of return, knowing full well that 'return' of any sort is an impossible ideal to achieve for a dislocated dismembered entity like her. Rejection of return, however, does not mean the rejection of her people, her long-lost home, her India, which was very different from this new post-1947 India. Rather, it is the acceptance of the bitter reality of Partition. Her old identity, her old name Pooro and the memories of her home are a figment of the past, like Salman Rushdie's old family photograph in black and white which he describes in "Imaginary Homelands". Like the photograph is for Rushdie, Hamida's original name 'Pooro' is always a reminder that it's her present which is foreign and "that the past is home, in a lost city in the mists of lost time" (Rushdie 2010: 1). Rushdie describes the alienation from homeland, the exilic position as something defined by a perpetual sense of loss, something which the writer tries to come to terms with through his writing, knowing full well that a return to the old 'home' is impossible:

> our alienation from India almost inevitably means that we will not be capable of reclaiming precisely the thing that was lost; that we will, in short, create fictions, not actual cities or villages, but invisible ones, imaginary homeland, Indias of the mind.
>
> *(Rushdie 2010: 2)*

Unlike the artist dislocated from her social cultural origin, Pooro has no space to renegotiate cultural identity; the only way she can overcome her feelings of homelessness and alienation is by accepting the altered circumstances of her life. It is through her acceptance of Rashida, her new family raised with him and hence her new identity, that the dislocated homeless Pooro comes 'home' as Hamida. Just as the artist creates a creative space fiction to renegotiate identity, to overcome his sense of dislocation; Pooro-Hamida creates the fiction of home on which can be based the fiction of 'belonging'.

Amrita Pritam's feminism has an integrative vision at its core and this is obvious in her portrayal of Rashida, the only male character in the novel who matches Pooro in nobility and kindness. Like Pooro, he too is a victim of patriarchal notions of honour and respectability. In the name of defending and restoring his family's 'honour', he is used by the upholders of patriarchal codes of religious and family honour for establishing the fact that cross-religious abduction of one woman in the past can only be avenged by doing the same with another. Rashida is a round character who shows remarkable growth as the narrative proceeds. The course of his journey is determined partially by his sense of guilt and partly by his own good nature and love for Pooro. His first and only act of insensitivity – Pooro's abduction – was no wanton act of impulse, like the killing of the albatross by the Mariner in Coleridge's "Rime of the Ancient Mariner". His action was the direct consequence of his socio-cultural liability as a male responsible for defending family honour, for which it was permissible to take any extreme measures. Throughout the novel, there is no single moment when Rashida is not found regretting this one villainous act against his own will or individual nature. Both Pooro and Rashida embark upon their own personal journeys together – while Pooro's journey is driven by the perennial sense of loss and homelessness leading to acceptance of her new identity, Rashida's is a journey from guilt to redemption. During those turbulent times when religious hatred was getting the best of humanity, Rashida risks his and his family's lives to rescue Laajo, the Hindu girl, and hands her over safely to her people. He is in full knowledge of the fact that Laajo's husband set his harvest on fire once, but he holds no grudges as this is for him an expectedly normal reaction from a brother to the abductor of his sister. This material loss caused by Pooro's brother, in fact, gives him a certain sense of calm, as he has always been haunted by his own misdeed of the past. He tries in every way possible to compensate for the injuries he once caused by forcefully abducting Pooro, but fails to completely absolve himself of his sins. It is only when Laajo, like many other Hindu women stranded in Pakistan and many such Muslim women stranded in India, returns to India, and Pooro-Hamida finds in every such woman a part of herself returning home that Rashida finally comes to peace with himself. Pooro's final decision to embrace her identity as Hamida and accept Rashida as the reality of her life is an act of kindness, not only towards Rashida but also towards herself. This is an act of forgiveness which brings peace to both the repentant offender and the distraught victim.

Unlike *The Ice-Candy Man*, where Bapsi Sidhwa keeps the denouement open with a promised ecstasy of reconciliation, Amrita Pritam's *Pinjar* tersely proceeds to the cessation like an arrow hitting the target. Pritam with her brilliant craftsmanship weaves the destiny of women with the destiny of the Nation and vice versa. Just as woman is made to live a double life, so is the Nation split into two; just as the Nation is dismembered and divided into two, its women's bodies, their souls, their identities are lacerated and scarred. The only way to survive this onslaught on their bodies, their psyches, their memories and their entire personas is by coming to a truce with their altered reality. This kind of acceptance, by no means, is a denial of agency to the female subject; rather it is a way of carving out several other forms of being, as Pooro-Hamida does in this novel.

Note

1 The skeleton is indeed the central metaphor, adopted by Amrita Pritam in her novel to explore the traumatic outcome, the horrible impact of the atrocities on women in the wake of Partition.

Works cited

Ali, Agha Shahid. "Farewell". In *The Country without a Post Office*. Haryana: Penguin Books, 2013.

Brownmiller, Susan. *Against Our Will: Men, Women and Rape*. New York: Ballantine Books, 1976.

Butalia, Urvahsi. *The Other Side of Silence: Voices from the Partition of India*. New Delhi: Penguin Books, 1998.

Butler, Judith. "Performative Acts and Gender Constitution: An Essay in Phenomenology and Gender Theory". *Theatre Journal*, vol. 40, no. 4, 1998, pp. 519–531. Retrieved from www.jstor.org/stable/3207893 (accessed on 31 August 2017).

Coleridge, Samuel Taylor. "The Rime of the Ancient Mariner". In *Fifteen Poets*. Oxford: Oxford University Press, 1941, pp. 257–275.

Flax, Jane. "Postmodernism and Gender Relations in Feminist Theory". *Signs*, vol. 12, no. 4, 1987, pp. 621–643.

Manto, Saadat Hasan. "Toba Tek Singh". Trans. Tahira Naqvi. *Manoa*, vol. 19, no. 1, 2007, pp. 14–15. Project Muse. Retrieved from doi:10.1353/man.2007.0041 (accessed on 1 October 2018).

Pritam, Amrita. *Pinjar: The Skeleton and Other Stories*. Trans. Khushwant Singh. New Delhi: Tara, 2015.

Rushdie, Salman. *Imaginary Homelands*. London: Vintage Books, 2010.

Sidhwa, Bapsi. *The Ice-Candy Man*. New York: Penguin Books, 1998.

13

HISTORY VERSUS (HER)STORY

A study of Jyotirmoyee Devi's *Epar Ganga Opar Ganga*

Jaydip Sarkar

Social memories evolve with various social, political and psychological purposes.

> In the public sphere, they might be evoked to legitimize or delegitimize the dominant power structure, or to distinguish one collective identity construct from another. In the private sphere, they might help people cope with individually experienced trauma. Social memories can be imposed, proclaimed, suppressed or hidden. They do not always form a coherent narrative, but might contain contradictory or repressed elements, gaps and denials. They are always fluid, however, as they evolve from a process rather than from an event with a clear beginning and end.
>
> *(Hartnack 2012: 249)*

In the recent past, researchers like Urvashi Butalia, Ritu Menon and Kamla Bhasin have elicited women's suppressed memories regarding their experiences of being marginalized and gendered by the Partition of British India. By making these accounts accessible in touching oral histories, these researchers have been instrumental in bringing about a shift in Partition studies. They have not only documented the hitherto unconceived brutality of physical violence on women's bodies during those days of political mayhem, but have also spelt out a paradox which characterized the social history of the feminine in the context of Partition. As Butalia notes:

> If colonialism provided Indian men the rationale for constructing and reconstructing the identity of the Hindu woman as a 'bhadramahila', the good, middleclass, Hindu wife and mother, superior of her men, Independence and its dark 'other', Partition, provided the rationale for making women into symbols of nation's honour.
>
> *(Butalia 1998: 192)*

144 Jaydip Sarkar

In both the cases, the female and the feminine were objectified, leaving very little space for independent and autonomous assertions of female subjectivity and self.

British India experienced a contrary movement in history; the progressive march towards freedom that was considerably non-violent and the consequent evolution of a two Nation-state, which was marked by communal violence, bloodshed and displacement. Butalia notes that the Partition of India was a heart wrenching saga of homelessness and displacement, where twelve million individuals had to exchange homes (Butalia 1998: 3). What is more, this terrible exchange happened within the constricted time period of a few months. Like flocks of cattle, individuals abandoned their habitus for an alien country, completely oblivious to what awaited them on the other side of the Radcliffe line. The greatest of human tragedies was being acted out, the only difference being that the pity and fear which the tragic evoked were inconceivable by spectators endowed with a historical consciousness. The humane was desanctified, with murder, abduction, rape and mutilation becoming the ethics of survival and the performatives of private and social identities. The long walk to freedom found a perfect visual enactment as the displaced travelled on foot in great columns or 'kafilas', trysting destiny with their mechanically performed projection of endurance, while in reality, a perceivable split had been created between 'surviving' and 'living' in the lives of the displaced subjects. These are but what Zamindar sums up as "Partition effects" (Zamindar 2008: 284), which are framed by remembrance, memory and lived experiences of the displaced and mutilated, the dead and the living dead. For Zamindar, an understanding of 'Partition effects' is essential and indispensible to lay bare the unheard histories of Partition, what Butalia refers to as the "underside of the history of Partition" (Butalia 1998: 349).

Jyotirmoyee Devi's *Epar Ganga Opar Ganga*, first published in Bengali[1] in 1967, is a representative text on a Bengali woman's experience of social hostility following her violation during Partition and her subsequent endeavor of rehabilitation and emancipation. A reading of the novel suggests how the discursive developments around "ideal" womanhood in Hindu cultural nationalism and the mystification of the sacrosanct feminine, bearing the burden of cultural valorization, played significant roles in the responses generated towards the female victims of Partition and how the idiom of violence was habitualized and naturalized, effecting, affecting and determining the nature of human relationship.

The novel opens with Sutara Datta, an Assistant Professor of History in a women's college in Delhi, who turns to her personal experience of pain during the Noakhali riots in the autumn of 1946. She, then an adolescent, had lost her parents in the communal fury: her father was murdered, her mother attempted suicide (and was eventually untraceable) and her sister Sujata was abducted. She herself lost consciousness in the course of an attack and was rescued by Tamizuddin—a Muslim family friend of theirs—and his sons. Recuperating in their care for six months, she was eager to be reunited with her surviving family members, i.e., her three brothers and a sister-in-law, and Tamizuddin and his sons escorted her to the "safety" of Calcutta where she joined her brothers and sister-in-law Bibha at the home of Bibha's parents where they had taken refuge to escape the violence of the riots.

However, the elderly women of the household, Bibha's mother and aunts, disapproved of Sutara's presence in the family because she had spent six months living among Muslims and was thus "polluted". She was sent to a Christian boarding school for women, a non-Hindu space where the student body primarily consisted of lower castes or low-caste converts and women in situations similar to hers. She was even unwanted at social events like marriages. On Bibha's sister Subha's wedding day, she was fed separately and hurriedly sent home to protect other guests from her "polluting" touch. Through the years, Sutara's brothers either witnessed her humiliation mutely or pretended that nothing had happened. Though Bibha's father, brother and sister protested occasionally, that could not bring about a significant change in the situation.

During the Partition, such incidents were numerous. In a large number of cases, the abused and/or converted Hindu women were not welcome in their original families. What happened in Noakhali in Bengal during Gandhiji's peace march in that strife-ridden area was narrated to political activist Madhu Dandavate by Sucheta Kripalani, who had accompanied Gandhiji in his peace march. One night, Sucheta received news that three young girls in Gandhiji's Peace Brigade were likely to be kidnapped. Along with the three young girls, she approached the Muslim landlord next door and requested him to protect the girls as his daughters. The Muslim landlord put his hand on the *Koran* and took a vow that he would fully protect the girls. After a few months, when peace returned to Noakhali and the members of Gandhiji's Peace Brigade returned to their respective homes, those three young girls who were protected by the Muslim landlord returned back home and were informed:

> "You have no place in our family, as you had stayed with a Muslim for three months, forgetting that you were Hindus." "What shall we do?" asked the girls. The parents' reply was "Go onto the streets and, if need be, become prostitutes, but our doors are closed for you."
>
> *(Dandavate, quoted in Mookherjea-Leonard 2004: 40)*

Disowned by their parents, the girls took shelter in Gandhiji's Ashram. They never married and later on died unsung and unwept. This reveals "the grim story of women who had to suffer only because of the communal prejudices of a tradition-bound society" (ibid.).

Unlike those three girls, however, Sutara completes her studies and becomes a lecturer of history at a women's college in Delhi, realizing painfully that she will never have a "home", not only because she has no place in her brothers' affections, but also, because her marriage prospects are bleak, as she is "polluted". Her correspondence and occasional meetings with her Muslim neighbors from the village, all of whom continue to cherish and admire her—especially Tamizuddin's wife and daughter Sakina—also come to an abrupt end when Tamizuddin's wife suggests a matrimonial alliance between her elder son Aziz and Sutara, with which she can not comply. In Calcutta, Bibha's brother Pramode expresses his resolve to marry

146 Jaydip Sarkar

Sutara, infuriating his mother, who has already arranged a match for him. Nevertheless, Pramode goes to Delhi and proposes marriage to Sutara. The novel ends with her bewildered acceptance.

The novel is structured in four parts; the last three, the "Adi Parva" (The Beginning), the "Anusashana Parva" (The Disciplining), and the "Stree Parva" (The Women Chapter), derive their names from books of the *Mahabharata*; and the first short section is titled "Sutara Datta". The second, third, and fourth sections plot Sutara's continuous migrancy; the locale for the second is a village in Noakhali, the third Calcutta, and the fourth Delhi. Further, towards the end of the fourth section, the author hints at a future possibility of Sutara's passage to England with Pramode. Within these larger changes of location there are smaller displacements too: Sutara is transferred from her original home to that of her (muslim-) neighbors' at Noakhali; from the residence of her extended family to the boarding school at Calcutta. Small or large, each of the transitions bears a permanent character, i.e., Sutara never returns to the original site, whether it is her parents' home, her Muslim neighbors at Noakhali, or to her brothers and their extended family at Calcutta. Her perpetual movements advance the feeling of homelessness, and each site becomes a new place of exile. Significantly, it is among the women refugees from West Punjab, residing at Delhi, that Sutara, for the first time, feels the bond of community owing to her identification with the victims of a shared history of violence.

The novel explores and engages with Partition from multiple dimensions, exploring the impact and influence of the catastrophe on the feminine subject. As a Partition novel, this text can be read and reread for several reasons. Jyotirmoyee Devi's depiction of physical violence on female victims of Partition is one of the most moving passages in the entire oeuvre of Partition Literature where the intensity is communicated in a prose marvelously restrained:

> Didi [elder sister, Sujata] suddenly let out a sharp, shrill scream, "Ma, Ma, Mother, oh! Baba," and kneeled over and fell to the ground. Their mother, unlocking the door to the cowshed, was shocked. Then she said, "I'll be there right away, dear."
>
> But Mother could not reach them [Sujata and Sutara]. Shadows had engulfed her. They were trying to seize her hand. But Mother freed herself and ran to the pond behind the house and leaped into it.
>
> The fire had set the whole area ablaze. One of the men tried to stop her, another said, "Don't bother. Let her go, that's the mother. Leave her." Didi was nowhere, had she died? What's the matter with Didi? Sutara did not see her again. She wanted to run to where Mother was, but her feet were caught in something and she stumbled.
>
> *(Devi 1991: 135–136)*

Jyotirmoyee Devi places the narrative beyond the binary politicized world of the self and the other, the commune and the alien, the friend and the enemy. She blasts the false legitimacy of the binary opposition which posits Hindus and Muslims as implacable enemies. Refusing to comply with the politics of appropriation, where the identity of the individual is contingent with the community (essentially religious), she seeks to explore the alternative paradigm of the milieu of Partition, where deviant subjects can essentially transcend the materiality of the self which he/ she derives from the commune. The text in its engagement with Partition, abstains from a xenophobic interpretation of the event. Devi is indeed critical of the presumptuous tendencies which identify the Muslim as a potent enemy and the Hindu as a compassionate empathizer of the marginal woman subject. It is true that the members of the majority Muslim community attack and kill Sutara's father, mother and elder sister, but what happens after this is that she is rescued by a Muslim family, whose head was a close friend and colleague of Sutara's father. Devi thus asserts that the history of the commune in the subcontinent is not essentially founded on the principles of religious exclusiveness. In doing so, she substantiates a critique of the essentialist reduction that the two-nation theory had inflicted on the shared histories of kinship, fraternity and love which were the founding ethos of the heterotopic commune. The implications of violence that accompanied Partition had extended beyond the material bodies of humanity, dismantling the ethos, ethics and founding principles of the spatial and lived histories. The violation of the subject is as much authentic as the violation of the foundationalities of selfhood, violating and shaming not just the immanent subject but also annihilating possibilities of resurrection, by deriding the labyrinth of the familiar from which the dispossessed subject can attempt to derive his/her essence of being.

Devi's fictionalized rendering of Partition relies on a biopolitical space where the changing times haven't compelled the commune to engage in an unmitigated violence directed against the other, with an amnesia of the past ordeals of kinship and fraternity. The act of rescue does not end with a forced marriage following conversion or with the usual dispatch of the Hindu girl to a rehabilitation center. On the contrary, Tamij Saheb, head of the family whom Sutara addresses as 'Tamijkaka,' his wife, their two sons Aziz and Moin and their daughter Sakina, school friend of Sutara, shower love and affection on her till she recovers. As Dasgupta points out, "This sensitive portrait of a Muslim family's love for a Hindu girl, even dangerous love at that point of time, enriched with minute details of affection, demolishes the deep-rooted opposition" (Dasgupta 2004: 9). Dasgupta further opines, while reading this part of the novel "we come to question the rationale of Partition itself" (ibid.: 10). Sutara's uncle, Tamij kaka, ponders:

> "She has been living for a long time in a Muslim household. Will she be accepted by her community? You know the Hindu society. How will they accept her? If they do not, where will the girl go?".
>
> *(Devi 1991: 151)*

Sutara's Muslim aunt says:

> You want partition, fight if you want. But why this humiliating assault on women, on their respect, honour, body? Does your religion sanction this? You, all of you, educated people of the village—lawyers, teachers—why aren't you raising your voices?
>
> *(Ibid.: 140)*

148 Jaydip Sarkar

This Muslim mother's accusation in Noakhali in the east is echoed in the confirmation of a Hindu refugee of the western part of the country who tells Ritu Menon and Kamla Bhasin:

> A woman has no religion … her only religion is womanhood. She gives birth, she is a creator, she is god, she is mother. Mothers have no religion, their religion is motherhood. It makes no difference whether they are Hindus, Sikhs, Muslims or Christians.
>
> *(Menon and Bhasin 1998: 243)*

Jyotirmoyee Devi situates Sutara within the "woman-as-nation" paradigm. Moreover, while she deems the obsession of women's bodily purity to be the cardinal cause of Sutara's miseries, she also indicates that its perpetuation was guaranteed by women who, as Nira Yuval-Davis and Floya Anthias caution, "actively participate in the process of reproducing and modifying their roles as well as being actively involved in controlling other women" (Yuval-Davis and Anthias 1989: 11). In the novel, Bibha's mother and aunts endorse the continuity of patriarchy and veto Sutara's presence because of her contact with the forbidden that disrupted her caste and religious practices. Bibha's mother monitors, with a reproving vigilance, the social and intimate contacts between family members. She orchestrates Sutara's alienation, both from her brothers and from the extended family, in the name of safeguarding the future for Bibha's daughters. When Bibha's mother's efforts to isolate Sutara are defeated by her idealist son Pramode's decision to marry her, she reproaches Bibha as it was she (Bibha) who restored Sutara to her extended family in Calcutta:

> After a long silence, [Bibha's mother] turned to Bibha, "I told you repeatedly not to bring that girl [Sutara] here. Don't. Don't get her. But you persisted! You let her stay here. Good for you! Saved your face from people's comments. A fine thing you did ruining my family; dug a canal and courted a crocodile into my backyard … What was the point in fetching her anyway, she who had lived with those unclean nonbelievers [Muslims]? Whatever happened was her misfortune. She should have stayed back. There are countless women like her in that country [Pakistan]. You think she retained her religion-caste purity living with them for such a long time? Who knows what she ate! And then, *what* had happened? *That* about which no one knows. She certainly could not have remained a Hindu living with Muslims!" Anger, disappointment, and revulsion swept through [Bibha's mother] and she burst into tears.
>
> *(Devi 1991: 243–44)*

It is only after Sutara escapes the supervision of her patriarchal family and community and migrates to a new space of economic independence that it is possible for her to establish some genuine social solidarity—a sisterhood with refugee women from West Punjab. Through Sutara, Jyotirmoyee Devi here illustrates the modalities of women's participation in social processes "as reproducers of the boundaries of

History versus (her)story **149**

ethnic/national groups; as participating centrally in the ideological reproduction of the collectivity and as transmitters of its culture; as signifiers of national differences" (Yuval-Davis and Anthias 1989: 1).

Sutara's experiences are disparate and multifarious. She cannot enter into a meaningful relationship with her Muslim neighbors through marriage despite the kindness and sustenance she receives from them, because engaging with Muslims would appear to be a betrayal of her parents' deaths, her sister's abduction, and her personal experience of violence. Studies (Butalia 1998: 188; Das 1995: 195) show that abducted women often married the men responsible for their abduction, bore children, and with time grew attached to their past abductors, but Sutara's is a different tale. In most of the cases, marriage between the abductor and abductee was made possible only because the women were mostly disempowered and were compelled to live at the abductor's mercy. But Sutara's situation in Delhi, when the marriage proposal arrived, was different. Perhaps Sutara would not have been able to resist it if Tamizuddin's family had abducted her or coerced her into marriage with Aziz while she was younger and living with them soon after the disaster. But years later in Delhi, educated and financially independent, her circumstances can no longer be compared with the helplessness of most of the abducted women. However, this point also should be kept in mind—that in rejecting the marriage proposal from Tamizuddin's family, Sutara treats them not as individuals who sheltered her, even enduring threats from their own community, but rather as part of the community that devastated her life. The familial personal is overruled by the tensions of the historic-political and Sutara fails to enter into a matrimonial relationship with the communal 'other'. Negotiating the burden of history becomes an impossibility for Sutara and marriage, which would have been an ideal reconciliation, is denied. Sutara isn't islamophobic, but the memories of devastation persist, intense enough to deny the possibilities of redemption and reconciliation through the trope of marriage. For her, formal correspondence and meetings with old Muslim friends are negotiable, but not the commitment of marriage, and here lies the complex dimension of the text.

The unforgettable trauma of rape, which Bibha's mother euphemistically refers to as "other problems", blurs Sutara's matrimonial possibilities. Debali Mookherjea-Leonard observes how sexual violence, in a twisted way, involves a process of removing the body from circulation within the libidinal economy. Sutara is no longer allowed to desire; she is a disenfranchised social subject, coerced into a circumstantial reality and materiality which she can transgress, only with greatest endeavors. It is significant that between her restoration to her extended family in Calcutta and her finding employment in Delhi, she has little textual presence by way of speech. Although her condition constitutes the problematic, and she is constantly acted upon, she rarely speaks. It can be argued that her silence is not a resistance but a metaphor for her loss of social agency through the "theft of the body" (Mookherjea-Leonard 2004: 43).

Sutara's silence is socially structured and policed by the family: her brothers' paucity of interaction with her; by the community: her presence is unwelcome in social events; and by the state: the prohibition on biographical exchanges between

150 Jaydip Sarkar

students at the residential school she attends. In reinserting Sutara back into the script of middle-class domestic sexual economy, the novelist "regenders her, by way of establishing a claim for a different destiny for gender, and eventually makes the details of people's lives matter once again" (ibid.).

However, unlike Veena Das's suggestion that marriage was "a strategic practice of the community through which some repatriated women were rendered invisible through absorption within the family" (Das 1995: 195), Pramode's wedding proposal to Sutara is neither a community game plan nor a fairy-tale ending, but rather an individual act of will. Pramode and Subha, Bibha's brother and sister, witness Sutara's repeated disgrace and disenfranchisement within their family. Both are sensitive, often even apologetic, to Sutara's distress. Hence, beyond simply constituting a "happy ending" at the level of the plot, Pramode's proposal has a sharp feel of a conscious, if slightly patronizing, act of good will by a responsible citizen.

Debali Mookherjea-Leonard rightly observes that separated from middle-class domestic life, Sutara with her colleagues and friends working in the college and residing in the dormitory constitute a community; a women's community that disregards regional differences and sustains a group-therapeutic function through a mutual support system. Writing in the 1960s, her recognition of the potentials of feminist solidarity is exceptional, although by ultimately distancing Sutara from the collective at the women's hostel, Jyotirmoyee Devi declines to advance a radical alternative to the family. While Sutara's entry into middle-class respectability marks a definitive break from the fixation with purity and routine rejections, it also weakens the possibilities of a life as a single, independent woman.

On the ending of the novel, Mookherjea-Leonard raises several questions:

> Does Sutara's reinstatement within the domestic space with its demands for women's chastity suggest potentials for its reorganization? Or, on the other hand, is the act in itself a subordination of the women's struggle to the struggle for the nation? Can it be because the nation still requires this construction to shore up its integrity?
>
> *(Mookherjea-Leonard 2004: 44)*

Such questions really bring to the fore a dialectic of trauma and triumph that distinguishes the lives of countless women struck by Partition. Bibi Inder Kaur, a victim of Partition in the west, thus described her victory to Ritu Menon and Kamla Bhasin:

> There are millions of women like me who want to do something but cannot. I managed because Partition gave me a chance. My husband feared that this would happen, that when I became independent I would be free and he was right … I gained much more than I lost. He only lost. I feel sorry for him but I never wanted to go back, back to that life. I had spread my wings.
>
> *(Menon and Bhasin 1998: 215)*

Shubho Ranjan Dasgupta rightly points out that a considerable number of contemporary historians, while highlighting "the rape, killing, the uprooting" of the days of Partition, fail to pay the required attention to this experience of struggle and triumph (Dasgupta 2004: 16).To that extent, their confrontation with the memory and paradigm of Partition really remains fragmented and misleading. Dasgupta rightly urges, "while confronting the many-layered reality and remembrance of Partition, we need to depend on what Sumit Sarkar proposed as 'many histories' which together try to capture the complexities of the total experience" (ibid.). In other words, we really need to expose the obvious limits of the nationalist meta-narrative, which concentrates only on the political at the expense of the human. Instead of clamoring for its outright rejection we have to complete it with the other histories which are true to the kindred points of loss and recovery, trauma and triumph. Jyotirmoyee Devi appealed for this completion in the novel by saying, "History is not a small matter. Only a single person does not write it … Further, history is not preserved merely in written pages … Which history has recorded the experiences of the weak and the suffering?" (Devi 1991: 131).

Note

1   The novel *Epar Ganga Opar Ganga* has been translated into English as *The River Churning* by Enakshi Chatterjee. It was published by Kali for Women in 1995. In this chapter, however, translations of selected portions of the text are taken from research papers by Subho Ranjan Dasgupta and Debali Mookherjea Leonard. I was first acquainted with the novel when, in March 2003, Prof. Jasodhara Bagchi presented a lecture on the issues of nationalism and sexuality at the Department of English, North Bengal University. This chapter contains several of her arguments and some of those found in the research papers of Subho Ranjan Dasgupta (who co-edited *The Trauma and the Triumph: Gender and Partition in Eastern India* with JasodharaBagchi) and Debali Mookherjea Leonard.

Works Cited

Butalia, Urvashi. *The Other Side of Silence*. New Delhi: Viking, 1998.

Das, Veena. "National Honour and Practical Kinship", in Das, Veena ed., *Critical Events*. Delhi: Oxford University Press, 1995.

Dasgupta, Subhoranjan. "*Epar Ganga Opar Ganga*: A Creative Statement of Displacement and Violence" (Occasional Paper). Kolkata: Institute of Development Studies, July2004.

Devi, Jyotirmoyee. *Epar Ganga Opar Ganga* in *Jyotirmoyee Devir Rachana Sankalan*, Vol. 1, Kolkata: Dey's and School of Women's Studies, Jadavpur University, 1991.

Hartnack, Christiane. "Roots and Routes: The Partition of British India in Indian Social Memories". *Journal of Historical Sociology* 25:2 (June2012). Retrieved from https://docum ents.pub/document/roots-and-routes-the-partition-of-british-india-in-indian-social-mem ories.html (accessed on 13 February 2020).

Menon, Ritu and Kamla Bhasin. *Borders and Boundaries*. New Delhi: Kali for Women, 1998.

Mookherjea-Leonard, Debali. "Quarantined: Women and the Partition", *Comparative Studies of South Asia, Africa and the Middle East* 24:1:2004.

Yuval-Davis, Nira and Floya Anthias. "Introduction". In *Woman-Nation-State*, ed. Yuval-Davis and Anthias. New York: St Martin's Press, 1989.

Zamindar, Vazira Fazila-Yacoobali. *The Long Partition and the Making of Modern South Asia: Refugees, Boundaries, Histories*. Karachi: Oxford University Press, 2008.

14

IMMANENT NEEDS, IMMEDIATE SOLUTIONS

Body and reconciliation in Manik Bandopadhyay's "The Final Solution"

Rupayan Mukherjee and Somasree Sarkar

In his essay "A Special Supplement: The Question of Machiavelli", Isaiah Berlin observes that the fundamental dispute that politics has with ethics is foregrounded in the general conviction that ethics is a sovereign discursive domain that lives in autonomy from Politics. Instead, Berlin argues that Politics is an alternative ethical condition, which isn't necessarily founded on the religio-moral principles and dictum but nevertheless, has a generic foundation and a tradition of its own. Berlin calls it "time-honored" and legitimizes his claim by revealing a heritage that dates back to Aristotle, which has valorized Politics as the "the art of living in a polis". Berlin argues:

> Politics – the art of living in a *polis* – is not an activity that can be dispensed with by those who prefer private life: it is not like seafaring or sculpture which those who do not wish to do so need not undertake. Political conduct is intrinsic to being a human being at a certain stage of civilization, and what it demands is intrinsic to living a successful human life.
>
> *(1971: 1)*

The human condition is thus an absolute and inevitable political condition, where the citizen precedes the self, the human subject precedes the human and almost unquestionably the "idion" is compromised with for the "koinon" (Arendt 1998: 24). What is more, it is the political condition that distinguishes the 'Man' from other natural subjects, the "bios" from the "zoe" (Agamben 1995: 1). It is the "bios politikos" (ibid.), i.e. the political life of the human subject, which ascertains him/her the sovereignty that in turn affirms the human subject as an autonomous being, promising him what the Greeks called 'eudemonia', i.e. a good life.

The political life in modern Nation states is often guarded by the fundamentals of a juridico-legal apparatus and that is what foregrounds the notion of the sovereign. Giorgio Agamben rightly points out that the condition of sovereignty is also paradoxically the condition of subjugation, whereby the natural life ('zoe') is accommodated within the political ('bios'). Foucault identifies this moment of appropriation of the natural by the political as the "threshold of modernity" (Foucault 1978: 143). He argues that modern man is primordially located within the economy of the political and escaping the political/politicos as a condition is an impossibility. The political is no longer a possibility that the man of antiquity chooses, it is instead an a priori condition which the subject can't avoid. Foucault writes: "For millennia, man remained what he was for Aristotle: a living animal with the additional capacity for a political existence; modern man is an animal whose politics places his existence as a living being into question" (ibid.).

The geo-political abstraction of the Modern State is thus founded on this principle of "inclusive exclusion" (Agamben 1995: 7) where the subject succumbs to the political condition or koinon in favor of the idion. The idion, however, isn't completely divorced from his being. Instead, it is appropriated and moulded within the greater condition of the koinon, promising, at least apparently, a modern bios–politikos that can accommodate the 'bare' or natural life with all its sanctity and valor.

Partition of the Indian subcontinent is one of the phenomenal incidents which was instrumental in ushering two Nations into an epoch of Modernity, i.e. a history of modernity in the Indian subcontinent would be incomplete without taking into account the socio-historical catastrophe of Partition. Zygmunt Bauman argues that modernity is a "condition of compulsive, and addictive, designing" (Bauman 2000: 30) and claims that the design of modernity inevitably produces "wasted humans … those who either could not or were not wished to be recognized or allowed to stay" (ibid.). The design of Indian modernity, which was simultaneous with the growth of Indian Nationalism, had systematically generated its own margin – a category of 'wasted humans' who remained passive, unrecognized and unrepresented in the discursive contours of the National imaginary. Partha Chatterjee depicts the hegemonic nature of Indian modernity and Nationalism, whereby the fragments of Indian society, i.e. women, dalits and religious minorities were often rendered silent, if not completely excluded, from the discourse of Nationalism, which was in turn largely dominated by the bhadrolok categories with the Indian National Congress serving as the dominant political structure of representation (Chatterjee 1993: 35).

The result of this unrecognition and exclusion was the validation of a two–Nation theory, based on the dictums of religion and communal ethos. The 'other', the 'waste' is now carefully rendered outside the paradigm of the National imaginary and is instead located within the economy of communal hatred and xenophobia. Anderson argues that modern Nation states are demarcated geographical paradigms based on the principles of exclusion and inclusion (Anderson 2006: 19) and the sovereign Nation, in context of Indian Partition, whose moment of birth collides with the moment of Partition, finds its intimate enemy, no longer in the political master but in the communal other. The sovereign Nation state thus becomes modern, not just in terms of an independent economy or an autonomous political ideal but in terms of its complete exclusion of the other; in its generation of 'waste', which it conceives as its enemy. The National imaginary, which is fundamental to any modern Nation State, finds a stable 'other', against which it fashions itself.

Partition of the Indian subcontinent generated a mass exodus of refugees, the 'wastes' of the Modern Nation state, who were rendered dispossessed within the newly conceived dictums of friend and foe, 'us' and 'them'. The making of the two nation meant that human subjects were subjected to a saga of displacement; the sovereign Nation state different from the native homeland. Hannah Arendt describes the refugees as "people who had indeed lost all other qualities and specific relation-ships–except that they were still human" (Arendt 1979: 299). It is, however, the transitional and liminal status of the refugee who is inhabiting that perilous locale of homelessness that makes them not a redundant waste to the sovereign State, but an identity conformed in an inclusive exclusion within the Nationalist discourse. Thus, the refugee stands as the manifestation of 'bare life' and problematizes the bio-politikos of the sovereign state. His/her identity is affirmed within an economy or paradigm of exception; he/she is a hyphen whose uncanny presence dismantles the grand narratives of citizenship in the modern State. Agamben argues that the refugee in relation to the sovereign state is "a limit concept" (Agamben 1995: 134), who "calls into question the fundamental categories of the nation-state" (ibid.). In his words:

> If refugees (whose number has continued to grow in our century, to the point of including a significant part of humanity today) represent such a disquieting element in the order of the modern nation-state, this is above all because by breaking the continuity between man and citizen, nativity and nationality, they put the originary fiction of modern sovereignty in crisis.
>
> *(Agamben 1995: 131)*

In the context of Indian Partition, it is the lived realities of the displaced refugees which perplex the grand narrative of independence and the moment of sover-eignty deeply. Their morbid experiences of displacement have lived on like a nightmare on the shoulders of progressive history of the Nation state and as such it has been relevant not just in the temporal context of the catastrophe, but also in terms of successive renderings of the trauma by the lived. It is thus that nationalist historiographers have often intended to understand the history of Partition as a "state of exception" (Agamben 1995: 109), which is best forgotten. It has been that chapter in Indian history, more precisely in the history of Indian independence, which evolved as an unavoidable supplement, as a surplus waste to the progressive history of India's Nationalism and her great march to freedom. Gyanendra Pandey claims "For too long the violence of 1947 ... has been treated as someone else's history – or even, not history at all" (Pandey 2003: 6). The deliberate ignorance and denial of conventional historiography to reclaim Parti-tion as a moment of loss and failure of the sovereign and its consistent attempts to declaim the event as a tertiary occurrence, an inevitability which is best to be forgotten, locates Partition in the underside of history and thus a 'state of exception' for the sovereign State.

The agony, the despair, the pathos, the sinister state of being which the refugee encountered persists till date, largely through the medium of representation. Such renderings of trauma are influential in creating what Marianne Hirsch has called "postmemory". Hirsch defines "postmemory" as "the relationship that the 'generation after' bears to the personal, collective, and cultural trauma of those who came before, to experiences they 'remember' only by means of the stories, images, and behaviors among which they grew up" (Hirsch n.d.: 1).

Fiction is foundational in the generation of postmemory and in its self referential relevance in culture, fiction has the possibility to usher history beyond the paradigms of the temporal and spatial. Hence, the neo-historiographers, in excavating the underside of history today, are increasingly reliant on fiction and validate it as an authentic historical source which has the possibility to unearth the other side of the happened. The refugee exodus, prompted by the Partition of India in 1947, had generated a wide range of literary and visual representations, which are relevant to date. The chapter, at this point, seeks to analyse a short story by the radical, avant-garde Bengali writer Manik Bandopadhyay, who is renowned for his critical interrogations into the human condition and his consistent literary endeavors to address the politico-social condition and its effect on the humane and humanity. Bandopadhyay's articulation of man is no longer a celebration of the ideals of humanity which his literary predecessor Tagore could bask in, rather his interest and motif lies in the depiction of the human subject as a discursive contingent of the age. The vision of humanity which Bandopadhyay cherishes is imbibed in the immanent and the immediate and has little regards for the sublime ideals of truth, justice, ethics which the transcendental man seeks to embody. A staunch Marxist, Bandopadhyay acknowledges his faith in the aesthetic as a medium that shares an irrefutable and undeniable proximity with reality. In his essay "Lekhaker Katha", Bandopadhyay reflects on how the "short simple annals of the poor" (Gray n.d.: 1), the "bare life" (Agamben 1995: 8) would often haunt his creative consciousness:

> and then villages would come floating from the banks of canals, rivers and forests – the tortured, tormented faces of farmers, boatmen, fishermen, weavers…and those faces – ordinary and rustic faces would relentlessly shout in my consciousness – give us words-give us words.
>
> *(Bandopadhyay 1974: 3)*

The immanent reality of the Indian Partition and the consequent aftermath that it evoked, in terms of displacement of the living and the consequent dehumanistion of the human subject, is the subject of Bandopadhyay's short story "The Final Solution". The story is centered around a refugee family which has taken shelter at Sealdah railway station in Calcutta and in all possibilities, has migrated from East Bengal, which post 1947, was incorporated into the geo-political milieu of East Pakistan. The plot ushers the readers into a sinister world of human exploitation as Mallika, the housewife, who is burdened with an ailing husband, a child and an unmarried sister-in-law, is lured into flesh trade/ prostitution by the pimp Pramatha. However, Bandopadhyay problematizes the structure of the story by refusing to present it as a mere chronicle of woman sub-jugation and exploitation, which has been an overt reality of Partition. Instead, he enhances the possibility of an emancipation of the feminine as with a climactic turn, the story ends with Mallika assassinating Pramatha and proclaiming to her sister-in law that she has found "the final solution" (Bandopadhyay 2011: 30) to her misery.

The story begins with a description of the plight of the refugees and portrays the hyphenated state that the displaced have been subjected to. They have constructed their homes on railway platforms – a heterotopic space where possibilities of recuperation are muted by the immediate and immanent dystopia, that the multi-tudes of displaced experience. Foucault defines heterotopias as "counter sites" (Foucault 1986: 24) "which have the curious property of being in relation with all the other sites" (ibid.) and yet they are outside the familiar place. The refugee infested Sealdah station becomes a heterotopia which is no longer the public space used for commutation. Instead, it is now a habituated space, accommodating multitudes of private space. In other words, it is a habitus of what we have pre-viously called, borrowing from Agamben, the "bare life" (Agamben 1995: 8). Hence, Bandopadhyay compares the dispossessed refugees to "herds of cattles and goats" (Bandopadhyay 2011: 19); the natural order of animal/bare life that is removed from the political dictum of citizenship. The geo-political locale of the railway platform, which is contingent within the politico-social epoch of Partition, is thus in a concurrent 'state of exception'.

It is this order of exception that suspends the juridico-legal apparatus and the normative structure of economy and polity. As the plot unveils, the chronotope of Partition reveals itself as a world turned upside down, where women become active agencies within the modes of production while the men, the dominant harbingers within the capitalist-patriarchal framework are rendered jobless. Jasod-hara Bagchi and Subho Ranjan Dasgupta have pointed this out in their introspec-tions on Partition and the subversive impact that it had, not just in the lives of individuals, but also on the social structure and ideologies. For instance, women, who had been, until then, largely confined within the sacrosanct precincts of home, were now suddenly exposed to the outside (Bagchi and Dasgupta 2003: 10–16). This outside, in a state of exception, is no longer protected by the juridico-legal apparatus that is an essential component of the sovereign. Hence, the feminine agency is susceptible to the ambiguous and simultaneously probable possibilities of abjection and emancipation.

Mallika, in the story, is offered employment by Pramatha, who is apparently a worker in the 'Help and Welfare Society', but a pimp in reality. He is a parasite who feeds on the apparent suspension of the juridico-political apparatus in this climate of exception and is the perfect manifestation of the petty bourgeoisie. The author describes him as a *pater familias*, one who safeguards the *law of the father* and the ideologues of patriarchy and seeks to protect or valorize the woman as the weaker sex. Yet, he is also the pimp who is contemplating to engage Mallika in the flesh trade and what is more, has located Mallika's femininity within the economy of desire.

The plot hence unleashes the many faces of patriarchy and constantly speculates an understanding of the feminine, largely within the discursive limits of patriarchy's conviction of womanhood. Mallika, the feminine subject is constantly framed and modeled within an economy of patriarchal gaze. On one hand, she is burdened by the liabilities of family and motherhood, which ascribes in her a "use value" (Irigaray 1985: 173). On the other hand, however, her identity of the refugee woman within the political state of exception, where the juridico-political apparatus stands suspended, makes her susceptible to commodification. Her possibilities of emancipation and her agency within the modes of production in economy are thus unmediatedly based on her exchange value, whereby she must commodify her sexuality in exchange of capital. Mallika seems to be aware of it, as the omniscient story teller narrates:

> Mallika could sense where the woman was being taken. She had known all about it in her days and nights on the railway platform, living among the multitudes ... She herself had seen how a girl or a woman returned alone – in a short time – an hour perhaps, clutching a few coins in her fists, filled with impotent rage.
>
> *(Bandopadhyay 2011: 25)*

This is, one might argue, the epiphanic moment of reconciliation in the short story. At a literal level, it is the protagonist's reconciliation with the state of exception and consequently the impending, immanent reality with which she must negotiate. However, it is also the problematic juncture in the story where the ideal of modernity which the colonized Nation, in its struggle for freedom and sovereignty, has so long nurtured, is compromised or revised. Partha Chatterjee has argued that the advent of modernity in India, whose harbinger was the middle class, relied on a sacrosanct distinction between the 'ghar' and 'bahir', the private and the public, where women were given the greater responsibility of preserving the transcendental traditional while the men would indulge in the immediacy of modern (Chatterjee 1993: 120). The dichotomy of man – immanent outside/ woman – sanctified transcendental inside, however, crumbles in the aftermath of Partition. Woman, who has so long been valorized (one might say falsely) as the mother and has been sanctified with the use value of motherhood steps into the contaminated economy of exchange, where her body is the only possibility through which she can affirm or assert her agency.

Herein lies the paradox where the woman is undoubtedly located within an economy of desire where her sexuality is commodified. Yet it is also the moment when the ideal of motherhood, which has been an over-nurtured ideology through which patriarchy has subjugated women, gives way to the agency of the feminine. Gerda Lerner locates the origin of patriarchy in the structure of the family which, in her words, "both expressed and constantly generated its rules and values" (Lerner 1986: 212). The structure of family is a historically stable, hierarchically organized foundational core of society which has been the faithful safeguard of patriarchy and its ethos. The catastrophe of Partition sets this otherwise stable nucleus called family in jeopardy, dismantling its hierarchical and stratified structure and desanctifying the

158 Rupayan Mukherjee and Somasree Sarkar

sacred locale of home. In a state of homelessness, the structure of family is dismantled, the hierarchies are turned upside down and it is within the previously discussed state of exception that the feminine becomes the immediate redeemer of family. Partition hence becomes a discourse of ambiguity. On one hand, it is the sublime tragedy of exploitation and violence, which was more often than not, inflicted upon the female body. Simultaneously, it is a breach in human history through which the patriarchy oppressed feminine self cherishes a possibility of emancipation.

Partition as the socio-historical calamity thus becomes not just a political state of exception in the newly founded sovereign state. It is also an ideological and ethical state of exception. It is within the greater political milieu of Partition that the woman subject realizes that she must devise alternative strategies of survival, which instead of being ethico-morally valid and transcendent, would be situational and contingent with circumstances. This is also the point in the story where the post-modern subject is born, one who doesn't have the a priori convictions of selfhood and subjectivity but instead relies on a discursive formulation of selfhood.

Mallika and her family are rehabilitated by the initiative and influence of Pramatha. In return though, Mallika is coerced to solicit him. This is a crucial epiphanic juncture in the story. The already commodified agency of Mallika fails to locate Pramatha as the client. She is disoriented and disturbed with the realization that she has now been unconditionally commodified as the fine balance between the client and the pimp no longer sustain. Both locate her sexuality within an economy of desire and this unconditional objectification of her sexual identity is a grotesque truth which she fails to negotiate with. Hence, in her fit of anger she hits Pramatha with the bottle and later strangles him to death. It is also the climactic moment where the feminine self seeks to transcend all economies of oppression, i.e. the ethical, the ideological and even the sexual. She is now a dehumanized self and yet it is in this state of being a bare subject, that she experiences and revels the possibilities of emancipation. Simone de Beauvoir notes that woman, within the discursive limits of humanity and culture, has essentially survived as the 'other', a "relative being" (Beauvoir 1956: 15) to man and masculinity, which has been a category as primordial as consciousness itself. Mallika's moment of dehumanization thus paradoxically becomes the moment when she finally transcends the ordeal of patriarchy, for history of humanity is genealogically patriarchal and phallogocentric. Lerner points out that history is the essence of civilization and the process of history making has largely been a practice of systematic exclusion of women. (Lerner 1986: 5) Mallika's act of killing Pramatha is inhuman, yet it is only in her complete departure from humanity that Mallika is able to emancipate her agency from the oppressive modes of sub-jugation and commodification.

Mallika's body thus becomes the only medium through which she can transcend the conditions and economies of oppression. Her sexuality is no longer confined within the possibilities of a governed transgression through which it can become her means of sustenance. Instead, her body becomes her final solution to the 'state of exception' which Partition has ushered her into. She triumphantly declares to her sister-in-law at the end of the story:

'We'll never be hungry again, thakurjhi never, ever … My son will have milk four times a day … I'll go to the railway station every evening in my frayed sari, the sharks will come again to pick me up, for sure … '

… 'But this time I'll be carrying a sharp knife with me, you understand, Thakurjhi. I'll hide it so that no one finds out … '

(Bandopadhyay 2011: 30)

The restoration of the maternal is promised by the libidinal, the recourse to the unethical can only enhance a restitution of ethics in this politico-social climate of subversion. It is also within this inverted paradigm of the unnatural that body becomes the contested locale of both violation and liberation. However, Mallika's emancipation is also one that is conditioned by the state of exception and hence one is left uneasy, pondering whether the female subject has truly emancipated her agency or whether it is one that is already predicted by the political state of exception. The woman in discussion seeks to explore her agency only as a reaction to the deviant politico-social milieu. Hence, one might argue that Mallika's agency is derived and contingent, whereby she becomes not a sovereign subject but one who is conditioned by the politico-social. That being said, the story celebrates a deviant femininity, and Partition as the backdrop of a socio-political state of exception, seeks to justify the deviant femininity and legitimizes Mallika's final solution.

Works Cited

Agamben, Giorgio. *Homo Sacer: Sovereign Power and Bare Life*. Trans. Daniel Heller-Roazen, Stanford, CA: Stanford University Press, 1995.

Anderson, Benedict. *Imagined Communities: Reflections on the Origin and Spread of Nationalism*, London: Verso, 2006.

Arendt, Hannah. *The Origins of Totalitarianism*, New York: Harcourt Brace Jovanovich, 1979.

Arendt, Hannah. *The Human Condition*, Chicago: University of Chicago Press, 1998.

Bagchi, Jasodhara and Subhoranjan Dasgupta, eds. *The Trauma and the Triumph: Gender and Partition in Eastern India, Vol. 1*, Kolkata: Stree, 2003.

Bandopadhyay, Manik. "Lekhaker Kotha". In *Manik Granthavali Vol. VII*, Kolkata: Jiyanta, 1974.

Bandopadhyay, Manik. "The Final Solution". Trans. Rani Ray. In *Map Making: Partition Stories from Two Bengals*. Ed. Debjani Sengupta. New Delhi: Amaryllis, 2011. 16–30.

Beauvoir, Simone de. *The Second Sex*. Trans. H.M. Parshley, London: Lowe and Brydone, 1956.

Berlin, Isaiah. "A Special Supplement: The Question of Machiavelli". *The New York Review of Books*, 4 November1971. https://www.nybooks.com/articles/1971/11/04/a-special-supplement-the-question-of-machiavelli (accessed on 16 August 2018).

Bauman, Zygmunt. *Wasted Lives: Modernity and Its Outcasts*, Cambridge: Polity, 2000.

Chatterjee, Partha, *The Nation and Its Fragments: Colonial and Postcolonial Histories*, Princeton, NJ: Princeton University Press, 1993.

Foucault, Michel. *The History of Sexuality Vol. I: An Introduction*. Trans. Robert Hurley,. New York: Pantheon Books, 1978.

Foucault, Michel. "Of Other Spaces: Utopias and Heterotopias". Trans. Jay Miskowiec. *Diacritics*, vol. 16, no. 1, Spring1986: 22–27.

Gray, Thomas. "Elegy Written in a Country Churchyard". Poetry Foundation, n.d. https://www.poetryfoundation.org/poems/44299/elegy-written-in-a-country-churchyard (accessed on 20 August 2018).

Hirsch, Marianne. "Postmemory.net", n.d. http://www.postmemory.net (accessed on 9 September 2018).

Irigaray, Luce. *The Sex Which is not One*. Trans. Catherine Porter with Carolyn Burke. New York: Cornell University Press, 1985.

Lerner, Gerda. *The Creation of Patriarchy*, Oxford: Oxford University Press, 1986.

Pandey, Gyanendra. *Remembering Partition: Violence, Nationalism and History in India*, Cambridge: Cambridge University Press, 2003.

15

THE APORIAC SELF

Feminine and the poetics of silence in Sabiha Sumar's *Khamosh Pani*

Sankha Ghosh

In his oft-cited essay, "Remembered Villages: Representation of Hindu-Bengali Memories in the Aftermath of the Partition", Dipesh Chakrabarty delineates the intricacies of traumatic memory, observing that it inevitably follows a trajectory opposite of historical narratives. Unlike historical narratives of Partition, which aim at a clinical analysis of Partition and its aftermath as a precise historical event, the traumatic memory of the displaced constructs it as an aberration; an unexpected and inexplicable act of violence. The economy of trauma personalises the historical and pits it against the nostalgia for the lost past, the sense of belonging which has been ruptured: "this memory, in order to be the memory of a trauma, has to place the Event – the cause of the trauma, in this case, the Partition violence – within a past that gives force to the claim of the victim" (Chakrabarty 1996: 2143).

Sabiha Sumar's *Khamosh Pani* (2003) at one level is a visual memoir of a rural Punjabi woman in Pakistan. Sumar originally conceived of it as a documentary but later decided to make a feature film as she felt a documentary would recall the memories of violence and thus unsettle her audience. Sumar says,

> I didn't want to do this as a documentary at all because it would mean scratching people's wounds. These women had been through the most awful violence one can imagine and a lot of women were now languishing in ashrams in India because their families had refused to accept them.
>
> *(Sumar 2005: n.p.)*

Ayesha's narrative is interspersed with the traumatic memory of the precise moment of her mortal danger; a set of sepia-toned flashbacks show young Veero, in the wake of communal violence in Pakistan during 1947, being coerced into jumping into the well along with other Sikh women by her father. The rationale was to embrace an honorific death in order to avoid the possibility of being raped by Muslim men. Uttering "No, not me", Veero manages to escape. Through fragmented flashbacks, Veero's inescapable plight is established; despite saving her life by refusing to jump into the well, Veero fails to evade sexual violence perpetrated by the Muslim assailants. Later, one of her abductors feels compassionate, offers her words of reassurance and eventually marries her. Veero converts to Islam and embraces the identity of Ayesha. The flashbacks are marked by their recurrence and fragmented nature. The fragmentation has been achieved by employing jump-cuts, which at once suggest the suddenness with which the snippets return to haunt her and how they dissolve abruptly. Critics who have archived oral narratives pertaining to women's experiences during Partition have recognised this absence of sequence as one of the features of recalling traumatic memory. Ritu Menon and Kamla Bhasin comment on their experience of retrieving the oral narratives by conducting interviews:

> recollection makes for a reliving of time past even as time present interrupts memory. Everyday time and life-time overlap, and each woman's story reveals how she has arranged her present within the specific horizons of her past and her future.
>
> *(Menon and Bhasin 1998: 18)*

The film thus weaves through a deeply personal memory, presenting it in flickers and whispers. Such non-synchronous renderings of the lived locates Ayesha's agency in a state of liminality which is suggestive of her disjunctured, problematic past. Simultaneously, it also has the possibility to unshed the burden of memory; which in her case isn't a stable, consolidated repertoire of the lost from which the displaced self can derive her sense of ontological being. Instead, it is negotiable, through a poetics of silence, which is not denial but a passive recognition.

Hence, Ayesha's memory does not conform to the logic that Chakrabarty presents in his essay. It is marked by an absence of any reference to the idyllic past which was ruptured by the event of trauma. Rather, we encounter a reversal here. Charkhi village has been projected as the idyllic present, a social milieu marked by peace and harmony. Nobody wishes to recall the atrocities of Partition; occasional implicit mentions are silenced by others. They have distanced themselves from any engagement with politics in a way that they remain unperturbed by the shift of political regime relegating it as a matter which does not concern the "naive villagers". At the barber's shop the radio announces that General Zia-ul-Haque is about to introduce Islamic law within six months. Unlike Rashid and Mazhar, the villagers hardly seem to be interested; rather, they share a trivial joke about the vain promise of election made by Zia-ul-Haque. The harmonious coexistence of the residents of Charkhi is portrayed in the scenes involving the villagers singing and dancing in a marriage ceremony at the house of the village Choudhury. In literary narratives, marriages often serve as a metaphor for new social formations (embodied by a set of young lovers who are getting married) replacing the older set of values of the previous generation. The inclusiveness of marriage ceremonies reasserts the

The aporiac self   163

ideals of social philanthropy. This film has a woman as its protagonist whose mortal existence as well as her identity has been rehabilitated by her marriage to a Muslim man. The film also traces the trajectory of prospective marriage and how its possibilities are thwarted. Initially, we encounter Ayesha's son Saleem and Zubeida, the young lovers who playfully discuss and contemplate the prospect of their marriage. Their exchange is preceded by a sensual scene involving Saleem playing a Sufi tune on his flute and Zubeida seeking him through a desperate pursuit of the strains of the melody. They are established as the vibrant young couple who harbour the dreams of a happy union. Ayesha wishes for the same and makes occasional teasing remarks to Saleem about the ideal daughter-in-law she wishes to have in the household. But Saleem eventually comes under the influence of Rashid and Mazhar and gradually the religious extremist ideals that he internalise, prompt him to believe that love marriages are contrary to the ethos of Islamic culture. Pavitra Sundar, in an insightful analysis of the soundtrack of the film, points out that Saleem's exposure to the religious extremist ideals puts his relationship to both Zubeida and his music under immense strain. She mentions a particular scene in this context: "During one argument, the once soft and charming Salim raises his voice and declares that he does not want to sit at home playing the flute, waiting for his wife to return from work" (Sundar 2010: 281). There is a reference to another marriage towards the end of the film after Ayesha's past of being a Sikh girl – a 'kaafir' – returns to plague the villagers; her neighbour and best friend asks her not to attend the marriage of her daughter. By this time, her son Saleem has already grown distant from her and this confirms how her immediate social milieu which has been reintroduced to communal tension has disowned her as well. A marriage that took place prior to the events of the narrative (between Ayesha and one of her abductors), villagers rejoicing at a marriage ceremony (at the house of the village Choudhury), a prospective marriage that is abandoned due to the transformation of the male lover (Saleem and Zubeida) and a marriage that will take place in the future where Ayesha cannot seek an entry, chart the fate of Charkhi. The idyllic social reality hinging on peace and harmony was realised as a new social formation by putting into oblivion the violence of Partition. It is ruptured not because the traumatic memory is reawakened but the religious extremist ideology that the youths of Charkhi have internalised operates along the same logic that had perpetrated endless violence in the past. The historical conditions of the two events, Partition of 1947 and the Islamization of 1979 may be different but the villagers realise the scepticism inherent in the two distinct historical occurrences and the possibility that the latter might echo similar atrocities. In order to avoid reliving that violence, the villagers refuse to accept Ayesha after her buried life is publicly exposed. It marks a shift from philanthropy to misanthropy; distrust, fear and contempt replace the bonds that the villagers shared earlier.

The fear and contempt that return to haunt the villagers implicitly elucidate their relationship with the past. As mentioned earlier, the film begins with an absence of any reference to the idyllic past prior to Partition and even an explicit mention of the event of Partition. The absence does not simply suggest an oblivion

164 Sankha Ghosh

which the temporal distance of three decades has achieved. One may argue that unlike other textual or visual narratives of Partition where nostalgic remembrance has an overbearing on the present, the locals of Charkhi are not subjects of spatial or geographical displacement. The lost materiality of 'home' does not reinforce itself upon them through memory and hence they are better equipped in coping with the violence of Partition. But the vulnerability that gradually takes hold of them after Ayesha's identity is exposed confirms that even if it is an act of collective forgetting, it has not been achieved merely by a temporal gap. It is a memory which has been deliberately silenced. A forceful muting so that it can be retrieved neither in speech nor in actions. Rather than forgetting, it is a deliberate refusal to remember. The moment the changing political climate forces them to confront issues pertaining to religious identity and its relationship to geographical space, the implications of the silenced past return to impose itself.

The deliberate act of silence or the refusal to remember has been the premise of the idyllic present of Charkhi. We encounter acts of hospitality and mutual respect shared between the residents of Charkhi and the Sikh pilgrims, visiting from India. It is one of the elderly villagers who discreetly informs Veero's brother, a member of the group of Sikh pilgrims, that her sister still lives there. Ayesha's identity is publicly exposed after her brother finds her and, handing over a locket she used to wear, confronts her about her past life. It becomes evident that the villagers belonging to the earlier generation who lived during the Partition knew about Ayesha's past identity. But, they did not choose to recall it until now. As mentioned earlier, the arrival of city-bred youths like Mazhar and Rashid and the extremist political ideology they preach gradually instils an anxiety among the villagers. Unlike the elderly, the young men of Charkhi who have begun to share Mazhar and Rashid's ideology harbour hatred and suspicion for the Sikh pilgrims. The public exposure of Ayesha's past identity thus accentuates the anxiety of the old and distrust of the young. Those who chose to maintain a careful reticence are now drawn into the public discourse regarding Ayesha's identity.

The question that remains is how this silence pertaining to an inexplicably violent past as well as anything preceding that violence has been achieved. A refusal to remember both the nostalgic and the traumatic presents us with a curious situation. It does not seek to re-establish the lost past but aims at constructing a social formation anew which refuses to lay any claim to its past. It is at this point we can employ the idea of forgiveness as the inherent logic of this deliberate act of silence. We can use Jacques Derrida's discussion of the concept of forgiveness as the analytical framework in this context. Derrida focuses on an irresolvable tension between the conditional and the unconditional act of forgiving in a lecture presented at Jerusalem in 1997 and later published in the journal *Studies in Practical Philosophy* in 2000. The text acquired a considerable amount of prominence after it was published by Routledge the following year as part of its "Thinking in Action" series. This chapter engages with the idea of unconditional act of forgiveness that is at work in *Khamosh Pani*.

The concept of forgiveness originates from the Abrahamic religions. Although it has emerged as a secular concept with time there exists a conflict between the ways in which the concept of forgiveness can be understood. Derrida writes,

> It is important to analyse at its base the tension at the heart of a heritage between, on the one side, the idea which is also a demand for the unconditioned, gracious, infinite, aneconomic forgiveness granted to the guilty as guilty, without counterpart, even to those who do not repent or ask forgiveness, and on the other side, as a great number of texts testify through many semantic refinements and difficulties, a conditional forgiveness proportionate to the recognition of the fault, to repentance, to the transformation of the sinner who then explicitly asks for forgiveness.
>
> *(Derrida 2001: 35)*

In Derrida's opinion, pure and disinterested forgiveness does not include the demand of an apology as a prerequisite and thus can be realised only by "forgiving the unforgivable" (Derrida 2001: 59). At the same time he distances forgiveness from forgetting, saying:

> each time that it [forgiveness] aims to re-establish a normality (social, national, political, psychological) by a work of mourning, by some therapy or ecology of memory, then the 'forgiveness' is not pure – nor is its concept. Forgiveness is not, it should not be, normal, normative, normalising. It should remain exceptional and extraordinary, in the face of the impossible: as if it interrupted the ordinary course of historical temporality.
>
> *(Derrida 2001: 32)*

The way that the villagers of Charkhi have dealt with their memories of the traumatic past evokes the sense of unconditional forgiveness. The silence has facilitated their disengagement from both the traumatic and the nostalgic. It therefore does not have a therapeutic effect nor does it have any aim of reconciliation with the idyllic past. It marks a disjunction with the past. The silence thus becomes a mode of forgiveness which is able to forgive the most heinous deeds of violence and does not hinge on an apology. The remarkable fact is that unlike other acts of forgiveness it is not mediated by language but silence. Derrida also explicitly mentions that unconditional forgiveness can operate only within two singularities, the guilty and the victim. Here we encounter a readjustment of this proposition. Here the unconditional forgiveness has been achieved only because there is no clearly laid-out distinction between the guilty and the victim, the Sikhs and the Muslims both were implicated in the act of violence. The "exceptional and extraordinary" act of pure forgiveness has been achieved only because the violation was an inexplicable event in itself. This unconditional forgiveness became the basis of the philanthropic present of Charkhi, which is ruptured at the wake of a political crisis. It is interesting to note that the religious extremists too embrace the rhetoric of forgiveness

166 Sankha Ghosh

in this film. But their idea of forgiveness is conditioned by clearly drawn categories of the guilty and the victim and an apology. Since they identify Ayesha as a 'kaafir', they want her to publicly admit that she is a true Muslim. Saleem on one occasion pleads with her, "All they say is that you stand in a public square and declare that you are a Muslim ... that you accept Islam and reject your false beliefs."

Water, the central motif in the film, too is invested in the thematic of forgiveness. Here we encounter another reversal. Water, in general parlance, often serves as the metaphor of life and sustenance. Unlike the familiar metaphor, water in this film is particularly unforgiving. It becomes the agent that devours everything. It does not distinguish between young Veero who escaped death by refusing to jump into water or Ayesha who chooses to commit suicide after being disowned by her community. The connotation of cleansing often associated with water too has been stripped off in this film. There is an apparently incongruous scene in this film that shows Saleem and his friend along with Rashid and Mazhar together washing their feet at a pond. The focus on their feet being cleansed by water recalls a curious religious association. Across religions, there exists a common practice of washing the feet of the animal that is chosen to be sacrificed before God. There is an explicit presence of violence and bloodshed in the act of the sacrifice. Here Mazhar and Rashid indoctrinate two youths of Charkhi with an ideology which symbolically places them at the level of the sacrificial animal. In this film, at the level of sustenance of communal life, the silence which is deliberate contributes to forgiveness, whereas the silence of the water which is unforgiving and unperturbed, comes to bear a metonymic relationship with the traumatic as it establishes the evocative dimension of silence, the past that the villagers attempted to disengage with.

Works Cited

Chakrabarty, Dipesh. "Remembered Villages: Representation of Hindu–Bengali Memories in the Aftermath of the Partition". *Economic and Political Weekly*, Vol. 31, No. 32, 10 August1996, pp. 2143–2145, 2147–2151. JSTOR, https://www.jstor.org/stable/4404497 (accessed on 19 May 2019).

Derrida, Jacques. *On Cosmopolitanism and Forgiveness*. New York: Routledge, 2001.

Menon, Ritu and Bhasin, Kamla. *Borders and Boundaries: Women in India's Partition*. New Delhi: Kali for Women, 1998.

Sumar, Sabiha. "Interview with Sabiha Sumar", 8 April2005. Asia Society. Retrieved from https://asiasociety.org/interview-sabiha-sumar (accessed on 19 May 2019).

Sundar, Pavitra. "Silence and the Uncanny: Partition in the Soundtrack of Khamosh Pani". *South Asian Popular Culture*, Vol. 8, No. 3, October2010, pp. 277–290.

POSTSCRIPT

Inverted prisms, imperfect histories: towards a Dalit historiography of India's Partition

Jaydip Sarkar

> History does not exist apart from our thinking it. Clearly, there are as many ways of experiencing history as there are histories to experience.
>
> *(Susan Crane, "(Not) Writing History")*

One is not just born into history, one also experiences history, both through the perceptions of materiality and the derivative hermeneutics of discursive knowledge. The ideals of discursively formulated knowledge depict just the recognised face value of history. On the flip-side lies experiential history, which is validated in doubt and legitimised in denial. The hegemonic hermeneutic design of governed history thus establishes the finitude of history and with it survives the spectres of 'unreliable histories', ungoverned and non-systematic, abandoned beyond the paradigms of acknowledgement.

Within the hegemonic discursive design of elitist Indian nationalist historiography, the catastrophic consequences of Partition have remained unacknowledged. Partition is rendered as an unavoidable by-product of Indian independence, a reality which is relevant only within the impending moment of sovereignty and which ought to be forgotten as a bad day in the office of the political. In fact, for a long period, Indian nationalist historians have remained silent on Partition violence with the conviction that this silence and consequent forgetting would help a peaceful co-existence and essential unity between the Hindus and Muslims living in India. It was only in the 1980s, a decade of terrible communal violence in India, with anti-Sikh riots taking place in Delhi and its surrounding areas in 1984, anti-Muslim riots in Bhagalpur in 1989, and the post-Babri demolition Hindu–Muslim riots in the country in 1992 that the historians began to seriously consider Partition in their work. Partition evolved as a contingent reality, as the extreme state of exception which could console the National unrest with the flickering hope, 'that has passed, so will this'. The body of scholarship we know as

168 Jaydip Sarkar

Partition Studies began to take definitive shape in the atmosphere created by these events; and as a result of this initiative, the corpus of Partition scholarship has expanded in recent years and has helped us to better appreciate, acknowledge, and share the tremendous and continuing impact of Partition on South Asia. Scholars have been diligent and innovative in uncovering and analysing the human experiences of Partition that are embedded in various locations and genres. Research has been conducted on literature, oral testimonies, letters, political pamphlets, parliamentary records, journalistic sources, memoirs, autobiographies, school history textbooks, sketches, painting, photographs, political cartoons, websites, cinema, theatre etc. Gyanendra Pandey observes: "If we do not examine how Partition was constituted by violence and how that violence unfolded, we will never know our past politics and will, therefore, be unable to control our future politics and prevent history from repeating itself" (Pandey 2001: 64).

Bengal had experienced the tremors of Partition deeply and thus a fertile oeuvre of Bengali literature has been deeply nourished by literary representations of Partition. However, its narratives of Partition mainly revolve round the émigré experiences of the so-called upper-class Bengali Hindus, and are

> totally dumb of those lower-caste Hindu people who lost their land, their food, rather their identity and from the platform of Sealdah were sent to Andaman or Nainital in the name of rehabilitation but got there nothing which they were ought to.
>
> *(Sikder 2013: 34)*

As Sikder elaborates, famous Bengali poet-novelist Sunil Gangopadhyay met with many Bengali refugees, settled in Dandakararnya and Malkangiri, but could not identify a single upper-caste Hindu among them. In fact, "the migrated upper-caste Hindus were given at least a sort of accommodation in 'west'-Bengal itself, while the lower-caste refugees were offered not only constitutional carelessness but a neglect from upper-caste Bengali-Hindu political intelligentsia, who sent them to Dandakaranya" (ibid.).

Partha Chatterjee observes that the institution of caste has been a salient characteristic that has distinguished Indian society from other social models and he observes that the caste system in India has evolved as a "unique Indian institution" (Chatterjee 1993: 173). The ambiguous locationality of caste within the economy of Nationalism, whereby it sustained as a simultaneous marker of both traditionalism (to an extent fundamentalism) and an essential imperative of Indianness, has deeply problematised political thought in India. As such, it has been simultaneously rejected and accepted by the discourse of Nationalism and owing to its lingering relevance as "ideological manifestations of a premodern social formation" (ibid.), caste system has persisted within the developing schema of Nationalism. Chatterjee draws our attention to this relevance of the discourse of Caste within the paradigm of Nationalism:

Postscript **169**

> The presence of a caste system, the assertion goes, makes Indian society essentially different from the Western ... Ideally, the caste system seeks to harmonize within the whole of a social system the mutual distinctness of its parts. This is a requirement for any stable and harmonious social order; the caste system is the way this is achieved in India.
>
> *(Chatterjee 1993: 174)*

The social structure of caste persisted in the aftermath of Partition and owing to its relevance as a relational and not an isolated truth, caste emerged as a determinant social identity for the displaced refugees, who were rendered homeless by the Radcliffe line. Ambedkar, in his insightful enquiry into the genesis of caste system, had observed the relevance of caste as a relational truth, "as a group within, and with definite relations to, the system of caste as a whole" (Ambedkar 2005: 5). The relational identity of caste for the individual subject is a part of the greater social relations that make up the grand narrative of cultural unity. Caste then, like class, evolves as an inseparable element of the social; it is oriented, valorised and prioritised within a matrix of hierarchy. Partha Chatterjee further extends this understanding of caste as a relational truth by arguing that the 'definition-by-self' within the matrix/ discourse of caste is immediately complemented by an implied 'definition-for-another' and thus the essence of caste is always determined within a schema of hierarchy, that which fixes "a universal measure of 'casteness'" (Chatterjee 1993: 176).

What is significant is that this matrix of hierarchy, which ethnographic scientists like Dumont have identified as "attribution of a rank to each element in relation to the whole" (Dumont 1970: 39), preserved its relevance even within a 'state of exception' like Partition. Karl Schmitt defines the 'state of exception' as "that which cannot be subsumed" and which "defies general codification" (Schmitt, quoted in Agamben 1998: 9). The epoch of Partition has often been considered as a 'state of exception' by Nationalist historiographers and political philosophers of the subcontinent since it was a clear deviation from the valorised progressive account of independence. However, the structure of modern State that was a formed in this state of exception was adherent to the fundamental hierarchy of Caste. As such, the rehabilitation design was construed with the caste quotient in mind – while the upper-caste elite refugees were rehabilitated in the metropolitan suburbs, the lower castes, the untouchables and even the religious minorities were abandoned to peripheral locales like the Sunderbans and Dandakaranya and even to Prison camps. As Ross Mallick points out: "... the land the Untouchable refugees were settled on in other states were forests in the traditional territory of tribal peoples, who resented this occupation" (Mallick 1999: 105).

Mallick explicates that while the displaced upper-class elites were subjects who had the ability to occupy "public and private land in Calcutta and other areas" (ibid.) and resisted all means and modes of evacuation, the lower-caste refugees were deeply dependent on government reliefs and aids of relocation. As such, the already marginal was further marginalised, where self-representation was a myth within the already existing political framework and a conformation to and not an opposition of the dominant political order could ensure a possibility of rehabilitation to the Dalit. The Dalit was denied agency and as such there were scarce possibilities of self-representation for the Dalit subject within the greater paradigm of the political. The pre-designed peripheral, both in terms of the political and the spatial, was the status that the modern Nation State had designed for the displaced Dalit subject.

Manoranjan Byapari's autobiography, *Itibritte Chandal Jiban* (lately translated as *Interrogating My Chandal Life: An Autobiography of a Dalit*) locates the Dalit subject in the backdrop of Partition and engages in an understanding of his marginality, which is a pre-conditioned, regulatory truth and which persists even in a deviant political order, in a *world turned upside down*. The book is indeed an interesting study, especially when read from an angle through which we often read Dalit personal narratives as critique of the grand narratives of Nation, national identity and standard national literature.

Byapari's autobiography informs the readers that he was born and brought up in a very poor family at Turukkhali, in the district of Barishal in the former East Pakistan. His father was a landless daily labourer and was steeped in poverty. Although his family surname was Mandal, his grandfather had engaged in business out of sheer curiosity, which failed miserably but had earned for him the surname of 'byapari' ('a businessman') – a title that was mockingly accorded to him by his neighbours. His grandfather had dared to step beyond the pre-discursive persona that the social-cultural had in store for him and this attempted endeavour to dismantle the hierarchical was criticised by the collective, through jest and ridicule.

India's physical frame was divided before the birth of Byapari. Most of the upper-class Hindus had already left East Pakistan or were about to leave it for a safe abode in India. Byapari's father, however, was unwilling to migrate, owing to his cordial relationship with the Muslim neighbours. But as all his relatives left the country, this destitute man had also no alternative.

Byapari states that after Partition, the migrated upper-class Bengali refugees took over the suburbs of Kolkata and formed colonies, around 150 in number, while the peripheral subjects within the hierarchical schema of caste, i.e. the Dalits and untouchables, were not allowed rehabilitation in those colonies. Byapari's family was shifted to the Shibmanipur camp in Bankura district. The dry arid climate and terrain of *raarh Bangla* was no match to the lush greenery of East Pakistan and like other rehabilitated Dalits, the Byaparis suffered from a lack of natural resources, the foremost of them being an insufficient, often scarce, water supply. The refugees, which also included women and children, had to wait for hours before they could ensure a scant amount of drinking water. Very soon, many of them were further displaced by the state to Andaman and Nicobar islands – the infamous *kaalapani* of British India.

Due to the continuing protests and voices of dissent from leftists, the systematic expulsion of refugees to Andaman was stopped and now it was time to send them to Dandakaranya where much like before, the environment, language and culture were completely alien. It was perhaps a calculated move by the State, which foresaw in these doubly marginalised subjects the possibility of unacknowledged manual labour. The Dalit refugees were engaged in deforestation and were further deployed to dig out natural resources. The refugees were used as the labourers for the development of that state. Yet again, the Leftists raised their voice and demanded that Bengalis be given place of rehabilitation in Bengal only.

Byapari recollects that from Dandakaranya, his father came to Marichjhapi in 1978. However, the pretensions of the Left regime in West Bengal, which had claimed to be considerate towards the Dalit refugees, were soon exposed. The settled refugees in Marichjhapi were subjected to unrestrained violence and gunfire by the State government. The refugees had attempted to make the occupied land a self-dependent colony and the then Communist government in West Bengal had intervened with its modes of repression. Byapari's autobiography perfectly captures the Dalit refugee's disillusionment with Communism and presents a vigorous criticism of the Jyoti Basu-led Communist government's stand on the refugee issues in Marichjhapi.

The state of homelessness is a perennial truth for the Dalit subject, and Byapari recounts his constant drift from one refuge into another. Coming out of the Bankura camp, Byapari's family would take shelter near an area in Bijaygarh, an unfamiliar territory where living conditions were hostile and dehumanising. The place was so unfit for living that even to enter the room one needed to crawl like a baby. Meanwhile, Byapari's elder sister died. Due to lack of clothes, his mother could not get out of the house. His grandmother would pick the left-over vegetables from the market areas left by the farmers. Here came Byapari's first job opportunity. He would graze the cattle of a middle-class farmer, but without pay – only in exchange for food and a new set of clothes once a year.

Byapari's recollections of this phase of life bring out the dynamics of caste politics of Bengal. The elemental matrix of Caste dominates all other considerations of social relations. The Dalit is a primordial marginal subject within this hegemonising and all-pervasive matrix of caste and as such, he/she is a social outcast in the practice of everyday and in discourses that concerns the social-cultural. What is surprising, however, is the systematic marginalisation of the Dalit by the strategems that were designed and devised by the juridico-political. The modern Nation-State, which had in theory valorised overarching dictums like 'secular' and 'socialist', was in its own way being governed by the pre-modern imperatives of caste in practice. The migrant refugees were systematically, yet unofficially, segregated on the principles of caste and the rehabilitation measures were qualitatively different for different castes. This qualitative segregation was done on the basis of the hierarchical structure that was an inseparable component of the caste system.

Byapari found his second employment at the house of a doctor, where he worked as a domestic help. This apparently progressive Doctor would invite all the Muslim leaders of the area in his house to enrich his social prosperity and to ensure social security. The doctor's wife would order Byapari, who, being an untouchable, was normally denied the entrance in the inner house of the family and even a clean plate to eat on, to clean up all the utensils and the plates that were used by the guests. In this case, Byapari "though treated by her as an 'untouchable', was ranked higher by her in comparison to the Muslims" (Byapari 2012: 52). Byapari's autobiography is saturated with such considerations and realisations about the salient nature of hierarchy

172 Jaydip Sarkar

and stratification which dominate and govern the middle-class Bengali subject. More importantly, it lays bare the obsession with *purity and pollution* that the traditional middle-class Bengali–Hindu subject has and which plays a considerable role in determining his/her ontological essence. The middle-class conscious self/subject needs an 'other' to formulate his/her essence of being and this devised other is often contingent in essence but constant as a category. It can unconditionally include both the Dalit and the Muslim and depending on the context, it can configure a hierarchy, where the Muslim becomes a bigger 'other' than the Dalit.

Byapari's torment continued as he was sexually exploited by a police man, escaped to Guwahati and finally got involved in the militant ultra-left Naxalite movement. When his father discovered that Byapari had become a Naxalite, he decided to go to Dandakaranya with thousands of new refugees of Bengal who emigrated from East Pakistan due to the 1971 war of liberation. His father earnestly hoped that if he went there, his son at least would survive. In Dandakaranya, they started living first at Paralcourt in the district of Bastar and later on at a nameless village, P.F.98. There they were provided with stipulated amount of rice and dal and 75 rupees per month, as approved by Government. With this inadequate food and money, the refugees failed to maintain their family. Hence, for earning more, they took up jobs that involve unskilled labour such as cleaning the forests, digging out soil, breaking stones, plucking *kendu* leaves and making dam. All these signify that there was in reality no process of rehabilitation at all.

Byapari's autobiography, of course, has other implications and experiences of marginality that the Dalit subject encounters and the almost inextricable affiliation that the Dalit has with deprivation. However, what is interesting to note is how the politics of caste and casteism remained intact even in a situation of political crisis like Partition, which has been previously phrased and substantiated as a 'state of exception'. Also, it is worth noting that the catastrophe of Partition was simultaneous with the birth of a modern Nation State – a Nation that had promised its citizens an altruistic ideal of 'Right to Equality.' However, the unbridgeable gap between theory and practice, the pedagogic and the performative, that to date haunts the Modern Nation State has been undauntedly depicted by Byapari. The accounts of his lived realities in the immediate aftermath of Partition provide the purview of a Nation State that boasts of modernity but is in reality, imbibed in non–modern social relations like caste. What is worse, the juridico-legal apparatus of this sovereign Nation State seems to be governed by considerations of caste and socio–cultural fundamentalism. As such, the very claim of sovereignty of this Nation state is jeopardised by the experiential realities of the marginal Dalit subject.

Works Cited

Agamben, Giorgio. *Homo Sacer: Sovereign Power and Bare Life*, trans. Daniel Heller- Roazen, Stanford, CA: Stanford University Press. 1998.

Ambedkar, B.R. *Castes in India: Their Mechanism, Genesis and Development*, Jullundur: Patrika Publications, 2005 (originally published 1916).

Byapari, Manoranjan. *Itibritte Chandal Jiban*, Kolkata: Kolkata Prakashan, 2012.

Chatterjee, Partha, *The Nation and Its Fragments: Colonial and Postcolonial Histories*, Princeton, NJ: Princeton University Press, 1993.

Crane, Susan A. "(Not) Writing History: Rethinking the Intersections of Personal History and Collective Memory with Hans Von Aufsess". *History and Memory*, Vol. 8, No. 1, 1996.

Dumont, Louis. *Homo Hierarchicus: The Caste System and Its Implications*, trans. Mark Sainsbury, Louis Dumontand Basia Gulati. New Delhi: Oxford University Press, 1970.

Mallick, Ross. "Refugee Resettlement in Forest Reserves: West Bengal Policy Reversal and the Marichjhapi Massacre". *The Journal of Asian Studies*, Vol. 58, No. 1, February1999. Print.

Pandey, Gyanendra. *Remembering Partition: Violence, Nationalism and History in India*, Cambridge and New York: Cambridge University Press, 2001.

Sikder, Ashrukumar. "Janoiko Chandaler Jabani", *Arekrakam*, ed. Ashoke Mitra, Vol. 7, No. 1, April2013.

INDEX

Abataranika (Mitra) 14–15
Adorno, Theodor 85
aesthetics and materials 85–86
Afro-Asian Writers Association 29
after-life aesthetic 85
Agamben, Giorgio 98, 113, 122, 152–153, 154, 156
"Alam's Own House" (Palit) 114–117
Ambedkar, B. R. 169
Andaman and Nicobar islands 170
Anderson, Benedict 21, 48
Anderson, Perry 102
Anthias, Floya 148
Anthropocene 121
"Anthropology of Pain, The" (Das) 34
aporia 32, 103–104, 122
Arendt, Hannah 154
Aristotle 86, 152
Arjun (Gangopadhyay) 7
Arnold, Kathleen R. 76, 78
Assam 1

Babri Mosque, demolition of 6, 36, 134–135, 167
Bachelard, Gaston 121, 122
Bagchi, Jasodhara 6, 156
Baig, M. R. A. 96
Bakultala P.L. Camp (Sanyal) 7
Bandopadhyay, Atin 7
Bandopadhyay, Manik 155–156
Banerjea, Surendranath 95
Bangladesh 1
Bangladesh war of Liberation 114

bare life 98
Baron in the Trees, The (Calvino) 63–64
Barthes, Roland 46, 97
Basti (Husain) 73–84
Basu, Buddhadev 93
Basu, Jyoti 171
Bauman, Zygmunt 153
Beauvoir, Simone de 158
Begum Jaan (film) 15
Bender, Barbara 85–86
Bend in the Ganges, A (Malgonkar) 42
Benegal, Shyam 6
Bengal Divided: Hindu Communalism and Partition (Chatterji) 3
Bengali Muslims 1
Bengali Partition films 13–15
Bengal Renaissance 24
Bengal Tenancy Act of 1928 8
Benjamin, Walter 98
Berlin, Isaiah 152
bhadralok 3, 10–11, 12, 13, 108
Bhagalpur riots 134–135, 167
Bhasin, Kamla 13, 22, 113, 143, 148, 150
Bhattacharya, Tapadhir 101
bildungsroman 48–54; as a genre 54; Moretti on 54
bios 98, 152, 153
bios-politikos 121–122, 152, 153
Biswas, Hemanga 22
body 51–52
Bordoloi, Gopinath 1
Bose, Subhas Chandra 49
British India Board of Education 25

176 Index

Brownmiller, Susan 136
Burgin, Victor 113
Butalia, Urvashi 22, 23, 47, 134, 143
Butler, Judith 32, 136
Bwadip (Roy) 7
Byapari, Manoranjan 170–172

Cabinet Mission Plan 2
Calvino, Italo 63–64
Campbell, Joseph 110
Caruth, Cathy 59
caste: Nationalism and 168–169; politics 171; relational identity of 169; social structure of 169
Chakrabarty, Bid 36
Chakrabarty, Dipesh 7, 82–83, 162
Chakraborty, Paulomi 14
Chatterjee, Partha 107, 126, 153, 157, 168–169
Chatterji, Joya 11, 96
"Chena Mukh" (Rajguru) 14
Chhere Asha Gram (The Abandoned Village) 7
Chowdhury, Sayandeb 13
Chughtai, Ismat 122
Cinema and I (Ghatak) 105
"Cinema and the Subjective Factor" (Ghatak) 85, 110
colonial rule 24–25
Communal Award of 1932 3
communal identity 9–10
communalisation of urban space 10–11
communal violence 6, 7, 123, 134–135, 139, 144, 161, 167
Communism 171
Communist Party 28
community identities 13, 40
Congress 26
consciousness 98; of ambiguity 98; historico-temporal 98; material 86–87
Crane, Susan 167
creative consciousness 155
"Crystal Goblet, The" *see* "Sfatikpatra" (short story by Ghatak)
cultural identity 74, 75–76
"Cultural Identity and Diaspora" (Hall) 74
cultural purity 13
Curzon, Lord 95, 96

Dalit 167–172
Dalrymple, William 59
Dandakaranya 169
Das, Jibanananda 93; "I Have Seen Bengal's Face" 94–97; "I Shall Return to This Bengal" 94, 97–99; *Rupashi Bangla* 94
Das, Veena 34, 150

Dasgupta, Subho Ranjan 6, 150–151, 156
Derrida, Jacques 92, 114, 117, 164–165
Desai, A. R. 26
Devi, Jyotirmoyee 7, 144–151
Dey, Arunima 30–31
diaspora 73, 74, 76, 79
diasporic nostalgia 74
Didur, Jill 36
Direct Action Day 10
displaced subject 112–114; home and 112–113; mourning 113–114; ontological disorientation 93
displacement 1, 93, 122, 154, 155; diasporic 73; material consciousness 87; spatio-temporal 73
docile body 52
Donald, James 113
Dumont, Louis 169
dystopia 48, 123

Earth 1947 (film) 6
East Pakistan 1, 10, 15, 73, 80, 81, 122, 155, 170, 172
Eco, Umberto 117
Elsaesser, Thomas 132
English educational system 24–25
Epar Ganga, Opar Ganga (Devi) 7, 144–151
essential enemy 117
eudemonia 152
exclusion 6; cultural violence of 82; ethics of 52; inclusive 153, 154; of the other 77, 153–154; politics of 78–80, 114; of women 158
exile 93–94

Faiz, Ahmed Faiz 92
Felman, Shoshana 60
feminism 52, 126, 127, 129–132, 140, 143–144, 156–159
"Final Solution, The" (Bandopadhyay) 155–160
Foreign Language Publishing House 29
forgiveness 164–166
Foucault, Michel 49, 51, 52, 153, 156
Frankl, Victor E. 56
Freud, Sigmund 57, 130

Gadar (film) 6
Gandhi, M. K. 43, 49, 122, 123, 125, 145
Gangopadhyay, Sunil 7
Garm Hava (film) 6, 122–132
gender identity 136
genocide 22, 31, 35, 42, 103, 107, 123
Ghatak, Ritwik 13, 14, 22, 101–111; literary representations 87; material

consciousness 86–87; realistic works 86; "Sarak" 88–89, 90; "Sfatikpatra" 88, 89–90
Ghosh, Amitav 5
Ghosh, Gour Kishore 8–10
Ghosh, Nemai 13–14
Ghosh, Ranjan 45
Ghosh, Shankha 11–13
Gledhill, Christine 131
Go-Between, The (Harley) 45
Great Calcutta Killing 36
Gujarat riots in 1992 36
Gulzar 62–68

Hagglund, Martin 90
Hajari, Nisid 37
Hall, Stuart 74, 75
Hamacher, Werner 99
Harley, L. P. 45
Hasan, Kamal 6
Hasan, Mushirul 4
hauntology 90
Hegel, Georg Wilhelm Friedrich 21, 46
Herodotus 86
heterotopias 49, 124, 156
Hey Ram (film) 6
Hindu Mahasabha 28
Hindus 2–11, 24–29, 35–42, 124–125, 134–135, 139; Bengal Renaissance and 25; Kohat riot in NWFP 3; myths 76, 79; refugee 148; upper-caste 3; women 145–151
Hirsch, Marianne 154
Historicism 23
historiography 2–4, 22; Dalit 167–172; Partition 23–24; postmodern tendencies 47; Subaltern 22
History of Sexuality, The (Foucault) 51
Hofer, Johannes 87
Holocaust 56, 57
home 121–122; displaced subject 112–113; memory of 112
homeland 93–94, 112
homeland-making 7–10
homelessness 122, 137; Dalit and 171; as moment of disenfranchisement 122; myth of 73–84; Partition and 144; political 79; structure of family 158
Homelessness, Citizenship and Identity: The Uncanniness of Late Modernity (Arnold) 76
homesickness 87
Hosain, Attia 5
human subject 97–98; consciousness 98; as politico-social subject 97
Huq, Fazlul 8

Husain, Intizar 73–84
Hutcheon, Linda 89
Huyssen, Andreas 48

Ice-Candy Man, The (Sidhwa) 48–54, 141
identity 36; agency and 52–53; communal 9–10; cultural 74, 75–76; gender 136; liminal 92; national 74, 75–84; political 53, 77–78; sexual 158; social 136
identity politics 77
"I Have Seen Bengal's Face" (Das) 94–97
illegal immigrants 1
imaginary 98–99
"Imaginary Homelands" (Rushdie) 112
immigrants 41; illegal 1; liminal space for 87; national identity 75; political otherness 76; potential 125; subjective experience 83
immigration procedure 6
imperfect histories 47
India, historiography of 22
Indian College in Calcutta 25
Indian National Army 49
Indian National Congress *see* Congress
Indian Peoples' Theatre Association (IPTA) 14, 29
Inoperative Community, The (Nancy) 21
Irigaray, Luce 157
"I Shall Return to This Bengal" (Das) 94, 97–99
Islamic brotherhood 38
Itibritte Chandal Jiban (Byapari) 170–172

Jalal, Ayesha 5
Jinnah, Muhammad Ali 2, 49, 50, 58, 64, 66, 122
Jones, Reece 7–8
jotedars 8
jouissance of return 97–99
Joyce, James 92

Kamra, Sukeshi 47
Kaur, Inder 150
Khamosh Pani (film) 161–166
Khan, Sir Syed Ahmad 25–26
Khan, Yasmin 3–4
Kobitar Kotha (Basu) 93
Kohat riot in NWFP 3
Komal Gandhar (film) 14, 103–109
Krishak Praja Party (KPP) 8–9
Krishna Sholoi (Rahman) 10–11
Kristeva, Julia 130
Kudaisya, Gyanesh 102

Lacan, Jacques 67, 123
Lahore Resolution of March 1940 2

178 Index

Lefebvre, Henry 86, 93, 121
"Lekhaker Katha" (Bandopadhyay) 155
Lerner, Gerda 157
Levinas, Emmanuel 52
liminal identity 92
liminal space 87
lower-caste refugees 169
Lukacs, George 48, 52

Mahabharata 146
Mahanagar (film) 14–15
Malaviya, Pt. M. M. 3
Mallick, Ross 169
Mammo (film) 6
Man's Search for Meaning (Frankl) 56
Manto, Saadat Hasan 4, 23, 62–66; "Toba
    Tek Singh" 56–60
Mapmaking: Partition Stories from Two Bengals
    (Nandy) 102
margin 153
material: aesthetics and 85; consciousness
    86–87; subjectivity 85–86; truths 86
Maus (Spiegelman) 48
Meghe Dhaka Tara (film) 14, 88, 103–109
melodrama 132
Memon, Muhammad Umar 74, 83
memories, of violence 23
memory: haunting 89–90; nostalgia 87–90;
    performatives of 113–114; trauma 56–60
Menon, Jisha 1
Menon, Ritu 13, 22, 113, 143, 148, 150
"Metropolis and the Mental Life, The"
    (Simmel) 93
Midnight's Furies (Hajari) 37
migrant refugees 171; *see also* immigrants
Mishra, Vijay 113, 114
Mitra, Narendranath 14–15
modern Nation State: Anderson on 21;
    evolution of 21; geo-political abstraction
    of 153
Montrose, Louis A. 23
Mookerjea-Leonard, Debali 6, 149, 150
Moretti, Franco 54
Morley–Minto reforms 3
Moses and Monotheism (Freud) 57
mourning 113–114; displaced subject
    113–114; nostalgic 89
*Mourning the Nation: Indian Cinema in the
    Wake of Partition* (Sarkar) 108
Muhammadan Anglo-Oriental College 25–26
Mukherjee, Srijit 15
Mukhopadhyay, Chandi 101
multiculturalism 48–49
Muslim League 9, 124; British policy and
    41–42; Congress *vs.* 10, 27–28; Direct

Action Day 10; elections of 1946 2;
    historiography of Partition 2
Muslim nation 26
Muslims: British-Indian 25; categorical
    identity 10; colonial rule and 24–25;
    identity 9–10, 25–26; identity crisis 25; as
    illegal immigrants 1; modern education
    and 24–25; nationalism 24, 25; reform
    programmes 25–26
myth: of homelessness 73–84; as
    semiological system 97

Nagarik (film) 14, 107
Nair, Neeti 35
Nancy, Jean-Luc 21, 46, 49, 114–115
Nandy, Ashis 101–103, 104, 107, 111
national boundaries 73–74
national identity 74, 75–84
nationality 24, 66, 113, 122
National Register of Citizens for the State
    of Assam 1
nativity 113, 122
Naxalite movement 172
Nehru, Jawaharlal 5, 49, 66, 122
Nehru–Liaquat Pact 1
New Historicism 23
Nietzsche, Friedrich 97, 98
Nihalani, Govind 5
Nilkantho Pakhir Khonje (Bandopadhyay) 7
non-actualised possibility 99
nonexpressive totality 130
Nora, Pierre 47
North East of India 1, 2
North Western Frontier Provinces
    (NWFP) 2
nostalgia 87–90
Novick, Peter 46

Of Grammatology (Derrida) 92
Ora Thake Odhare (film) 14

Pakistan 2, 49
Pal, Bipin Chandra 7
Palit, Dibyendu 114–117
Pandey, Gyanendra 2, 3, 11, 22, 35, 154
Panigrahi, D. N. 41
Paris massacres of 2015 45
Partition 1; Bengali literature 6–7; historical
    cataclysm of 93; historiography 2–4;
    literary and filmic representation 4–6;
    political history 2–4; scholarship 168; as
    socio-historical calamity 158; as state of
    exception 169
Partition of Bengal and Its Aftermath, The
    (Baig) 96

"Performative Acts and Gender Constitution: An Essay in Phenomenology and Feminist Theory" (Butler) 136
performatives of memory 113–114
Pinjar (film) 6
Pinjar (Pritam) 5, 135–141
political identity 53, 77–78
politics: Berlin on 152; in modern nation states 152–153
Portrait of the Artist as a Young Man (Joyce) 92
postcoloniality 73, 82
"Postcoloniality and the Artifice of History: Who Speaks for 'Indian' Pasts?" (Chakrabarty) 82
postmemory 155
postmodernism 47, 137, 158
post-structuralism 47
Premnath, Gautam 73
Prem Nei (Ghosh) 8–10
Pritam, Amrita 5, 135–141
Pritchett, Frances W. 74
Progressive Writer's Association 29
Punjabi Hindu Sabha 3
Punjab Land Alienation Act 2–3

Radcliffe Commission 96
Radcliffe line 86, 90, 96, 115, 122, 144, 169
Radhakrishnan, R. 73
Rahman, Anisur 62, 67
Rahman, Mijan-ur 10–11
Rai, Lala Lajpat 3
Rajguru, Shaktipada 14
Rajkahini (film) 15
rape 2, 22, 35, 53–54, 135, 136, 144, 149, 161–162
Ray, Iraban Basu 101
Ray, Satyajit 14–15, 105
reconciliation 157
refugees 122, 169–171
religious affiliation 35
religious exclusivism 115
religious fundamentalism 35
religious identities 24, 28, 115
"Remembered Villages: Representation of Hindu-Bengali Memories in the Aftermath of the Partition" (Chakraborty) 7, 161
"Remembering Fanon, Decolonizing Diaspora" (Premnath) 73
right to equality 172
Rigney, Ann 47
riots 1, 36
Ritwikcharcha: A Bengali Collection of Essays on Ritwik (Mukhopadhyay) 101

"Road, The" *see* "Sarak" (short story by Ghatak)
Roy, Ram Mohun 25
Roy, Rituparna 37
Roy, Sabitri 7
Rupashi Bangla (Das) 94
Rushdie, Salman 94, 112, 140

Sahni, Bhisham 5, 6, 23, 27, 29–31
Said, Edward 93–94
Salesian College, Sonada, Darjeeling 67
Sanyal, Narayan 7
"Sarak" (short story by Ghatak) 88–89, 90
Sarkar, Bhaskar 108
Sarkar, Sumit 151
Sathyu, M. S. 6, 125–128
schizophrenia 110
Schmitt, Karl 169
Scientific Society of Aligarh 25
self 32, 34; consciousness of 122; material disposition of 85–86; ontological essence of 86; violation of 53–54
self-purification 68
self-representation 169–170
semiological system, myth as 97
Sen, Mrinal 36
sexual identity 158
sexual violence 57, 136, 149, 162
"Sfatikpatra" (short story by Ghatak) 88, 89–90
Shadow Lines, The (Ghosh) 5
Shaikh, Farzana 24
Sidhwa, Bapsi 48, 49, 53–54, 141
Sikh extermination in 1984 36, 167
Sikh women, violence against 31
Simmel, Georg 93, 115
Singh, Bir Bahadur 36
Singh, Khushwant 4, 135
Skeleton and Other Stories, The (Singh) 135
social identity 136
social memories 143
Soja, Edward 121
South Asia 102
sovereignty 152–153
"Special Supplement, A: The Question of Machiavelli" (Berlin) 152
Spiegelman, Art 48
Spivak, Gayatri 92–93
state of exception 169
Studies in Practical Philosophy (journal) 164
Su, John J. 86
Subaltern historians and schools 22
Subarnarekha (film) 14, 103–109
sublime narrative 45, 46, 47, 63–68, 155, 158

180 Index

Sumar, Sabiha 161
Sunderbans 169
Sunlight on a Broken Column (Hosain) 5
supplement 92–93
Supuribaner Sari (Ghosh) 11–13
Svensson, Ted 34, 79–80
Swaralipi (Roy) 7

Tamas (Sahni) 5, 6, 23–32
Tamas (tele-serial) 15
Tan, Tai Yong 102
Tennyson, Alfred 135
Thomson, E. P. 22
"Toba Tek Singh" (poem by Gulzar) 62–68
"Toba Tek Singh" (short story by Manto)
    56–60, 139
Todorov, Tzvetan 13
Train to Pakistan (film) 6
Train to Pakistan (Singh) 4, 35–43
trauma 56–60; concept of 56–57; displaced
    subject 112; economy of 161; incubation
    period/latency 57; return of the
    repressed 60
*Trauma and Triumph of Partition, The: Gender
    and Partition in Eastern India* (Bagchi and
    Dasgupta) 6
Trauma: Explorations in Memory (Caruth) 59
traumatic memories 59–60, 161
two-nation theory 42, 66, 134, 147, 153
Tyabji, Budruddin 26

Unclaimed Experience (Caruth) 57
United Provinces 5
untouchables 169

upper-caste elite refugees 169
urban space, communalisation of 10–11

Veer Zaara (film) 6
violence 2, 3–6, 96; against women 30–31;
    communal 6, 7, 123, 134–135, 139,
    144, 161, 167; culture 29–30, 82;
    gender-based 31; ideology of 34–43;
    masculine displays 51; memories 23;
    narratives 22; nature of 29; reconciliation
    and 54; self-determination 78; sexual 57,
    136, 149, 162; terror 59; trauma of 56–60

Wavell, Lord 41
Weber, Samuel 78
Whitehead, Anne 111
"Whose Homeland? Territoriality and
    Religious Nationalism in Pre-Partition
    Bengal" (Jones) 7
Willemen, Paul 108
women 32; colonial India 135; exclusion of
    158; experience of Partition 136; rape 2,
    22, 35, 53–54, 135, 136, 144, 149,
    161–162; relational and marginal identity
    127; sexuality 52; violence against 30–31;
    see also feminism

Yuval-Davis, Nira 148

Zamindar, Vazira 127
zamindari system 8
Zia-ul-Haque, Muhammad 162
Žižek, Slavoj 45–46, 68, 98–99
'zoe' 98, 152, 153